THE SAVAGE EMPIRE

FORGOTTEN WARS OF THE 19TH CENTURY

IAN HERNON

SUTTON PUBLISHING

First published in 2000 by
Sutton Publishing Limited · Phoenix Mill
Thrupp · Stroud · Gloucestershire · GL5 2BU

British Library Cataloguing in Publication Data
A catalogue record for this book is available from the British Library.

ISBN 0 7509 2480 2

Dedication

For Pauline, Joanna, Kim, Barbara,
Jimmy, Jamie, Mary and Douglas

Typeset in 10/12pt Plantin Light.
Typesetting and origination by
Sutton Publishing Limited.
Printed in Great Britain by
Bookcraft, Midsomer Norton, Somerset.

Contents

Acknowledgements

It is not my intention here to chronicle the broad sweep of imperial history during the nineteenth century. There are bigger and better books for that. Rather, as with the first volume, *Massacre and Retribution*, I aim to throw some light on the darker corners which are too often forgotten, and to do so with the eye of a reporter rather than an academic. These are simply great stories. For the sake of the participants, on all sides, they should be remembered.

In writing this book I have repeatedly been confronted with a variety of spellings of names and places, largely due to the phonetic translation of eastern and other ethnic languages which may not share the English alphabet. I have generally opted for those spellings most commonly used in dispatches home. I hope that in doing so I have not caused offence or bruised sensibilities. That was certainly not my intention.

Many people have given me encouragement and practical help for which I am most grateful. They include my workmates David Healey, John Smith and Peter Willoughby; my agent Mike Shaw of Curtis Brown; Jonathan Falconer, commissioning editor at Sutton Publishing; and Sarah Cook. And, as always, my family.

Introduction

The Roman Empire was never at peace, from the beginning of its history to the rule of Augustus and, as Victoria foresaw, war became part of the everyday British experience, too; war of a small and distant kind, it is true, but none the less real for that – none the less noble for those who saw it as an instrument of greater ends, none the less exhilarating for those who loved the smell of the gunsmoke, nor the less tragic for those, friend or foe, who had not yet learnt to ask the reason why.

James Morris

In his *Inquiry into the Nature and Causes of the Wealth of Nations*, published prophetically in 1776, Adam Smith wrote:

> The discovery of America, and that of a passage to the East Indies by the Cape of Good Hope, are the two greatest and most important events recorded in the history of mankind. Their consequences already have been very great, but in the short period of between two and three centuries which have elapsed since these discoveries were made, it is impossible that the whole extent of their consequences can have been seen. What benefits, or what misfortunes to mankind may hereafter result from these great events, no human wisdom can foresee. But uniting, in some measure, the most distant parts of the world, by enabling them to relieve one another's wants, to increase one another's enjoyments, and to encourage one another's industry, their general tendency would seem to be beneficial. To the natives, however . . .

It was a big however. During the subsequent century the various empires of the west subjugated, conquered, exploited, evicted and even wiped out entire races. By the standards of the time the motives were often 'pure' – the propagation of Christianity, trade, remorseless imperial conquest, glory, riches, social advancement – but the results were still fire-blackened villages, scorched hunting grounds empty of game, the destruction of civilisations older than our own, mass slaughter, epidemic, social inferiority and poverty.

As with *Massacre and Retribution*, to which this is a companion volume, it is not the intention of this book to judge or condemn the part the British Empire played in such worldwide suffering. To do so, in any case, would be irrelevant. It is unfair to impose today's standards on a century which preceded ours. And bigger books by better historians have already covered the social and political forces involved in creating a global empire. My purpose is simply to tell some more stories of martial glory and disgrace which have been broadly forgotten by several generations of writers, readers and teachers. Taken together they form a patchwork which, I hope, can help to explain the broader sweep of perhaps the most dynamic century in history.

Smith's work was published in the same year as Britain lost America, with the result that British ambitions turned away from the New World. Traders, explorers and soldiers looked instead to the south and to the east. The century began with Britain fighting the Napoleonic Wars which, on land at least, were largely confined to Europe; it ended with the imperial pink scattered across the globe, in Asia, Africa and Australasia. Of course Britain had settled those continents before, but generally only as trade centres, ports and islands on the main sea routes. As the century progressed vast territories were opened up. For much of that time the British public were only vaguely aware of such imperial expansion. Unlike the conquest of the North American continent, in which the drive west was remorseless and unstoppable, there was no grand plan, no Manifest Destiny. In *The Climax of Empire* James Morris wrote: 'The acquisition of it all had been a jerky process. Absence of mind it never was, but it happened so obscurely that to the ordinary Briton the rise of the Empire must have seemed like some organic movement rather than the conscious result of national policies. One thing simply led to another.'

Successive British governments, preoccupied by expensive wars against France and Russia and by social turmoil at home, tried to rein in the expansion when it involved costly administration. Time and again they were thwarted by officials on the spot, trade moguls with an eye to a quick profit, and military men hungry for glory. Gradually the empire seeped into the consciousness of the British nation and became part of its national identity. Denis Judd noted: 'It also provided manifold opportunities for personal, financial and sexual aggrandisement. It introduced strange and exotic foods, foreign flora and fauna, useful words, outlandish philosophies, new sports, other cultures, and a whole host of unfamiliar experiences into the British way of life.'

What it did to the rest of the world was equally profound. The most beneficial aspect, in terms of humanity, was the part Britain's armies and navies played in the abolition of slavery and the policing of that veto. It can be argued that it too often replaced chains and whips with economic slavery, destabilised ancient societies and was spurred on by profit rather than by genuine humanitarianism. That may have been true in some cases, but not in others. British power was actively engaged in stamping out an evil trade many decades before it was outlawed in America.

The empire also freed many people from petty princelings and brutal local dictators. Much of the empire was carved out by collaboration with the local populace rather than by outright conquest. Britain may have plundered the world, but it built much that has lasted on great continents and in far-flung corners. Nevertheless the technological advances which led to bridge-building and an industrial society hungry for materials also created weapons of mass destruction. As the century continued they were used with sanctimonious ferocity by the civilised against foes who became increasingly defenceless.

The courage of British soldiers fighting far from home, in malarial swamps and dense jungle, against enemies who refused to play according to the white man's rules of the game of warfare, should never be despised. The terrors they faced in alien landscapes were very real. Ensign Thomas Lucas, writing about a Xhosa massacre in South Africa in 1851, recalled the terror of butchery and torture committed by 'primitive' people:

Stretched out in fantastic positions across the path, lay the bodies of thirteen infantry soldiers in hideous array, horribly mutilated, the agony expressed in their glassy upturned eyes showing that they had met with a lingering death by the sharp assegais of the Kaffirs. Painful experience has since taught me that this peculiar horror of expression always attends death when produced by sharp weapons.

But it is difficult to see how such terror can compare, as the century progressed, with that imposed on native people by the western technology of war. Steamships and railways were used whenever possible to transport well-armed troops and artillery as close as possible to the startled enemy. Repeating rifles, machine-guns and shell-firing cannon became the weapons of choice against enemies armed with spears, single-shot muskets and raw, naked courage. Lawrence James noted:

In pitched battles, native warriors still relied on such traditional close-combat weapons as thrusting spears, swords, clubs and bows, arms which had rarely been seen on European battlefields since the end of the Middle Ages. Fighting with these weapons, the native had either to wait in ambush for his adversary so as to take him unawares or else rely on his own courage or religious faith and charge him in the open. His success depended upon his physical strength, fitness and skill at arms and on his being in a countryside he knew better than his enemies.

British blood-lust was evident in conflicts where well-educated officers and ignorant men faced races they considered inferior; the slaughter of such peoples was often likened to sport. At Ulundi in 1879 an NCO described a cavalry charge against fleeing Zulus: 'We had a glorious go in, old boy, pig-sticking was a fool to it.' Officers who prized their sharpshooting skills described their personal body-counts as 'bags'. A civilian observer during the 1885 Sawakin campaign wrote: 'It was a pretty sight seeing a good shot at work, and what awe the Arabs stand in of a first-class rifle shot.'

The use of firepower to murderous effect was a deliberate strategy, a way of bringing troublesome peoples to the imperial heel. An outrage, real or manufactured, against the British Crown and its representatives was inevitably followed by a lesson in brute power. A senior officer told defeated chiefs in Sierra Leone in 1887: 'The Queen has shown you her power by sending her force and taking the country which now belongs to me and the governor. When people make war, those who have been conquered have to suffer for their misdeeds.'

During that remarkable century it was not just aboriginal natives who faced Britain's technological superiority, but also older civilisations in Spain, Persia, Burma and China. All fell before the shell splinters, high explosive and massed firepower concentrated with ruthless effect. Too often these were not isolated skirmishes but the harnessing of technology for mass murder. In that sense Britain's was a 'savage empire'. And that, too, should not be forgotten in the tumult of imperial flag-waving.

★   ★   ★

CHAPTER ONE

The Capture and Loss of Buenos Aires, 1806–7

'Success to grey hairs but bad luck to white locks.'

Lieutenant-Colonel Lancelot Holland wrote painfully in his diary:

> We were ordered to march out without arms. It was a bitter task, everyone felt it, the men were all in tears. We were marched through the town to the Fort. Nothing could be more mortifying than our passage through the streets amidst the rabble who had conquered us. They were very dark-skinned people, short and ill-made, covered with rags, armed with long muskets and some a sword. There was neither order nor uniformity among them.

Their ordeal marked the humiliation in South America of British arms, not once but twice, at the hands of a ragbag army of soldiers, civilians and gauchos quite different to the disciplined armies of Europe currently embroiled in global conflict. That shame resulted in the court martial of the senior officer involved but British pride quickly recovered on the glorious battlefields against Napoleon, and a bizarre adventure in South America was just as quickly forgotten. But on the southern continent it marked the beginning of the end of Spain's greedy grasp and the pride felt at the humbling of Britain led eventually to revolution and the making of Argentina.

★   ★   ★

In 1493 Pope Alexander VI decreed that the New World between California and Buenos Aires belonged to Spain, to be plundered and settled for the benefit of the kings of Castile. English mariners and freebooters challenged that decree from the start and the vast continent of South America became the bloody focus of global power politics.

The settlement of present-day Argentina began after Amerigo Vespucci discovered the Rio de la Plata in 1501. He was followed by such renowned explorers as Ferdinand Magellan and Sebastian Cabot. The land was disputed between Spain and Portugal but a 1535 expedition led by the Spaniard Pedro de Mendoza founded a new town: Nuestra Senora Santa Maria del Buen Aire, or Buenos Aires. Mendoza died on the journey home but his lieutenants pushed the boundaries of the new territory a thousand miles up the Plata and Paraguay rivers. Buenos Aires was neglected in favour of a settlement at Asuncion which became the main centre for Spanish expansion for fifty years.

Buenos Aires, re-established in 1580, was isolated from the more settled northern part of the country, and in 1725 had a population of only 2,000. It relied on Indians working the corn and potato fields, and on cattle and horses imported from Spain. The whole of Argentina, less prosperous than other neighbouring Spanish colonies, was a subordinate part of the viceroyalty of Peru until 1776. By then Buenos Aires was fast coming into supremacy thanks to a shift in trade eastwards as the silver mines of Peru declined. It was becoming a bustling cosmopolitan city in which Europeans mingled with gauchos and Spanish merchants, traders with freebooters, priests with intellectuals. It was made the capital of the new Spanish viceroyalty of La Plata which incorporated present-day Argentina, Uruguay, Paraguay and southern Bolivia. The port of Buenos Aires was opened to transatlantic trade which increased its wealth immensely. It also increased the smuggling trade with Spain's traditional enemies, Portugal and Britain, and with France. The city boasted teachers of dancing and music and a French-built organ for its cathedral. By 1800 the population had swelled to 45,000. The spirit of independence grew with it, boosted by the imported ideas of European Enlightenment, the example of the French Revolution and the increasing numbers of fiercely self-reliant gauchos known as the 'centaurs of the pampa'. Encouragement came from Britain, Spain's old foe.

In 1790 a plan was put to Prime Minister William Pitt to overthrow the Spanish yoke by force and gain independence using British support. The architect of the plan was Francisco de Miranda, a Venezuelan who had gone to Spain at the age of seventeen to become an army officer. When Spain and France decided to help the American colonists in their war of independence against Britain, Miranda's unit was sent to cooperate with the French. His experiences gradually inspired him with the enthusiastic desire to emancipate his own country. At the close of the American war he resigned his commission and travelled through a Europe aflame with revolutionary thinking. In Russia he became a favourite of Prince Potemkin and the empress, who circulated letters to her ambassadors putting him under imperial protection. She threw in a gratuity of £4,000, presumably for services rendered. Miranda had to flee revolutionary France after a tribunal acquitted him of spying but left him dangerously under suspicion.

In London he produced his plan to free his country. An army of 10,000 troops would be raised in North America while Britain furnished money and ships for the expedition to oust the Spanish authorities. Pitt was keen on the idea. In return for Britain's assistance, the colonists that Miranda represented pledged £30 million, and Florida would be ceded to North America. They wanted a defensive alliance between themselves, Britain and the USA, and a treaty of commerce with Britain; in return they promised the opening up of the Panama isthmus via Lake Nicaragua, and a link between the Bank of England and those of Lima and Mexico, giving Britain command of the precious metals in those regions. But the American President Adams was tardy in agreeing terms and the plan was postponed indefinitely. However, Spain's hold on its South American possessions weakened year after year. Blockades, famine and the falling silver output all contributed to the dissent. In an effort to control the spread of nationalism, Spain eased its veto on

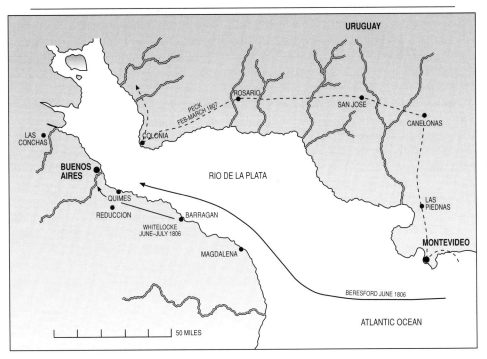

Buenos Aires campaigns, 1806–7.

trade with America and Portugal and even permitted the supply of jerk-beef to British colonies in the Caribbean.

In 1895 war broke out between Britain and Spain, now allied to Napoleon's France. Six years later the Miranda plan was revived, only to be halted by the peace of Amiens. Renewed hostilities in 1804 gave Miranda his best chance yet. Lord Melville and Sir Home Riggs Popham acted as liaison between Miranda and the British Government, but once again he failed to reach an agreement and the operation was again suspended under pressure from the Tsar of Russia, who hoped to win Spain over to the coalition against Napoleon.

Miranda tried once more in the United States, taking with him letters of credit from Mr Pitt and the good wishes of the British Cabinet. At New York in February 1806 he embarked upon the hired warship *Leader* with 200 volunteers, mainly young South American exiles of good reputation. The expedition did not get off to a good start. Another ship supposed to bring reinforcements was seized by American officials under pressure from the Spanish and French ambassadors. The Spanish were ready and waiting for his little force when it arrived off Caracas in a heavy gale. Some 500 soldiers and 700 Indian levies poured a heavy but ineffectual fire on Miranda's troops as they landed at dawn. However, a few determined volleys from the landing parties threw the defenders into panicked retreat. Miranda marched on the town of Coro and took it without bloodshed, but failed to win over the citizenry to his cause. Sympathetic British naval officers promised him support and a ship of the line and two frigates were actually sent to give every assistance to Miranda's 'little army' which by now numbered 500 men. But the expedition then came to a standstill. When rumours reached Miranda of a peace deal between Britain and France he was thrown into despair and returned with his followers to Trinidad. Sadly for him, the rumours were false. The affair may have ended in shambles but it cemented in the minds of senior British officers the possibility of breaking Spain's stranglehold on a rich continent. Foremost among them was Admiral Sir Hope Popham, Miranda's former intermediary.

Popham had been born forty-four years earlier at Tetuan in Morocco where his father was consul. He was his mother's twenty-first child and she died giving him life. As a young naval officer he saw action off Cape St Vincent but it was as an entrepreneur, commercial adventurer and technician that he thrived. He made important friends while serving in Calcutta but his fortunes almost foundered when a trading mission to China was stopped by the British because some of the cargo was believed to be French-owned. Popham lost £40,000 and was only partially recompensed after a lengthy lawsuit which finally cleared him of illegal embargo-breaking. Returning to naval service he soon made important royal connections while attached to the army serving in Flanders under the Duke of York. The duke praised his 'unremitting zeal and active talents' and ensured his protégé's promotion. Popham won friends at court and in the government and Pitt selected him to command the abortive missions in support of Miranda's dreams of an independent South America. Popham met Miranda many times and was fired both by his enthusiasm and by the promise of riches and glory.

During the last years of the eighteenth century Popham revamped Britain's sea defences from Deal to Beachy Head, commanded the naval part of an expedition to destroy the sluices of the Bruge Canal, arranged the embarkation of Russian troops for service against the Dutch, was made a Knight of Malta by a grateful Tsar, and provided efficient naval support for an ill-fated army assault on the Alkmaar Canal. In 1800 he was appointed commander of a small squadron ferrying troops from India and the Cape of Good Hope to Egypt. During that service he was accused of running up 'enormous and profligate' refitting expenses, a charge he was not cleared of until 1805. On his exoneration he was appointed commodore to an expedition against the Dutch in the Cape in cooperation with a land force under Sir David Baird.

Popham's squadron arrived near Robben Island on 4 January 1806 and the troops were fully disembarked by lunchtime on the 7th. The landing was not easy because of a violent swell, and a capsized boat cost the lives of thirty-five Highlanders. Enemy sharpshooters on nearby heights caused only a few casualties. The British force of about 4,000 men, with two howitzers and six light field guns, crossed the Blue Mountain and made contact with the main Dutch body of 5,000 men, most of them cavalry. The Dutch at first held their position with obstinacy but broke and ran from a charge by the Highland Brigade. Dutch losses were put at 700 men killed or wounded while British losses were 'very inconsiderable but consisting chiefly of officers'. The march on Cape Town was hampered by thorn scrub, the burning sun and a lack of water, but on the 10th the Dutch garrison surrendered and Baird took possession of the town. The brief campaign was over. Brigadier-General William Beresford was detached to occupy the countryside and secure the passes. In recognition of a gallant defence the Batavian troops were not treated as prisoners of war but were instead sent back to Holland under oath that they would not take any action against Britain or her allies until they arrived home. The whole of the settlement of the Cape, with all its South African dependencies, was given up to the British.

In April Popham was told by Captain T. Wayne of the American slave-ship *Elizabeth* that the people of Buenos Aires and Montevideo were 'groaning under the tyranny' of their Spanish masters and would welcome a British expedition to free them. Popham, long an advocate of British intervention in the region and still smarting over the failure of successive attempts to support Miranda's aspirations, was all too ready to believe such unsubstantiated reports. He had also just learnt of the setbacks the allies had suffered at the hands of Napoleon's armies, culminating in the battle of Austerlitz. He persuaded himself that the reason for Pitt's failure to embark on a South American adventure – the hope that Spain might switch sides and join the confederacy against France – no longer applied. He also heard that the French Admiral Villaumez was sailing his squadron to the West Indies rather than the Cape and no longer seemed a threat to Britain's new South African possessions. Popham convinced Baird that here was a golden opportunity to counter European setbacks with a glorious, and easy, victory across the Southern Atlantic. With no authorisation whatsoever he proposed a British invasion, launched from the Cape of Good Hope, to liberate the people of La Plata from Spanish rule. He signalled his intentions to the Board of Admiralty who remained happily unaware of his maverick enterprise until long after it was too late.

Popham persuaded Baird to lend him 1,200 men under Beresford and sailed westwards, leaving the newly acquired South African settlement with no naval force for its defence. One verdict on his actions, published a year later in the *Annual Register*, said:

> In every point of view his conduct was unwarrantable. If an officer is to permit himself, either through desire for fame or cupidity, to undertake remote expeditions not within the bound prescribed in his orders, the most able minister may be perpetually counteracted by the mistaken zeal of the persons whom he employs. The best combined system of policy may be frustrated by the mischievous activity of a general or an admiral, who thus presumes to deviate from his line of duty, and arrogates to himself the functions which belong only to the united deliberations of a Cabinet.
>
> It is most completely evident that he was invested with no discretionary powers; but his imagination was so much fired with the ideas of conquest, wealth and rewards, that he resolved to risk every danger to realise the splendid reveries that dazzled his understanding; to overleap every obstacle, and vault into the possession of imaginary consequence. The benefit of his country might unquestionably be amongst the most powerful motives that influenced him in this resolution; yet it is the duty of subordinate characters, when they have no

express latitude of action allowed them, to reflect that their best merit is to perform the services required at their hands. It is also possible that Sir Home thought that success would atone for his deviating from the strict import of his orders. Success may captivate popular applause, and popularity screen an individual from reprehension; but success cannot alter the nature of right and wrong, nor make amends for the destruction of a single link of that chain of combined duty which is so material to the welfare of the state.

★   ★   ★

Popham arrived off Cape Santa Maria on 8 June 1806 on board the 32-gun frigate HMS *Narcissus*. After calling at St Helena for some infantry reinforcements, his fleet arrived in the Rio de la Plata a week later with 1,460 rank and file on board under Beresford's command. The soldiers were mainly from the 1st Battalion, 71st Highland Light Infantry, under 34-year-old Lieutenant-Colonel Dennis Pack. There were also 300 marines, a dragoon squadron and an artillery company with eight field guns. The fleet consisted of the 64-gun frigate *Diadem*, the smaller frigates *Raisonable* and *Diomede*, the brig *Leda* and four transport ships, as well as *Narcissus*.

Major-General William Carr Beresford, the illegitimate son of the Earl of Tyrone and the younger brother of a vice-admiral, was thirty-eight and had one empty eye socket as the result of a shooting accident in Nova Scotia. He saw action against Napoleon in the Mediterranean, won a battlefield promotion after leading the storming party against the tower of Martello in 1794 and was present at the captures of Bastia, Calvi and San Fiorenzo. The following year he took command of the 88th, or Connaught Rangers. He had served alongside Baird and Murray in India and Egypt before the Cape expedition.

Popham and Beresford agreed that their first target should be Buenos Aires itself, the capital of the province, rather than Montevideo. Troops, marines and some seamen were transferred from the line-of-battle ships into the transports and *Narcissus*. Adverse winds and currents, thick fog and the treacherous shoals at the mouth of the great river delayed the landing for eight days. During that time Popham's flagship *Diadem* blockaded the port of Montevideo while the *Raisonable* and the *Diomede* cruised before Maldonado as a diversion.

The main force disembarked near the point of Quilmes on the 25th, watched by around 2,000 Spanish soldiers lining the brow of a hill, who did nothing to oppose them until reinforcements arrived the following morning. Then an ill-directed fire was opened up which did little damage to the invaders. The British marched in cool formation to well within musket range and sent the Spanish into retreat with just one volley. Popham reported: 'We had the satisfaction of seeing from the ships near 4,000 Spanish cavalry flying in every direction, leaving their artillery behind them, while our troops were ascending the hill with that coolness and courage which has on every occasion marked the character of the British soldier.' The Spanish soldiers, mainly poorly trained militia led by confused and incompetent officers, burnt behind them a wooden bridge over the smaller River Chuela and formed up behind hedges and houses on the opposite bank of the river.

Beresford ordered his men to cross over by raft and pillaged boats at dawn the following morning. Again, they met little effective challenge. Beresford reported: 'The opposition was very feeble and the only difficulty was the crossing of the river to get at them.' The British quickly discovered that the Spanish troops had abandoned Buenos Aires. Beresford's entire casualties in the landing and subsequent skirmishes and in the capture of a great South American city totalled one man dead and thirteen wounded, including Captain Le Blanc whose leg was amputated above the knee.

The Viceroy of the Province, Rafael, Marques de Sombremonte, had been among the first to flee, much to the disgust of his subjects. With him went the city's leading merchant, Manuel Belgrano, who later became a military commander and national hero. Brigadier-General Jose Ignacio de la Quintana was left to agree surrender terms. These were rather more generous than was customary at the time, as the British commanders regarded their action as a liberation rather than a conquest. Beresford pledged that all private property would be unmolested by his soldiers, all private citizens protected, local magistrates would continue to raise taxes as usual, the Catholic religion would be honoured, and captured vessels in the harbour should be restored to their owners along with their cargoes (valued at one and a half million Spanish dollars). Official reports described Beresford's conduct as 'exemplary'. The British, however, did seize public property belonging to the Spanish Crown. The huge sum of 1,086,000 dollars was sent back to London on the *Narcissus*. Munitions captured included 45 cannon, 41 mortars and howitzers, 550 whole barrels of powder, 2,064 muskets with bayonets, 616 carbines, 4,019 pistols, 31 musketoons and 1,208 swords. Merchandise snatched consisted mainly of stores of Jesuit bark and quicksilver. Beresford proclaimed that Britain intended to open up free trade with South America and to reduce duties bearing too heavily on traders. In a letter to Lord Castlereagh he said: 'I trust the conduct adopted towards the people here has had its full effect, in impressing upon their minds the honour, generosity and humanity of the British character.'

Popham sent dispatches to London stressing the importance of the colony and the immense profits which it could offer to English corporate traders. Long before his enthusiastic and self-serving narrative reached London the situation had changed dramatically.

Beresford's terms may have been generous but they did not amount to the declaration of freedom that had been expected by at least some of the region's people, most especially the poor, the gauchos and 'people of colour'. Sorely disappointed, they listened eagerly as Pueridon, a municipal member and agitator, secretly preached insurrection. Weapons were stockpiled and hidden in various parts of the city. Meanwhile Santiago de Liniers y Bremond, a Knight of the Order of Malta in the service of Spain, collected men from the countryside around Colonia. Spaniards and gauchos from the outlying districts realised the numerical weakness of the British and began mustering outside Buenos Aires. On 1 August 550 soldiers under Pack, with six field guns, sallied out and defeated an irregular force. The following day Pueridon, having 'thrown off the mask', advanced on Buenos Aires with 1,500 men. They were halted by Beresford's cannon.

Offshore Popham tried unsuccessfully to prevent Liniers' force of 2,500 men crossing the Plata to link up with the 'insurgents' on its right bank. Popham's squadron was buffeted by stormy weather and Liniers made good use of the thick fog to blanket his crossing of the river. He and his men crossed unobserved by the British warships. Torrential rain fell for three days making the roads impassable for the British foot soldiers and cannon but not for the local cavalry and gauchos.

Liniers marched through the cold driving rain to the outskirts of Buenos Aires, installed siege artillery and threw a cavalry screen around the city. In a tough two-hour fight on 5 August the British were pushed back from their outside encampments, suffering 157 casualties compared with 205 on the Spanish side. The British troops found themselves besieged within the city they had captured so easily just weeks before.

On 12 August the enemy's forward posts began a smart fire which was returned by British cannon placed in the main avenues radiating from the central square. The firefight prompted large numbers of city dwellers armed with muskets to crowd the flat roofs of surrounding houses, which were protected by parapets. They opened up a murderous fire on the British troops and gunners below. Those without firearms poured down torrents of scalding water and boiling fat, and hurled stones and bricks at soldiers huddled in doorways or sheltering under what little protection they could find in the blood-spattered streets and alleys. A dispatch recounted: 'Reinforcements crowded the tops of all the houses commanding the Great Square, and our troops were considerably annoyed by people they could not get at.'

Heavily outnumbered, and having lost nearly 180 men in the desperate action, Beresford decided to capitulate. He and his small army were taken prisoner. At first, Beresford and his officers were interned near the city but later they were dispersed to remote provinces for greater security. Many of the ordinary troops were disarmed and, under oath not to flee or to cause trouble, were given the freedom of the city. Many lodged with local families favourably disposed towards Britain.

Popham and his ships were powerless to help except by mounting a blockade. A small reinforcement arrived from the Cape in October under Lieutenant-Colonel Backhouse who, together with Popham, tried to take Montevideo by assault. They found the waters too shallow to allow the ships close enough to the town for an effective cannonade and the plan was abandoned.

More successful was an attack on 29 October when 400 men under Lieutenant-Colonel Vassal assaulted the coastal village of Maldonado. Backhouse reported: 'To the cool intrepidity of our little column much praise is due, as it advanced with the utmost steadiness and alacrity, and without firing a shot, until sufficiently near to make a certainty of carrying both the guns and the town, which was principally done by the bayonet, notwithstanding the advance was made under heavy discharges of grape and musketry.' The 240 defenders, both regulars and militia, fled leaving behind 50 dead and wounded and two field guns. At a cost of two dead and four wounded Backhouse's force then overwhelmed a 12-gun battery at Punta del Este while Popham seized without bloodshed the fortified island of Gorriti with its 20-gun battery. The British at least now had a convenient winter station for the troops and ships, but Popham was faced with the problem of feeding both his own men and the Spanish prisoners taken from captured vessels. Rather than simply putting them ashore, where they might join the Spanish forces, he stranded 200 of them on the small uninhabited island of Lobos in the mouth of the Plata. In what was later described at home as an act of 'inhumanity scarcely credible' he left them without shelter, water or food. Forty of the castaways managed to swim ashore with the help of inflated sealskins and a Spanish vessel was sent to rescue those left behind.

Popham's callous action aroused fury in the province and two British officers being held as prisoners were murdered. Beresford protested to Colonel Liniers, who had assumed chief command of La Plata, and the Frenchman agreed to guarantee the security of all British prisoners of war. In his correspondence Liniers stressed the respect that he and the people of the province had for Beresford, and also the disgust with which Popham was regarded.

★   ★   ★

Back in London, because news took long months to cross the Atlantic, everyone was blissfully unaware of the disaster which had overtaken Popham's dangerous enterprise. *The Times* of 15 September proudly reported the capture of Buenos Aires:

> The circumstances which attended this success are in the highest degree honourable to the British name, and to the character of our brave army . . . By our success in La Plata, where a small British detachment has taken one of the greatest and richest of the Spanish colonies, Buonaparte must be convinced that nothing but a speedy peace can prevent the whole of Spanish America from being wrested from this influence, and placed forever under the protection of the British Empire.

When *Narcissus* arrived at Portsmouth a few days later and disgorged six wagon-loads of booty, the newspaper reported: 'The procession was followed by vast numbers of seafaring persons in this port; the population of the town turned out to witness it, rending the air with their patriotic acclamations in honour of the bravery of their countrymen and of the triumph and treasure they have gained from the foe.'

Popham's dispatch stressing the value of his prize sparked a frenzy among the mercantile community, speculators and adventurers. Ships were quickly fitted out for the four-month journey and loaded with cargoes expected to appeal to the South Americans. The *Annual Register* reported: 'Enthusiasm revelled in imaginary wealth. The fortunate individual who could command a vessel, and the no less happy trader who was admitted as a sharer in joint concerns, equally expected to see their warehouses filled with the produce of Spanish opulence, or crowded with the ingots of Potosi and Peru.' The speculators did not trouble to consider that most British manufactured goods, with which they were filling their ships, had long been available to the South Americans, either through official Spanish merchants or through the extensive contraband trade. The British Government did not deter the commercial armada and the Treasury relished the prospect of fixed duties of 12½ per cent on exports sold.

Government ministers were initially furious at hearing of Popham's unauthorised expedition, and regarded his actions as contemptuous of their authority. But he had, they still believed, delivered them an unexpected victory. They decided to send out reinforcements to support Beresford and hold the province. On 9 October an advance force of 4,800 men under General Sir Samuel Auchmuty set sail while preparations were made for a bigger expedition to follow.

Auchmuty was a fifty-year-old warhorse, the son of a New York lawyer. Barely out of his teens, he had fought with the loyalists at the battles of Brooklyn and Whiteplains, for which he was given a lieutenancy without purchase. In England he found it impossible to live on his pay and exchanged into the 52nd Regiment then under orders for India. He saw much action, serving in the war against Hyder Ali, the 1790 and 1791 campaigns against Tippoo Sultan and at the siege of Seringapatam. Having left England a penniless lieutenant, he returned fourteen years later a lieutenant-colonel with powerful patrons. After being sent to Egypt to help subdue the French there, he and Baird became popular heroes following their heroic, if over-romanticised, march across the desert and passage down the Nile. He was knighted, made a general and for three years commanded the garrisons on the Isle of Thanet.

Auchmuty's force, comprising men of the 40th Regiment of Foot and the 95th Rifles, embarked in ships commanded by Rear-Admiral Charles Stirling. Delayed by leaky transport vessels, they were forced to put into Rio de Janeiro for water; there they learnt of the recapture of Buenos Aires and the imprisonment of Beresford and his army. Undeterred, the fleet arrived in the Rio Plata in early January and found Popham's garrison in Maldonado close to starving and without artillery or supplies: some 400 enemy horsemen blocked all their attempts to forage. Auchmuty decided to abandon Maldonado, judging it indefensible, but left a small garrison on Gorriti. Stirling meanwhile superseded Popham and ordered him home to England to face a court martial.

Auchmuty determined to attack Montevideo and on 13 January landed in a small bay 9 miles from the town. Although the enemy were present in large numbers on the heights they did not contest the landing and the British were able to form a bridgehead a mile deep. After a few days they moved out under a heavy fire of round and grapeshot and established advance parties in the town's suburbs which were hastily evacuated by the Spaniards.

Inside the city were 10,000 inhabitants and 3,500 troops under Governor Pascual Ruiz Huidobro. Outside another 2,500 riders mustered under Sombremonte. Around 1,300 Spanish soldiers and levies, supported by cavalry and two field guns, attacked the British vanguard in two columns. They were defeated with heavy losses after a spirited fight and a devastating flanking manoeuvre led by Lieutenant-Colonel Brownrigg. Auchmuty reported that one British charge 'was as gallantly received and great numbers fell on both sides'. The general had a horse shot from under him in the action but the Spanish retreated within the city ramparts with

Major-General William Carr Beresford. (National Army Museum)

100 casualties. Many of the area's armed inhabitants, serving as cavalry, now dispersed, allowing the British forces to encircle the town walls.

Huidobro sent out 2,300 troops to attack again, supported by 1,700 riders under Sombremonte. Their aim was to cut off Auchmuty's force from the sea. On 20 January the Spanish infantry collided with the British left flank at Cristo del Cordon. Auchmuty deployed his light brigade and the 95th Rifles in cornfields along the line of march, catching the Spanish in a lethal cross-fire. The Spanish fled after suffering heavy losses: 200 dead, 400 wounded and 200 captured; the British casualties totalled 149. Sombremonte's cavalry watched the slaughter from a safe distance but did nothing.

The British did not have enough trenching tools to make a direct approach and after several days of bombarding the town with cannon on shore batteries and from ships offshore their supplies of powder ran low. The town's southern rampart was breached, however, and Auchmuty ordered an assault at 3 a.m. the following day, 3 February. Before dawn his troops came under destructive cannon and musket fire before discovering that during the night the defenders had barricaded the 11-ft breach with cow-hides. In the darkness the head of the column missed the gap and blundered around under constant fire for fifteen minutes. Eventually the disguised breach was spotted by Captain Renny of the 40th Light Infantry, who was shot dead trying to scale it. His men rushed to the breach and forced their way into the town. At the top of the main streets the enemy had positioned cannon which for a short time did great execution. But the British troops streamed in from all directions, some clambering over the town walls rather than searching for the breach, cleared a passage with their bayonets and overturned the guns. By daylight the British had possession of all key points except the main citadel where the defenders made a show of resistance until the sun's rays revealed their hopeless position, and they surrendered. Auchmuty noted in dispatches:

> The gallantry displayed by the troops during the assault, and their forbearance and orderly behaviour in the town, speak so fully in their praise that it is unnecessary for me to say how highly I am pleased with their conduct. The service they have been engaged in since we landed has been uncommonly severe and laborious, but not a murmur has escaped them; everything I wished has been effected with order and cheerfulness.

The victory was costly. During the brief but savage action Auchmuty lost 134 rank and file, several sergeants and drummers, and eight officers killed. Lieutenant-Colonels Vassal and Brownrigg, who had displayed great courage on several occasions, died of their wounds. A further 335 men, 20 sergeants, 6 drummers and 28 officers were wounded. Auchmuty had effectively lost one-eighth of his army. According to British accounts, the Spanish lost around 800 dead, 500 wounded and 2,000 taken prisoner. Another 1,500 escaped in boats or hid themselves in the cellars and attics of the town. Stirling seized 57 ships in the harbour plus 15 sloop-rigged gunboats and 6 row-boats armed with guns. Despite such booty an observer noted: 'The vigour and resolution with which Montevideo was defended proved the error of the persuasion that any port belonging to the Spanish in South America would be an easy target.'

The stout Spanish resistance had not included the Marques of Sombremonte who, having fled Buenos Aires when Beresford approached, similarly deserted Montevideo before Auchmuty attacked. He remained in the area, however, and Auchmuty wrote to him demanding that the British prisoners in the capital be released. After some confusion it was finally reported back that the Marques was himself barred from the city he had deserted and had no authority to make any bargains. Liniers, who now commanded Buenos Aires, sent out a detachment which arrested Sombremonte and took him prisoner.

Auchmuty dispatched Pack to take Colonia, which he did without opposition. A surprise but half-hearted assault on his garrison a few weeks later by 1,500 men was repelled with single-figure casualties on both sides.

Meanwhile, hearing of the fall of Montevideo, Liniers sent General Beresford under guard 300 leagues inland. Beresford, aided by two Spanish officers of noble birth who wanted to negotiate with the British, escaped with difficulty and, after hiding for three days, reached a British vessel. He, like Popham before him, was sent home.

Auchmuty, through correspondence with the capital, considered that there were two parties in Buenos Aires:

> The party in power were mostly natives of Spain, in the principal offices of church and state, and devoted to the Spanish Government. It had been their policy to inflame the minds of the lower orders against the English, by every species of exaggeration and falsehood, and to lead them to such acts of cruelty as might preclude the possibility of any communication with them . . . The second party consisted of natives of the country, with some Spaniards who were settled in it. The oppression of the parent state had made them most anxious to shake off the yoke of the mother country; and though from their ignorance, their want of morals, and the barbarity of their disposition, they were totally unfitted to govern themselves, they aimed at following the steps of the North Americans and erecting an independent republic.

Auchmuty believed, however, that he would need 15,000 men to retake even such a divided city. His own force was depleted by battle and disease, his supplies were running low, and the countryside was hostile to his foraging parties. He sensibly decided to keep his army in Montevideo and await reinforcements.

*   *   *

Before Auchmuty's dispatches reached London the British Cabinet had agreed another expedition to capitalise on Popham's supposed success. Consequently, four thousand men, including two companies of artillery, under 43-year-old Brigadier-General Robert Crauford, embarked in a fleet under Admiral George Murray. Their

General Sir Samuel Auchmuty.
(National Army Museum)

orders were to gain a British foothold on the Pacific coast of South America in Chile. They were to limit their operation to securing the peace and goodwill of the local inhabitants, improving the lot of Negroes, halting the importation of slaves and establishing a line of posts across the Andes to enable communications with Buenos Aires. As soon as Auchmuty's news of Beresford's surrender reached London the sloop *Fly* was sent to overtake Murray with orders for the fleet to wait at anchor off the Cape of Good Hope. A further force of 1,630 men, including a company of horse artillery, was sent to join them.

General John Whitelocke was appointed overall commander with the mission to recapture Buenos Aires, free the British prisoners and send into exile those officials responsible for the city's 'insurrection'. Whitelocke arrived at Montevideo on 10 May with an army composed mainly of the 88th Regiment and the Light Brigade, with 350 horses and 16 field guns. He immediately took command from the battle-scarred Auchmuty whose successes in such difficult circumstances were hard to follow. Whitelocke could not match them.

Now aged fifty, Whitelocke had obtained his first commission through well-connected friends of his family. His brother-in-law, Matthew Lewis, was deputy secretary of war while Whitelocke advanced his military and diplomatic career in Jamaica. In 1793 he suppressed San Domingo but saw many of his men die of yellow fever. Major Sir Brent Spencer described him as an officer 'who carries with him such universal approbation and so well earned applause'. He was made colonel of the 6th West India Regiment in 1795, Brigadier-General in Guernsey in 1798 and Lieutenant-Governor of Portsmouth in 1805. He had not seen any action in the main theatres of war. He began to make preparations for an attack on Buenos Aires. Sloops of war and other light vessels were sent to reconnoitre the southern bank of the river Plata. They discovered that the water was too shallow to allow a landing under cover of warships anywhere to the west of the city. The closest place to the east was the bay of Barragon, almost 30 miles from the capital.

Crauford now arrived with his diverted expedition, bringing Whitelocke's total force to 9,400 men. Meanwhile, on 7 June, Pack and fewer than 1,000 men marched quietly out of Colonia to surprise Colonel Elio's encampment at San Pedro. After a four-hour march they confronted 2,000 forewarned Spanish in battle array with sixteen guns deployed. But Pack and his men drove through the line without pause and scattered Elio's army; they lost 5 dead and 40 wounded. Spanish losses were much greater: 120 dead, hundreds wounded and 105 taken prisoner, while 8 cannon and 250 muskets were also captured.

Whitelocke, aware that heavy rains made July and August the most unfavourable months for campaigning, decided to press on without delay rather than wait for more reinforcements. Leaving a garrison of 1,300 men at Montevideo he sent his forces up-river in small divisions because navigation was notoriously intricate. The troops suffered many delays because of foul winds but the landing at Barragon on 28 June was unopposed.

His army in the field now consisted of 7,822 rank and file, including 150 mounted dragoons. It was supported by eighteen artillery pieces with ammunition conveyed by 206 horses and mules. In the ships was the reserve artillery of heavy pieces, mortars and howitzers, together with entrenching tools for 1,000 men, six pontoons with their carriages, and provisions for two months. Great difficulty was encountered in getting the guns and supplies across a morass which ran parallel to the shore and it was a very fatigued army that reached the Chuelo. On the river's left bank the enemy had constructed batteries and a formidable line of defence. Whitelocke decided to split his men into two columns which would by-pass the Spanish defences, cross the river higher up, and reunite in the suburbs of Buenos Aires.

General Crauford, with the light infantry and the 95th Regiment, made contact at the Corral de Miserie ranch with Spanish forces under Liniers strongly positioned behind hedges and embankments. A bayonet charge dislodged the enemy in five minutes and Liniers fled to the city leaving behind 60 dead, 70 prisoners, 9 guns and a howitzer. It now became clear that Whitelocke had blundered by splitting his force. If the main body had been present the city could have been taken that evening, according to some witnesses. Instead Crauford's force made camp to await the rest of the army, giving Liniers precious time to organise resistance in the city's barricaded streets.

On 3 July an ultimatum was sent to Liniers: all British citizens detained should be given up and 'all persons holding civil offices dependent on the government of Buenos Aires' and all military officers should become prisoners of war. All arms, ammunition and public property should be surrendered but protection would be given to religious and private possessions. Not surprisingly, Liniers rejected the demands.

Whitelocke and his main force, further delayed by an incompetent guide, did not arrive until that afternoon. He quickly formed his line. Auchmuty's brigade was on the left, extending towards the convent of the Reciketas 2 miles away, with the 36th and 88th Regiments on their right, Crauford's brigade in the centre, and the dragoons and the 45th Regiment on the right of the whole, towards the Residencia. The rains had already begun, making any further delays unwise. Whitelocke decided against a general bombardment, partly because of the difficulty in getting his artillery into place in the sodden conditions, and partly to avoid unnecessary civilian loss of life which would set the entire populace against him. At 6.30 a.m. on

The storming of Montevideo. (National Army Museum)

5 July Whitelocke sent eight battalions, totalling 5,800 men, into the city streets in thirteen columns.

The town and suburbs of Buenos Aires, with a Spanish garrison of 7,000 and a civilian population of 42,000, was divided into sections which formed enclosed squares of about 140 yards on each side. The houses had flat roofs, making each square a potential death-trap. Auchmuty's objective was the Plaza de Toros. Other columns were to fight their way through the barricades in the main streets and take the Residencia. Two corporals, equipped with tools for breaking down the doors of the houses, were placed at the head of each column. All the troops were ordered to rush on with unloaded muskets, and no firing was permitted until they had reached their appointed targets. A cannon shot down the central avenue was the signal for the army to advance.

Whitelocke had previously remarked on the defensive suitability of Spanish towns, with their flat roofs and narrow alleys, which were ideal for ambush – but he appears to have ignored his own advice with his plan of attack. The *Annual Register* noted: 'The indecision of General Whitelocke upon several occasions, in the march from the heights of Barragon, had been remarkable; but it is singular, notwithstanding his apprehensions regarding the weather, that he should have adopted a plan which seemed to militate against all his own ideas on the subject of the attack.'

Inevitably the British troops quickly found themselves exposed to fire of the most destructive kind. An official report noted:

The streets were intersected by deep ditches, behind which were planted cannon that poured showers of grape-shot on the advancing forces. Independently of the enemy's troops, a great proportion of whom acted on the roofs of the houses, all the inhabitants, with their negroes, defended their dwellings which were, in fact, so many fortresses, the doors of them being so strongly barricaded that it was almost impossible to force them. Discharges of musketry, hand grenades, bricks and stones saluted the British soldiers, who were also torn to pieces by grape-shot at the corners of streets.

Auchmuty's column took the strong-points of the Retiro and the Plaza de Toros, along with 32 cannon and 600 prisoners after a vigorous fight which saw heavy casualties on both sides. The 5th Regiment met comparatively little opposition and captured the convent and church of Santa Catalina. The 36th and 88th Regiments, commanded by Brigadier-General Lumley, reached their targets after beating back stiff resistance. But the 88th, being closest to the Spanish fort, suffered so many casualties that they were overpowered and captured. This disaster exposed the flank of the 36th and that regiment, together with the 5th, retired to Auchmuty's post at the Plaza de Toros. During the retreat the grenadier company distinguished themselves by attacking 500 of the enemy and spiking two of their guns. The two British six-pounders deployed down the central streets met with superior fire and four troops of carabineers supporting them failed to capture the Spanish battery despite several charges.

The left division of Brigadier-General Crauford's brigade, under the gallant Pack, fought through almost to the river and then turned to seize the Jesuit college. But that stout building proved impregnable and, after suffering heavy losses, one part of the brigade took refuge in a house; this proved untenable and they were forced to surrender. The other part retired on the right division commanded by Crauford himself. His men had reached the river and turned towards the great central square and fort 400 yards away. Learning of the fate of his flank Crauford took refuge in the convent of San Domingo. There he and his men mounted a 'most gallant resistance against superior numbers'. The enemy surrounded the convent on all sides and attempted to seize a British three-pounder in the street outside. Part of a company of light infantry under Major Trotter – described as an officer of great merit – charged out. Most, including Trotter, were killed 'in an instant'. The official dispatch noted: 'The brigadier-general was now obliged to confine himself to the defence of the convent, from which the riflemen kept up a well directed fire upon such of the enemy as approached the post; but the quantity of round shot, grape and musketry to which they were exposed at last obliged them to quit the top of the building.' The enemy brought up cannon to force the wooden gates of the convent and Crauford, cut off and persuaded by the absence of gunfire close by that the other columns had also failed, capitulated at 4 p.m. The 45th Regiment, the furthest from the enemy centre, took and held the Residencia without too many problems. The shooting dwindled as night approached. The day had cost the British 311 killed, 679 wounded, 208 missing and 1,600 taken prisoner.

Throughout the day's fighting Whitelocke had waited with the 1,000-strong reserve in the suburbs at the Corral de Miserie ranch. After remaining passive all day he returned to his headquarters to dine and sleep. He did not realise the scale of the disaster until he received a dispatch from Auchmuty the following morning. He joined his battle-weary subordinate at the Plaza de Toros which the British still held along with the Residencia and much of the city centre.

Liniers proposed a mutual exchange of all prisoners, including Beresford's defeated army, provided that the British agreed to evacuate the Rio Plata and Montevideo within two months. He hinted that, given the mood of the civilian population, he could not guarantee the safety of the prisoners if hostilities did not cease. Whitelocke could have ignored the offer. His forces commanded a sizeable part of the city and he still had 5,400 effective fighting men. Captain Fraser of the artillery pledged to have thirty cannon aimed at the city by the following morning. But Whitelocke agreed to Liniers' terms, much to the disgust of many of his men. The British left the city in the circumstances described by Lieutenant-Colonel Holland.

Alongside Spanish and Creole graffiti celebrating victory, British soldiers scrawled obscene messages directed at Whitelocke. A favourite toast among officers became 'Success to grey hairs but bad luck to white locks.'

In his dispatch to London Whitelocke robustly defended his decision. He claimed that the whole male population of Buenos Aires was actively employed in its defence. He played up the danger to the British prisoners taken in the two battles for the city and added: 'Influenced by these considerations and reflecting on how little advantage would be the possession of a country, the inhabitants of which were so absolutely hostile, I resolved to forgo the advantage which the bravery of the troops had obtained, and acceded to the annexed treaty.' He was supported by Rear-Admiral George Murray who reported back that the treaty had achieved the prime objective of releasing British captives. He added that Whitelocke 'saw no prospect whatever of establishing ourselves in this country as there was not a friend to the English in it'.

On 24 July General Ackland, with more than 1,800 troops, arrived at Montevideo but in the light of the British débâcle and the demeaning treaty signed by Whitelocke they moved on to India a week later, along with the 47th and 87th Regiments. On 9 September Whitelocke left Montevideo for the last time, arriving in England with his dispirited men on 7 November. It was not a glorious home-coming.

*   *   *

The shameful news had preceded Whitelocke. *The Times*, which a year earlier had so joyfully reported the capture of Buenos Aires, said that the disaster was 'perhaps the greatest which has been felt by this country since the commencement of the revolutionary war [with France and her allies]'. A thorough official investigation was promised into the 'apparent mismanagement' of the commanders. Whitelocke was lampooned in cartoons while Popham's claim for a share of the spoils taken early in the first campaign was ridiculed.

On 28 January 1808 Whitelocke faced an array of charges at a general court martial at Chelsea. He was accused of measures ill-calculated to effect the conquest of Buenos Aires, of enraging the population by declaring that civilian officials would be taken prisoner, of splitting his force at a crucial time, of sending his troops into heavily defended streets without proper support, of failing to show leadership by holding himself back in reserve, and of shamefully surrendering his army's position by agreeing to Liniers' terms. Such conduct was 'tending to the dishonour of his majesty's arms, and being contrary to his duty as an officer, prejudicial to good order and military discipline, and contrary to the articles of war'.

There was much to say in Whitelocke's defence. His expedition had been conceived by others under the profoundly wrong assumption that much of the local population would be friendly. He faced huge problems from the swampy terrain and the onset of the rainy season. And it was argued that if Crauford had fallen back on the Residencia, as Pack had advised, Buenos Aires might have surrendered the following day. But such a defence could not disguise Whitelocke's incompetence throughout the campaign. He too easily listened to conflicting advice. He was prone to dithering, but always determined when it came to asserting his own authority. And his behaviour in wining, dining and sleeping without bothering to discover what had happened to his men was indefensible.

After a seven-week trial the court of nineteen officers, all of them lieutenant-generals, found him guilty on all counts save for the part of one charge which related to his order that the columns should not begin firing until they reached their allotted targets. The court agreed that precautions had been needed to prevent the unnecessary discharge of weapons. But that did not take the sting out of the overall verdict. The court decreed that Whitelocke be cashiered 'and declared totally unfit and unworthy to serve his majesty in any military capacity whatever'. The king confirmed the sentence and ordered that it be read at the head of every regiment and inserted in every orderly book 'with a view of its becoming a lasting memorial to the fatal consequences, to which officers expose themselves, who, in discharge of the important duties confided in them, are deficient in that zeal, judgement and personal exertion which their sovereign and their country have a right to expect from officers entrusted with high commands'.

Whitelocke spent the rest of his life in retirement and died in 1833 at Hall Barn Park, Buckinghamshire, the seat of his son-in-law. He is buried in the west aisle of Bristol Cathedral.

Popham, the architect of the original ill-judged adventure, escaped similar ignominy. The previous year he had been arrested on his return to England and suffered a three-day court martial on board *Gladiator* in Portsmouth Harbour. He was charged with withdrawing his squadron from the Cape of Good Hope without orders to pursue his maverick plan, leaving that newly won colony in great danger from French attack. He argued forcefully that Cape Town was not threatened and that it was his duty to seize any opportunity to distress the enemy, as he had tried to do in South America. He claimed that his command was, by its nature,

General John Whitelocke, the subject of savage caricature. (National Army Museum)

discretionary. He pointed out that Admiral Rooke had no direct orders when he took Gibraltar. Neither did Lord St Vincent when he attacked Tenerife. And neither did the illustrious Lord Nelson when he pursued the French fleet to the West Indies and back. Popham also claimed that his assault on Buenos Aires had been approved in private interviews with the late Mr Pitt. The court found him guilty of highly censurable conduct and issued a severe reprimand but decided against any further action.

The City of London regarded Popham's adventure as a gallant attempt to open up new trade markets to enrich its coffers, and presented him with a sword of honour. Even in the Royal Navy the reprimand did little to impede the wily admiral's career. The following year, to the horror of many senior officers, he was appointed captain of the fleet in the expedition against Copenhagen and helped to settle the terms by which all Danish men-of-war were surrendered. In 1812 he had command of a small squadron on the north coast of Spain, co-operating with the guerrillas ashore. In 1814 he was made rear-admiral and from 1817 was commander-in-chief of the Jamaica station. His health broke and he died at Cheltenham shortly after returning to England in 1820. In naval circles he is best remembered as the adaptor of a code of signals used for many years. Popham was a greedy, unscrupulous adventurer. He was also a superb navigator, a cautious surveyor and a commander who preferred to use guile than to risk unnecessary bloodshed. According to some naval experts, the best-selling novelist C.S. Forester used Popham, at least in part, as the inspiration for his fictional sea-dog Horatio Hornblower. In 1999 the historian John Grainger, after researching the *Naval Chronicle*, wrote: 'The parallels between their careers are clear, becoming in the end almost identical.'

Beresford was also untarnished by the South American shambles, and enjoyed a long and distinguished military and political career. After being wounded in Portugal, he reorganised the Portuguese army and was knighted for his services at the battle of Busaco. He showed poor leadership at the battle of Albuera, however, and was best regarded as an organiser. He commanded with greater distinction during the invasion of France. Back home he enjoyed rich rewards, sitting in the House of Lords. He was governor of Jersey from 1820 until his death, aged eighty-five, in 1854. Wellington said that he would have once recommended Beresford to succeed him in command of the entire British Army, not because he was a great general, which he was not, but because he alone could feed an army.

Auchmuty, whose abilities in South America had put Whitelocke to shame, became commander-in-chief at Madras. In 1811 he captured Java despite stubborn resistance from the Dutch defenders. For the second time he received the thanks of Parliament, and he was made a Knight of the Bath and colonel of the 78th Regiment. In 1821 he was appointed commander-in-chief in Ireland but did not enjoy that high command for long. The following year he was killed when he fell from his horse in Phoenix Park and he was buried in Christchurch Cathedral. The *Dictionary of National Biography* noted: 'His great merit is shown by the high rank which he, the son of a loyal and therefore ruined American colonist, without money or political influence, had managed to attain.'

The sense of dishonour felt in Britain was profound, not least among those merchants who had been told about a profitable new market, only to see it closed to them. A third British expedition under the Duke of Wellington was proposed to salvage some national pride but had to be abandoned when developments on the Iberian peninsula demanded that he stay in Europe.

The main impact of the two failed British invasions was to weaken Spain's authority in the province of La Plata and breed a new, proud spirit of independence among the Argentine people. It was they, not Spain, who had defeated the British and united the previously squabbling factions. The regular Spanish army had been defeated by Beresford. Sombremonte and Belgrano, the leading citizen, had both fled Buenos Aires at the first whiff of danger, leaving the people to look after themselves. That the people had successfully united to capture, repel or otherwise defeat the invaders was a matter of great and lasting pride. A poem written to celebrate the British defeat gave wide currency to the name Argentina.

To the local populace the real heroes were Liniers, who had created an 8,000-strong militia, and Martin de Alzaga, a Basque from a poor family, who had been one of the leaders of the uprising against the British. Liniers became interim viceroy and, to help bankroll his militia of largely common folk, opened up trade with the British merchants who had followed Whitelocke and whose ships were still waiting with their cargoes off Montevideo.

The position changed in 1808 when Napoleon installed his brother on the throne of Spain and the Spanish patriotic *junta* opposed him, aided by the British. Old enemies became allies and *vice versa*. Liniers came under suspicion because of his French background and Alzaga attempted a *coup d'état* on 1 January 1809. Among the militia his rebellion was supported only by Spanish units but these were quickly disarmed by the large native section made up of Argentine-born artisans, farmers, gauchos, creoles and blacks. Spanish rule nevertheless continued, in name at least, until 1810 when the *cabildo*, or city forum, in Buenos Aires set up an autonomous government to administer the region until the restoration of King Ferdinand VII. In the event, Ferdinand proved to be a terrible monarch and an assembly on 9 July 1816 declared an independent nation, the United Provinces of Rio de la Plata.

Years of hard fighting continued, with Spanish armies threatening the borders, and one by one the outlying regions of Paraguay, Bolivia and Uruguay were lost. But the regions which had successfully beaten off the British, despite the weakness of their Spanish masters, became the core of modern Argentina. Thus an adventure conceived by a pompous British admiral indirectly gave birth to a nation.

★   ★   ★

CHAPTER TWO

The First Burma War, 1824–6

'The invading army of rebellious strangers.'

The conflict which first robbed Burma of large chunks of its territory has been called the worst managed war in British military history, but that judgement may be too harsh when compared, for example, with the later horrors of the Crimea. For the British statesmen, generals and administrators it was an almost total victory which greatly extended the empire. But for the men who fought an exotic and underrated foe, it was a nightmare of malarial swamp, dense jungle, blistering heat, hunger and thirst. For too many of them a sweat-drenched and sordid hospital cot was their place of dying, rather then the field of battle.

★   ★   ★

Ptolemy mentioned Burma in the second century AD, but the country and its people remained largely unknown to the outside world for a millennium. Civilisation came from India, although the Burmese shunned many aspects of Indian culture, most notably the caste system. The kingdom of Pagan, which included what became Lower Burma, was overrun by the Mongol hordes and then for several centuries remained divided into states under Shan princes. The sixteenth century saw the rise of the Toungoo dynasty which until 1752 was occupied largely with internal conflict, beating off encroachments by China, and with unsuccessful attempts to invade Siam. The kingdom of Ava was also conquered and its chief city on the Irrawaddy became the seat of power.

The first European known to have visited Burma was the Venetian merchant Cesar Fredericke in 1455, but the country's physical position adjoining Bengal and Assam made contact with Britain inevitable. In 1586 the English prospector Ralph Fitch sailed up the Irrawaddy River, which bisects Burma longitudinally. In his memoirs he described great gilded pagodas, royal white elephants fed from silver dishes, and Buddhist monks in yellow robes. The women were 'white, round-faced with little eyes'. The missionary Father Sangermano also reported the celestial white elephants which were an important part of Burmese court and ceremonial life. When such a beast was caught in the forest of Pegu, he said, it was bound with scarlet cords and waited on by the highest mandarins. A silken net was draped over it as protection from mosquitoes and, once aboard the specially constructed boat designed to ferry it to the royal palace, gold-embroidered silk protected it from the sun.

The East India Company made contact in 1617 and both it and its Dutch counterpart opened depots. Trade was initially not good, as the westerners failed to fully comprehend Burma's natural riches. They used their footholds largely to repair and build teak ships. Visitors were nevertheless entranced by the lush tropical forests, the exotic buildings, the tinkle of the temple bells, the smells of spice and strange fruit, and, above all, by the colours. Much later Rudyard Kipling wrote of 'lilac, pink, vermilion, lapis lazuli, and blistering blood-red under fierce sunlight that mellows and modifies all'. The American traveller Frank Vincent described the Burmese as 'a simple-minded, indolent people, frank and courteous, fond of amusement and gay-coloured apparel, friendly amongst themselves and hospitable to strangers. They appreciate a quiet life, smoking, and gossiping, and sleeping throughout the day, and listening to wild music and singing throughout half the night. Stern ambition is among them, indeed, a very rare trait of character.' He remarked on the red and yellow fabrics worn by both sexes, loosely wrapped so that one of a woman's legs was always immodestly exposed; on the tattoos sported by the men from hips to knees; and on the enormous cigars wrapped in green leaves incessantly smoked by men, women and children. 'Burmese boys take to smoking even earlier than do the youth of this country,' he wrote. 'I have frequently seen babes at the mother's breasts alternating the nourishment of Nature's Nile with pulls and puffs at their cheroots.' Legend suggested that the bare legs of the women and the tattoos of the men was a ruse dreamt up by an ancient queen disgusted by male infidelity so that 'by disfiguring the men and setting off the beauty of the women, the latter may regain the affections of their husbands'. Vincent added: 'Burmese laws on the whole seem wise, and evidently are calculated to advance the interests of justice and morality; but they very often prove futile, owing to the tyranny and rapacity of the king and the venality of many of his officers.'

The kings of Ava were generally despotic tyrants and each succession was marked by the massacre of hundreds or thousands of potential rivals, their families and followers. Western powers, including Britain, wrongly assumed that the Burmese people would welcome the overthrow of such rulers, but they did not appreciate the populace's devout belief in kingly divinity. The Burmese rulers, in turn, misunderstood western attitudes. One snorted in disgust, 'These hat-wearing people cannot bear to see or hear of women being beaten or maltreated.'

In 1755 the Peguan rulers of Burma were overthrown by a chieftain of military genius who assumed the royal title *Alaungpaya*, or 'Embryo Buddha'. He suspected the British of aiding the Peguans and promptly burnt the Company trading post at Negrai. He slaughtered thousands of Burmese whose loyalty he distrusted and deported thousands more. His invasion of Thailand was ended when he died of an accidental wound during the siege of a city.

His successor, King Bodawpaya, continued his policy of aggressive military expansion. Thailand was again invaded, the kingdom of Mon was savagely destroyed and rebellions bloodily suppressed. Territorial conquests, however, were largely lost as armies had to be pulled back to beat off Chinese attacks in the north. The constant blood-letting led to a regular trickle of refugees to neighbouring states, but the trickle became a flood after the conquest of the coast region of Arracan. Many refugees headed for British-held Chittagong, and used it as a base for counter-invasion sorties. Burma now had a common frontier with British India and border incidents were inevitable. Dispatches to London referred to the 'violent and

A Buddhist monastery, engraving by James Thomson.

haughty character' of the Burmese people. Anglo-Burmese relations were further soured in 1795 when a small Burmese force entered Chittagong in pursuit of robbers. The friction sparked flames in 1820 when the Burmese generalissimo Maha Bandula conquered Assam and neighbouring Manipur, sending even more refugees fleeing into Bengal.

Britain strongly suspected that Bandula planned to strike at Calcutta, and their fears were strengthened when the Burmese seized the island of Shapuri. A small guard of sepoys was driven off with the loss of several lives. In 1824 Lord Amherst, Governor-General of the East India Company, sent a note to the new Burmese king, Bagyidaw, with a stern reprimand, and demanded the removal of his forces from the island. In fact, this had already occurred and it was reoccupied by British naval soldiers, but they found the island so unhealthy that they withdrew shortly afterwards. Bagyidaw regarded the note as an act of weakness and became even more pugnacious. Two British naval officers from the Company schooner *Sophia*, who had been sent to help define the Burmese border in a British bid to avert war, were kidnapped and sent to the interior for imprisonment, although they were later freed unharmed. Amherst felt he had no option but to declare war formally on 5 March 1824.

Justifying his decision, Amherst said:

The Burmese Government, actuated by an extravagant spirit of pride and ambition, and elated by its conquest over the petty tribes by which it is surrounded, has ventured to violate the British territories, to attack and slay a party of British sepoys, to seize and imprison British subjects, to avow extensive schemes of mischievous aggression, and to make hostile preparations on our frontier.

The war had already started before the formal Declaration. Burmese troops moved into the small state of Cachar, a British protectorate, and threatened the frontier of Sylhet. The Burmese excused their action by claiming to be in pursuit of bandits and criminals. They demanded that the rajah of Sylhet acknowledge submission and allegiance to the king of Ava. Their planned invasion was, however, halted by the advance of British troops.

In Cachar they constructed stockades on the principal mountain passes and high roads, palisades of teak beams and bamboo, behind which were earth entrenchments with cannon batteries, further protected by deep ditches. Early in February a detachment under Colonel Brown marched on strongly defended stockades at Doodpatlee. The Burmese occupied a narrow slip of flat land flanked by steep hills and the River Soorma, with a ditch about 14 feet wide in front of a cannon-proof fortified wall. Solid redoubts and spiked bamboo strengthened the defences while the road approaching it was so steep that 'a few determined men might bid defiance to hundreds'. Several spirited attacks were made under cover of heavy fire from three six-pounders, but each failed in turn. At the end of a long, gruelling day the British gave up and retired to Juttrapore. Captain Johnson of the 23rd and four other officers were hurt, while around 150 sepoys had been killed or wounded in the inglorious action. One officer reported that the Burmese, estimated at 2,000 strong, 'defended themselves with great bravery and their losses must have been considerable'.

This early defeat convinced some British officers that the enemy was not to be despised, but their commanders in India continued to underestimate the calibre of the Burmese and the strength of their defences, often with fatal consequences. Early reports confirmed the dismissive attitude of the Calcutta generals: the Burmese forces were a loose concoction of tribal fighters, numbering just 15,000 men, of whom barely two-thirds had firearms, the rest making do with spears and swords. Nevertheless Calcutta speedily sent reinforcements into the provinces of Sylhet and Assam, which they reoccupied with little trouble. The main British effort was, however, to be directed in the south. The first target was the important seaport of Rangoon. From there naval power would be harnessed to take troops up the mighty Irrawaddy to deliver a knockout blow aimed at Ava itself.

A joint army and naval force assembled in May 1824 at Port Cornwallis in the Andaman Islands. There were 63 ships and 11,500 British and Indian troops, including a royal regiment of cavalry and two of infantry. The ships included *Diana*, a 60 horsepower paddle-steamer with a funnel almost as tall as the masts of more conventional vessels. She was the first steamer to be employed in the British forces and her appearance provoked wonder among the natives. The whole force was under the command of Lieutenant-Colonel Sir Archibald Campbell of the 38th Regiment.

Campbell came from a prosperous but not wealthy Perth family; now aged fifty-five, he had been a serving soldier since he was eighteen. He saw extensive action in

India, Mysore, Cochin and Ceylon. His gallantry at the first siege of Seringapatam ensured rapid promotion. Despite faltering health he served with distinction during the Peninsular War and commanded Portuguese regiments at the battles of Albuera, Vittoria, the Pyrenees and the Nivelle, when he was mentioned in dispatches. Further battle honours followed until the end of the Napoleonic Wars saw him knighted and serving as aide-de-camp to the Prince Regent before being posted to India as colonel of the 38th.

As the main expedition set sail from Port Cornwallis, a force of Bengal Marines on board the warships *Slancy* and *Mercury* took the island of Cheduba off the Arracan coast with only 'trifling' losses. The rajah, who paid allegiance to Ava, was imprisoned and seven companies of sepoy infantry garrisoned the island, which they described as of 'uncommon fertility'. At the same time another detachment, consisting of the 17th Madras light infantry, sailed against the island of Negrai at the mouth of the Irrawaddy, which they intended to use as a stepping stone for an attack on the town of Bassein further up the river. The Burmese were dug in behind a strong stockade on the island. The Indians took it by frontal assault, but their officers considered it too precarious to hold against counter-attack, and it was abandoned.

The main expedition reached the Rangoon River on 10 May and the following morning took the town itself with ease. Barely a hundred inhabitants were found: the rest had fled, leaving stockpiles of ammunition. Several artillery pieces were also captured, although they were poorly regarded by the invaders. Some soldiers found large stocks of brandy in a merchant's house and quickly became drunk. According to one officer 'they went rambling from house to house with lighted torches, and as may be fully anticipated, the town was set on fire and a great portion of it consumed in consequence'. Despite such poor discipline, the first stage of the operation had gone smoothly, but the British were about to suffer a major setback in the north.

A detachment of British troops had been posted at Ramoo, in advance of Chittagong, with the intention of preventing any further Burmese encroachments into Bengal. On 13 May, after several days of skirmishing, a 5,000-strong Burmese force advanced on the British positions and entrenched on the south side of a nearby river. The following day a party under Captain Trueman, with two six-pounders, bombarded them out of their positions and drove them into the surrounding hills. The day after that the Burmese reformed within 300 yards of the British ranks. On 17 May they captured several outposts, deserted by panicked provincial troops. All hopes of reinforcements had by this time been dashed, the British flanks were exposed, and the defenders were demoralised by thirst, hunger and fatigue. The commanding officer, Captain Noton, ordered a retreat which was conducted in good style for the first mile, but then became disorganised flight. The enemy cavalry pressed them hard while sharpshooters harried the column, and stragglers were cut down. Most of the British officers, including Noton, were killed. The Burmese were seen to be using mainly European muskets. They also deployed *jinjal* guns tied to tree trunks. A dispatch recorded: 'The event of this encounter, though obviously accountable by the great numerical superiority of the enemy, considerably shook the courage of our provincial allies in this quarter, and it was not for some time that they could be induced to face the enemy.'

A freed Bengali soldier later delivered a letter from the Burmese commanders to the British commandant at Chittagong. It said: 'Our master of the Lord of the White Elephant, the Great Chief, the Protector of the Poor and Oppressed, wishes that the people of both countries should remain in peace and quiet.' It claimed that the British were the aggressors, that sepoys had fired on a delegation bearing a flag of truce and that they had taken pains not to assault the local population. 'Our soldiers injured none of the poor inhabitants, and committed no oppression, and destroyed no habitations, yet the English gentlemen, with the Bengalee Sepoys, began firing on us from muskets and cannon,' the letter continued, '. . . a battle ensued, many were wounded, and many put to flight. The people of Ramoo set fire to their own village, and burned it.'

Meanwhile, the British in Rangoon were threatened by large Burmese forces assembling behind stockades encircling the town. On 10 June Campbell sent out a column of 3,000 men to attack the enemy's fortified camp at Kemmendine with four eighteen-pounders, four mortars and several light field guns. Two divisions of ships were sent up-river to block the Burmese escape route. Two miles from the town the column bombarded a strongly built stockade and within half an hour breached its walls. Men of the Madras European Regiments, supported by the 41st, poured into the breach, while on the other side companies of the 13th and 38th Regiments scaled the 10 foot high defences. Every one of the 150 men found inside the stockade was killed. The column moved on for another mile and then, linking up with the naval flotilla, hacked their way through the riverside jungle to assail the main Burmese stockade. During that night the British forces were occupied erecting batteries, while the defenders inside were heard exhorting one another to resist to the death. At daybreak the cannon and mortars opened fire. The bombardment lasted two hours. When a breach was observed a detachment was sent forward, only to find that the enemy had fled, taking their dead and wounded with them.

The king of Ava, irritated rather than alarmed at this setback, ordered a general attack on Rangoon towards the end of June. Spies forewarned Campbell and their intelligence reports were confirmed by sentries who observed large bodies of Burmese troops crossing the river above Kemmendine. On 1 July three columns, each about 1,000 strong, crossed the front of the British positions and moved towards their right. They came into contact with the piquets of the Madras Native Infantry which held steady under attack but were unable to stop the enemy advancing between their posts. The Burmese occupied an old pagoda and several houses on a hill, from which they commenced a 'feeble and harmless' fire. Campbell instantly moved to the point of attack. Supported by a gun and howitzer from the Bengal artillery, three companies charged the hill and drove the Burmese out at the point of the bayonet. The enemy fled into the comparative safety of the jungle, leaving about 100 dead.

The war now became one of attrition, with the British constantly frustrated by the elusiveness of their enemy. Most seasoned officers still held to the textbooks of the Napoleonic Wars and expected their foes to stand and fight. The Burmese could not see the point in defending positions once they became untenable. Their mode of warfare in many ways appears to have a twentieth-century flavour. Each infantryman, armed with a musket, long spear and short sword, carried entrenching

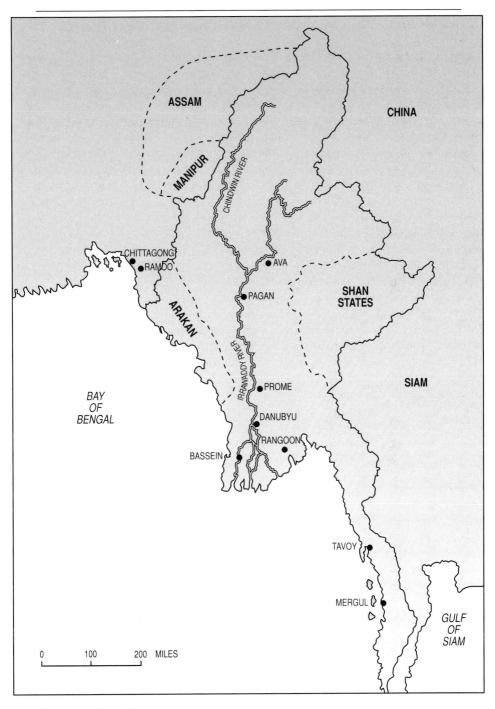

The First Burma War, 1824–6.

tools. Once they took up a position they dug neat foxholes, each capable of holding two men with their supplies of food, water and firewood, which protected the occupants from both enemy fire and the elements. Above their trenches they built observation platforms in the treetops, with guns lashed to the trunks. Their stockades were so well-built they could withstand light cannon.

Campbell went on the offensive. On 8 July he launched a general attack on the enemy lines and his men took ten stockades by assault. The artillery was bloodily effective and estimates of enemy losses, although perhaps inflated, were of over 800 dead. In all, 38 pieces of Burmese artillery, 40 swivel-guns and 300 muskets were captured. Campbell lost 4 men dead, and an officer and 38 rank and file wounded. The Burmese withdrew a greater distance from the British lines but lack of provisions and the onset of the rainy season prevented Campbell from following up his successes. His army settled down in Rangoon until the end of the year. In the meantime they launched sporadic attacks on enemy stockades, while warships burnt Burmese river-craft. On 4 August a successful attack took the town and temple of Syriam. Troops dug holes under the pagoda, searching, with little result, for the valuable offerings presented annually by devotees at the shrine of divinity.

One expedition did, however, see the British checked. A detachment moved against the pagoda of Keykloo but had to stop to deal with entrenchments intersecting the road. The troops took each with charges but were exhausted by the time they reached the main Burmese stockade, which was more formidable than any

The storming of the stockade outside Rangoon. (National Army Museum)

of the others encountered so far, and even boasted a cannon behind a strong parapet. The Burmese held their fire until the British were within 50 yards and then opened a steady and well-directed fusillade. The sepoys were forced to throw themselves flat on the ground. Their commanding officer waited in vain for a supporting column which had been misdirected by disloyal guides. A retreat was ordered but the sepoys, herded together from all sides, became a confused mass. A second expedition was mounted a few days later and the pagoda was taken with some loss of life.

At around the same time expeditions were fitted out against several Burmese sea-ports. A force commanded by Colonel Miles took Tavoy and Mergul, two of the most important stations on the Tenasserim coast. Another under Colonel Sir Henry Godwin had a harder fight at Martyaban. His seaborne expedition set off on 14 October but was delayed by calms and contrary currents, and by the ignorance of the pilots, and it did not reach its target until 29 October. The town was guarded by rocky cliffs and a 2-gun battery behind masonry walls up to 20 feet thick. The stockade ran along the shore for more than three-quarters of a mile and joined a large pagoda which projected into the water to form a bastion. It was a strong position garrisoned by over 3,000 troops but it was stormed by 220 men of European and native regiments with the loss of 7 killed and 40 wounded. The booty included many cannons, 150 wall-pieces, 500 muskets, 7,000 round iron shot, 1,500 grapeshot, saltpetre and sulphur. Most of the munitions were destroyed when Godwin ordered the magazine to be blown up. The remainder of the long, narrow Tenasserim territory submitted to British protection, and British garrisons occupied the whole coast from Rangoon eastwards.

The court of Ava ordered a general conscription of men to drive the invaders into the sea. A grand army consisting of almost 60,000 of the best Burmese troops, including the Imperial Guard, moved towards Rangoon under the command of General Bandula and accompanied by two royal princes. In the height of the rainy season Bandula led his cumbersome army down the Arracan coast, over a mountain range and through dense jungle. As a military feat it was comparable to Hannibal's crossing of the Alps. He arrived outside Rangoon at the end of November, along with a train of artillery and Cassay cavalry, and drew his lines in front of the great pagoda of Dagon. For five days his men busily erected stockades and batteries, and suffered losses in continual skirmishing. Before their lines were fully fortified Campbell directed an attack on the left wing. In the early morning light two columns, one of 1,100 men, the other of 600, supported by cavalry of the Governor-General's guard who had arrived from Calcutta only the night before, broke through the enemy lines and drove them from the field with 'great slaughter'. The victory was not followed through, and Bandula was able to spend the night and the following day rallying his men and reinforcing his right and centre lines. He pushed forward towards the great pagoda and closed on the British trenches and breastworks. He prepared a general attack but at 4 a.m. on 8 December all the British batteries opened up with a 'most murderous' fire of grape and rockets, while a column sallied out to attack the Burmese left flank again. Bandula's men initially held their ground but soon broke and fled in every direction, leaving behind almost all their artillery, stores and ammunition. Burmese casualties were reckoned by the victors to have been 5,000 dead and wounded. Total British losses were said to have not exceeded 200 and Campbell jubilantly reported the 'total defeat' of Bandula.

Despite the severity of his losses, Bandula, an inspiring commander, largely succeeded in rallying his army and five days later took up positions near the village of Kokine, roughly 3 miles from the British advance posts. He had constructed the usual defensive stockade with such judgement as to the best position as, Campbell himself noted, 'would do credit to the best instructed engineers of the most civilised and warlike nations'. The 20,000 men behind the stockades were still panicky, however, and a column of 1,300 British infantry took the position at the first assault. The defenders fled, offering no resistance, and leaving their baggage and ammunition behind. Marines destroyed 200 Burmese fireboats. It was the last major action of the year.

The *Annual Register* reported: 'The result of the campaign was to give us the command of some of the most important maritime stations of the Burmese; and, what was perhaps of more moment, to impress upon them a salutary sense of our military superiority.'

In the north the preceding months had been much quieter. The Burmese were forced to evacuate most of their occupied territories but remained in Ramoo for several weeks and took the stockade of Tek-Naaf owing to the timidity of the 150 provincial troops garrisoning it. In August Colonel Innes took command of the Sylhet frontier and, slowly but steadily, cleared the province of Cachar of Burmese invaders by the end of October. Over the same period Assam province was also liberated, although the British commander there, Brigadier MacMorine, died of cholera along with many of his troops. His campaign was completed under the command of Sir Edward Paget. But Britain's military top brass were then shaken by an event potentially more shattering than any battlefield defeat.

Three native regiments, the 26th, 47th and 62nd, stationed at Barrackpore, were ordered to march to reinforce troops employed in driving the Burmese out of Assam and Cachar. Discontent grew within the ranks over several days. On 31 October they were ordered to draw up in marching order for an inspection of their knapsacks. A large number refused to put on their knapsacks, claiming that the carrying of baggage was degrading to their caste. The commanding officer, Colonel Cartwright, addressed each company in succession, pointing out the draconian penalties for mutiny. Some finally obeyed the order, but most left their knapsacks on the ground. Another parade was ordered for the following morning in front of General Dalzell. Fewer than 400 men, including all the native officers and NCOs, lined up. The remainder held back, their muskets loaded. Dalzell rode up to remonstrate with them but they drove him off and compelled most of the obedient soldiers, apart from the officers, to rejoin them.

Some shots were fired and that evening 130 men of the 62nd and 20 of the 26th seized their colours. Paget arrived with the Royals, the King's 47th and the artillery and the next morning his troops were drawn up in position. The mutineers did likewise and were solidly determined not to give in. They said that they had taken an oath not to surrender, and intended keeping it. Two signal guns were fired and artillery opened up from the rear on the mutineers, lined up in dense ranks. A volley from the Royals sent them running for cover in every direction. Around 100 were either killed on the parade ground or drowned attempting to cross the adjoining river. Most of the rest were captured. Twelve of the supposed ringleaders were executed but the sentences of the rest were commuted to fourteen years' hard labour in irons.

News of the mutiny, a foretaste of a much greater affair, caused alarm in England where it was seen as evidence of wider discontent in the entire Indian army. The price of East India Company stock nose-dived but then recovered.

*   *   *

The British forces in Rangoon did not enjoy the occupation and illness began to reduce their numbers dramatically. From the start their billets were far from ideal and the lack of supplies was a constant problem. One officer wrote:

> Deserted as we found ourselves by the people of the country, from whom alone we could expect supplies, unprovided by the means to move either by land or water, and the rainy monsoon setting in – no prospect remained to us but that of a long residence in the miserable and dirty hovels of Rangoon, trusting to the transports for provisions, with such partial supplies as our foraging parties might procure from time to time by distant and fatiguing marches into the interior of the country.

Campbell's army had few pack animals to help them forage, and a march further into the interior would have been impossible even without the rains. After barely a month two-thirds of Campbell's garrison was unfit for anything but the lightest of duties and of the incapacitated an alarming number of both Europeans and sepoys were seriously ill.

One of the transports ran down *Diana*, throwing the steam engine out of level and badly injuring the only engineer. She was repaired only through the efforts of 32-year-old naval officer Frederick Marryat, who had previously served on St Helena until the death of Napoleon. It was Marryat who had first suggested the deployment of *Diana* and who had overcome intense hostility to the idea of bringing along such a new-fangled vessel. Later in the operations, when the naval commander, Commodore Grant, became ill, Marryat took responsibility for the entire squadron, most notably organising the drinking water for the fleet.

In January 1825 Campbell urged the local inhabitants to return to Rangoon. He could not help boasting of his victories: 'The ancient kingdom of Pegu has become a desert from the rage of war. The most powerful armies possible for your court to get together have been sent against us; we have dispersed them like chaff.' He said that Britain only wanted peace, that Burmese property would not be looted and the townspeople would not be abused in any way, provided they behaved themselves. He added: 'It only remains for me to carry the victorious English arms, not only to your capital, but to the remotest parts of your kingdom, till your court is brought to a proper sense of that justice, honour and policy, due from one neighbouring state to another.' His appeal was partially successful and large numbers of the inhabitants did return to Rangoon. Campbell hoped that the people of Pegu would become allies to throw off the yoke of Ava.

Early in February Lieutenant-Colonel Godwin dislodged Bandula's advance division at Tantabain. That allowed Campbell, now supplied with mules and oxen to haul the field pieces and supplies, to move with a large force towards Prome. His column met no opposition for 50 miles and a strong Burmese division under Maha Silwah, which had been occupying an old Talian fort, melted away before the British advance. The local population appeared grateful at the expulsion of the Burmese troops and brought the British column supplies of rice and buffaloes, and even helped with road-building.

A substantial Burmese force remained at Danubyu, a fortress commanding both the water route to the north and Ava, and the vital road from Rangoon, from which Bandula sent out sorties to harry the British. Campbell described one such attack by Burmese using elephants as fighting vehicles:

> . . . a scene at once novel and interesting . . . Seventeen large elephants, each carrying a complement of armed men, and supported by a column of infantry, were observed moving towards our right flank. I directed the [Governor-General's] bodyguard, under Captain Sneyd, to charge them, and they acquitted themselves most handsomely, mixing boldly with the elephants; they shot their riders off their backs, and finally drove the whole back into the fort.

Campbell directed 42-year-old General Willoughby Cotton, a commander with a growing reputation for mediocrity, to take a river-borne force up the Irrawaddy to attack the Danubyu stronghold. The river could be both placid and turbulent, spiked with hidden obstacles, mudflats and rapids. The soldiers looked on a changing scenery of gigantic elephant grass, sandy beaches, villages constructed of bamboo and palm mats, brightly dressed Burmese gazing silently at the 'barbarians', ornate pagodas and the crumbling ruins of more ancient civilisations, banana plantations, and dense jungle foliage with tendrils trailing in the water.

At Teesit they destroyed three abandoned stockades. Two men of the naval light division were killed when fired upon from the bank. Their comrades stormed an enemy breastwork to take revenge. The flotilla anchored out of gunshot range of the stockades of Panlang and during the night the Burmese floated fire-rafts among the British ships, but to no effect. The following morning a strip of land was occupied close to the extensive stockades and a battery of four mortars and two six-pounders erected within an hour of landing. Shortly before dusk the steam-vessel *Diana* arrived and anchored between two stockades while columns of infantry advanced along both sides of the river. But as the attacks were launched each stockade in turn was found to be deserted.

The enemy was protected by a succession of formidable stockades, beginning at the pagoda and increasing in strength until reaching the main work surrounded by a deep *abatis*. Their guns seemed to be numerous and the garrison crowded the walls.

A prisoner was sent in under a flag of truce with a demand to surrender the place. The Burmese refusal was 'civil but decided'. Bandula replied: 'We are each fighting for his country, and you will find me as steady in defending mine, as you in maintaining the honour of yours. If you wish to see Danubyu come as friends, and I will shew it to you. If you come as enemies, land.'

Covered by a light division and some sharpshooters in rowboats, 160 men of the 89th beat back an enemy outpost dug into a bank of the river. The British boats advanced under incessant fire from about thirty heavy Burmese cannon. Their accuracy gave substance to reports that Bandula had been practising his artillery crews for some time. Cotton's force had only 600 infantry available to assail a fortress which held perhaps 12,000 Burmese, well-furnished with artillery and muskets. Rather than attempting a suicidal frontal attack on the main positions, Cotton decided to knock out the successive stockades one by one, while the flotilla kept up a strong fire from the river.

At dawn the following day he landed 500 men with two six-pounders and a small rocket battery to attack the white pagoda. All were exposed to a heavy fire which was kept up to the last 'with perseverance and spirit'. The pagoda stood in a narrow gorge and the Burmese had no way of escape except over their own defences. They stood their ground until overwhelmed. The cost to the British of taking this first line of defence was 20 men killed or wounded; the Burmese lost 400.

The second stockade, about 500 yards away, proved a tougher nut to crack. Two more six-pounders, four more mortars and a fresh supply of rockets were brought up and placed in position at a bamboo and teak house. After an apparently devastating bombardment, 200 men of the 89th under Captain Rose advanced in two storming parties. They were greeted by a destructive fire from the stockade which forced the two columns to diverge and take refuge in a ditch. This was found, too late in many cases, to be laced with sharp spikes. Those who managed to find cover between the lethal spikes discovered the ditch was cunningly scarped to expose it to fire from the stockade. Every man who tried to get out was knocked down. Rose, already wounded, was felled by a second shot while struggling to maintain the attack. Other officers were killed or wounded while the losses among the men were 'extremely heavy'. They were ordered to retire if they could. More cannon and mortars were brought up to increase the battery, but the enemy strengthened their works and towards evening brought their own heavy guns to bear. Cotton reckoned that taking the stockade would cost so many lives that it would threaten his ability to storm the main defences. He decided to retire and await reinforcements. Captured enemy cannon were spiked and the British artillery reshipped. British losses were 129 killed, wounded or missing.

Campbell and his main army, who had been moving northwards towards Ava, spent three weeks marching to join Cotton. On 1 April his bombardment of the stubborn stockade began and continued to the following morning. As the British advanced, the enemy's small rearguard was found in full retreat towards the jungle. The main fortifications had been evacuated during the night after Bandula, Burma's greatest general, had been killed by a rocket while he was engaged on his daily round of inspection. Other chiefs who wished to carry on the fight could not stem the panic-stricken flight of the garrison troops towards Lamina. Within the defences the British found sufficient stocks of grain to feed themselves for several months.

Elsewhere British operations met with less costly success. In the north the Burmese capitulated at the siege of Rangpoore, their last foothold in Assam. In Cachar progress was slower because of the savage terrain and because heavier than usual rains made road construction almost impossible. A series of brilliant operations in March gave General Morrison full possession of the coastal province of Arracan. General Macbean occupied without resistance the islands of Ramiree and Sandowey.

Campbell made his headquarters at Prome where his army was trapped until November by the rainy season. Here, Campbell was faced with the greatest problem of the campaign – his men began to die at an alarming rate. The army had been poorly equipped by a Calcutta administration almost entirely ignorant of the climate and terrain of inland Burma. Sanitary conditions were appalling, and the men had few means to keep dry. Cholera, malaria, dysentery and jungle rot all took their toll, although precise numbers appear to have been covered up by the authorities, afraid of both mutiny and public scandal. The captured grain supplies ran out, while the Burmese employed a precocious scorched-earth policy to deny the British supplies from the surrounding country. Scarce provisions were moved laboriously up-river from Rangoon, about 150 miles away, by a flotilla of small boats under Captain Alexander of the *Alligator*. Despite his efforts, the supply was erratic and insufficient. The rains continued to fall with mounting ferocity and much of the nearby farmland was flooded, increasing the epidemic. The Burmese constantly made small-scale raids which whittled down the numbers of fit men, and swiftly disappeared into the jungle when they were counter-attacked. Those British and Indian troops who dared follow them faced not just ambush, but swamps infested with leeches and the *Anopheles* mosquito.

In the meantime peace negotiations were held at Meeady between senior British officers and envoys authorised by Saha Menjee Maha Mengom, the king's first minister at Ava. A ceasefire was agreed for 17 October along with articles providing for a demarcation line between the two armies. As a result Campbell met the Burmese Commissioners Kee Woongee and Lay Mayn Woon for a parley at Nemben-zick. Compliments and courteous speeches were passed on both sides. The Burmese envoys politely asked after the health of the British king. The following day more chiefs came from Ava; having failed to persuade Campbell to withdraw all his forces and territorial claims, they asked for an extension of the armistice to 2 November so that they could consult with King Bagyidaw. Campbell agreed, and invited twelve chiefs to dine with him. Toasts were drunk to the royal house of Ava and one chief, referring to the differences between their two nations, said, 'the sun and moon are now eclipsed, but when peace is restored they will dazzle the world with increased splendour'.

The war, however, was not over.

★   ★   ★

British troops entering Rangoon, 1824. (Monro's *Burmese Empire*)

The extended armistice allowed Campbell time to see his depleted army through the rainy season and for the less seriously ill to recover. The Burmese authorities used the time to collect and prepare new military forces. Neither side was prepared to give in.

King Bagyidaw, on hearing of the British demands to annexe much of the southern part of his realm, flew into 'the most intemperate bursts of impotent passion'. Thanks to the vigorous preparations a new army of over 50,000 men had been gathered. To lead them the King sent Maha Nemiow, a general of great experience, though previously overshadowed by Bandula. Nemiow attached to his army 8,000 Shans, men of 'high character' and an envious reputation for gallantry, who had yet to meet the British in battle. Along with them were three high-born women believed to be endowed with the gifts of prophecy and the miraculous ability to turn aside musket balls and bullets. The agreed demarcation line was swiftly crossed and the Burmese laid waste the countryside almost to the walls of Prome, broke British supply lines and threatened communications between Campbell's military HQ and Rangoon. The king's envoys rejected the peace proposals and sent Campbell a laconic ultimatum: 'If you wish for peace, you may go away; but if you wish either money or territory, no friendship can exist between us. This is the Burmese custom.'

The army of Ava moved along the banks of the Irrawaddy against Prome, then held by fewer than 6,000 British and sepoy troops. Nemiow split his army into three columns, each marching along parallel routes. His tactics were seriously flawed. Hills, ridges and dense jungle separated the columns and prevented them from supporting one another. Nemiow took personal command of the left division, 15,000 strong including the Shan horsemen, marching inland from the eastern bank. The central column, over 25,000 men headed by the royal minister of state, marched along the river bank supported by a large number of war-boats. The third column, 15,000 men under Sudda Woon, moved up the opposite bank of the Irrawaddy. The three divisions moved slowly, risking no general engagement and encircling Prome at a distance.

Colonel McDowgal with two brigades of native infantry was sent to dislodge Nemiow's advance guard at the village of Watti-goon, 16 miles to the north-east of the town. One division approached the enemy, while two more circled around the flank and rear. The British plan for a simultaneous attack from three directions was thrown awry by the Burmese who moved forward to meet the frontal assault head on, bringing up large numbers of Cafray cavalry. The British force beat them back but McDowgal was killed in the action. The central division, seeing no sign of the other two, was then forced to retreat with heavy casualties. Three more British officers and 61 men had been killed, 40 were missing in the dense jungle and 120 were wounded.

Nemiow was emboldened by this victory to move closer to Prome, but at a snail's pace, building earthworks and barricades at every stop. By the end of November his central column was visible, stockaded on the Heights of Napadee, which ran along the river bank 5 miles above Prome, with another column dug in on the opposite bank. Nemiow's column moved up to the stockade at Simbike and Kyalaz on the Narwine River, where they threatened the British river traffic. Despite his initial success, Nemiow was proving himself an unskilled tactician. His army was still divided into three, each separated from the others by wide or fast-flowing river waters or by thick forest. Campbell decided to go on the offensive by attacking each component in turn with his much smaller force.

At daybreak on 1 December Campbell left four sepoy regiments to defend Prome and marched the rest out to attack Nemiow's corps on the Narwine River, while his river flotilla and some extra sepoys mounted a diversionary assault on the Napadee Heights. Campbell split his force into two columns. One, under General Cotton, advanced along the left bank of the river while the other, under Campbell himself, forded the river and moved up the far bank. The idea was that whichever column reached the enemy first would instantly attack, while the other would block the Burmese retreat. Despite difficult and unfamiliar terrain, the tactic worked, with Cotton engaging first. One report noted:

> In less than ten minutes every stockade was carried, the enemy completely routed, and the second column had only an opportunity of cannonading his panic-struck masses as they rushed fast through the openings of the jungle in front. Everything had been confusion within the stockades from the moment

that General Cotton's column entered them; the very numbers of the enemy, crowded within their works, disabled them for effective resistance. The Shans alone maintained their character, and fought bravely. Animated by their young prophetesses, and the example of their *chobwahs*, or chiefs, they maintained the contest until the greater part of them were cut down. One of the prophetesses received a mortal wound, and old Maha Nemiow himself fell, encouraging his men in the hottest of conflict, to desperate resistance.

The Burmese left column was completely dispersed and Campbell now turned his attention to the centre column on the Napadee Heights. He gave his men just two hours' rest before marching them back to the hamlet of Zeouke to bivouac for the night. During that day they had performed a harassing march of 29 miles and fought and won a battle. At daylight on the 2nd they were again on the move. Dense jungle forced them to take a road leading to the front of the fortified ridge which was inaccessible on three sides. The British artillery opened up on the lofty stockades, backed by cannon fire from the flotillas under Commodore Sir John Brisbane on the river below. Brigadier Elrington was directed to advance through the jungle to the right where 'the enemy opposed him with great gallantry and resolution, defending every tree and breast-work with determined obstinacy'. Six companies of the 87th drove the Burmese outlying posts to the bottom of the ridge, clearing the valley floor. The main hilltop complex of stockades and earthworks, all filled with musketmen, extended for 3 miles and there was only one narrow road up to them. Once the artillery and rockets had silenced several enemy guns, the 1st Bengal Brigade was sent in to make the frontal assault, while the 38th hacked their way through the jungle to the right. An officer recorded:

Nothing could surpass the steadiness and resolute courage displayed in this attack. Scarcely a shot was fired in return to the enemy's continued volleys. The 38th, which led, first entered the enemy's entrenchments of the heights, driving him from hill to hill, over precipices which could only be ascended by a narrow stair, until the whole of the formidable position was carried.

During the attack Brisbane's flotilla pushed past to capture all the Burmese army's boats and stores.

Both the Burmese divisions which had advanced on the eastern side of the Irrawaddy were now scattered, leaving only the right column under Sudda Woon, stockaded on the western bank. That general had kept his men so quiet and well concealed that Campbell at first thought he had retreated silently. A rocket brigade and mortar battery was set up during the night on a small island in the river, opposite the enemy works. They opened fire early on the 5th as troops under General Cotton were ferried across the water. The Burmese retreated from their riverside positions to much stronger stockades half a mile into the interior, the walls mounted with heavy guns. Cotton, supported by reinforcements, plunged ahead and the position was swiftly taken. The enemy fled in all directions, leaving behind 300 dead and 350 muskets.

Captain Frederick Marryat. (Royal Naval Museum, Portsmouth)

The *Annual Register* reported: 'Thus, in the course of four days, the immense army of Ava, which had threatened to envelope Prome and swallow up the British army troops, had melted away like vapour, and Sir A. Campbell was at liberty to march upon the capital, still distant about three hundred miles.'

After a day's rest, Campbell began that march in two divisions. The first, under his personal command, advanced in a curve to sweep up the remaining enemy river defences and to prevent a rally by the Burmese. The second, under Cotton, marched parallel to the river to act in co-operation with the flotilla. The early stages were through thick and tangled jungle which ruined provisions and drenched the men. Cholera again broke out on the route and several men died before healthier, higher ground was reached. The two columns reached Meeady, the supposed Burmese rallying point, after thirteen days' hard slog but found it just evacuated. The remainder of the Burmese army retreated to Melloone, a town on the right bank of the Irrawaddy, and regrouped. Some 12,000 strong, once again they constructed strong stockades on fortified heights with 600 yards of fast-moving river in front of them. The two armies sat watching each other from opposite sides of the stream. On the 26th the Burmese sent across a messenger under a flag of truce, bearing letters from the chiefs stating their desire to end hostilities. A minister had arrived from Ava with full authority to negotiate and ratify a peace.

After several false starts a truce was agreed and the Burmese provided two warboats to act as pilots for Brisbane's flotilla which was having difficulty negotiating the river channels. A peace conference opened on 1 January 1826 with a new Burmese negotiator, Kolein Menghi. To the first British demand for war indemnity, he said that they did not grow rupees but might be able to pay a million baskets of rice within a year. Alternatively, the British might cut down and take away fine teak timber in lieu of cash. The Burmese would not give up Arracan, 'not on account of its value, for it was rather a burden to Ava than a source of profit, but because the nation was proud of the conquest which had been achieved by the valour of their ancestors, and the national honour was engaged not to yield it'. Campbell stuck rigidly to his demands and, faced with British cannon ranged upon the Burmese positions, Menghi agreed after three days' palaver and a treaty was signed by both sides. Under its terms the four provinces of Arracan, Mergui, Tavoy and Zea were to be ceded to the East India Company; the kingdoms of Assam, Cachar, Zeating and Munnipore were to be placed under princes named by the British Government; British ships would be allowed entry to Burmese ports and could land their cargoes free of duty; and Ava was to pay the Company a crore of rupees (ten million rupees) by instalments to cover some of the costs of the war. The treaty document had to be ratified by King Bagyidaw and returned to Campbell within fifteen days.

During that period the British observed the Burmese in Melloone, under Prince Memiaboo, strengthening their defences in violation of the truce. On the fourteenth day three Burmese officers claimed there had been unexplained delays in getting the treaty to the king and begged for an extension. They offered to pay a cash instalment and present hostages if the British army would retire to Prome. Campbell regarded that 'a proposal too extravagant and absurd for any court but that of Ava to make'. He stuck to the agreed deadline and said that if the treaty were not ratified and returned by midnight on the 18th, hostilities would recommence.

When that hour passed work immediately began on constructing batteries and landing heavy ordnance from the flotilla. The operation was so zealously performed that by 10 a.m. the following morning twenty-eight heavy cannon were in positions threatening the full mile's length of the enemy works across the river. An hour later the batteries and rockets opened up while troops were embarked in boats to cross the torrent. The current and a strong breeze carried the first brigade under Lieutenant-Colonel Sale to the attack point well ahead of the rest of the force. Sale was wounded in his boat, but the men of the 38th rushed on and swiftly took the earthworks facing them. The second brigade landed in time to cut off the escape route of the Burmese troops. In spite of the initial confused landing, the British lost only 9 men killed and 34 wounded in the assault.

In Prince Memiaboo's house they found 30,000 rupees in specie and

A Sepoy of the Madras Native Infantry, from a contemporary lithograph.

both the English and Burmese copies of the treaty which, having been signed, had never been sent to Ava. When Campbell later sent a note to the chief minister suggesting sarcastically that he supposed it had been left behind in the hurried departure from Melloone, the minister coolly replied that, 'in the same hurry he had left behind him a large sum of money, which also he was confident the British general only waited an opportunity of returning'.

On 25 January Campbell resumed the march on Ava. Six days later his army was met by an American missionary, Dr Price, and Assistant-Surgeon Sandford, who had been taken prisoner some months before and who had been released by the king to act as messengers of peace. Bagyidaw was asking for terms and Campbell stuck to those agreed at Melloone. He refused to halt his onward march but agreed as a gesture to pause for two days at Pagahm-Mew, ten days' march ahead and halfway to the capital. When the British approached that neighbourhood they found 16,000 Burmese troops, including refugees from Melloone and fresh levies from Ava. Their commanders were pledged to defeat the 'Invading Army of Rebellious Strangers'.

Campbell decided to assault their positions both in the Logoh-Nunda pagoda and within the old walls of the city. On the morning of 9 February the British troops, including Cotton's men who had marched all night to catch up, left camp for the assault. For the first time in the entire war they found the Burmese forces outside their defences, ready to meet them on open ground. The Burmese commanders, Ta-Yea-Soogean, Woon-dock and Ne-Woon-Breen, had chosen their ground well. It was overgrown with prickly jungle which made it difficult for regular troops to manoeuvre while concealing large numbers of irregular troops. The Burmese were lined up in a crescent, hoping to engulf the British in its 'horns'. The British, however, were in larger numbers than expected, thanks to Cotton's forced march, and the Burmese tactics failed. Campbell led the 13th light infantry and four guns on the right attack; the 38th attacked on the left; and the 43rd Madras advanced on the banks of the Irrawaddy. The Burmese held their ground for some time but were forced back under the rapid fire of their more disciplined adversaries. A large number took refuge in a well-constructed field-work but the sepoys were so close on their heels that they did not have time to form themselves into defensive lines. Between 300 and 400 Burmese died, either on the point of the bayonet or by plunging into the river in a desperate effort to escape.

The main Burmese force was still intact; believing that the British centre was unoccupied, they pushed forward along the main road until checked by the sight of the 39th in reserve. Throughout the day the Burmese cavalry charged in fruitless bids to turn the British right, but they were repulsed every time. Gradually they were beaten on all sides and left Pagahm-Mew, with all its arms, stores and personal possessions, in British hands. The Burmese commander Nee-Woon-Breen, who had persuaded the king to launch this last, ill-fated attack on the invaders, carried the news of the disaster back to Ava. He was executed on the spot.

There was no effective force left between Campbell's army and the capital. Their onward march was, for the first time, through country not devastated by the enemy's scorched-earth policy. The soldiers passed through rich and well-cultivated fields, thick with copses and pretty villages. Temples and pagodas glittered along the river banks.

Storming the stockade at Kemmedine. (National Army Museum)

The army had reached Yandaboo, within four days' march of Ava, when on 24 February Dr Price again appeared with more freed British prisoners, the stipulated first instalment of war compensation and the treaty ratified by King Bagyidaw. The war was over. Campbell and some officers visited Ava where they were met with every honour by the humbled monarch. The army retraced its steps to Rangoon. They no longer faced Burmese ambush but a much more hostile enemy – disease – continued to reduce their numbers.

★   ★   ★

The financial cost of the war to Britain was £13 million, of which £1 million was recovered from the Burmese in indemnity. The human cost was far, far greater. Accurate figures of the death toll from disease and exposure are difficult to obtain. One estimate suggests that of the 40,000 British and Indian troops engaged in total, including those on the northern frontiers, around 15,000 died. Of the 3,586 British and European troops who first occupied Rangoon, 3,115 perished in Burma – but only 150 of them were killed in battle.

There was no great public outcry in England. The largest numbers deployed, and therefore those with the highest casualties, were sepoys whose deaths were not even counted in the British press. The death rate had shocked the Calcutta administration, but Amherst and his pen-pushers were not eager to expose the incompetence and bad planning which left troops without adequate food, medicine and other supplies. And, after all, Campbell had delivered a significant victory which enriched and extended British rule. Under the treaty Arracan, Assam and Tenasserim were ceded to the British, while King Bagyidaw undertook not to interfere in Manipur, Cachar and Jainta. Trade with Burmese ports was opened to fill the coffers of the Company and other English merchants. The outcome of the war, rather than the cost, was greeted with great public enthusiasm in London.

Campbell was voted a gold medal and an income of £1,000 a year by the Company board of directors and he received Lord Amherst's official thanks. For three years he governed the ceded provinces of Burma and Siam, but ill-health took him home in 1829. He was treated like a hero when he arrived and was later created a baronet, with a special coat of arms bearing the title 'Ava'. From 1831 to 1837 he was Lieutenant-Governor of New Brunswick and was nominated commander-in-chief in Canada. In 1839 he was offered the command of India but turned it down owing to his failing health. He died in 1843.

Frederick Marryat and *Diana* had proved the worth of steamships in military campaigns and the little craft had many successors in the waters of the Irrawaddy. Marryat retired from the navy in 1830, at the age of thirty-eight. For the next eighteen years, until his death, he devoted himself to writing stirring adventure novels, mostly set at sea. His most famous are still read: *Mr Midshipman Easy*, *Peter Simple* and *The Children of the New Forest*.

General Sir Willoughby Cotton served in Bengal, Jamaica and Afghanistan. In the latter arena, after thirty years' service, he had still not learned to send out reconnaissance patrols while leading his troops through country crawling with hostile Sikhs. At the outbreak of the Crimean War, Cotton, despite his self-confessed 'advancing years and unwieldy figure', unsuccessfully applied for a fighting command. He died in 1860, aged seventy-seven. Lord Amherst was made an earl and subsequently served as Governor-General of Canada. He was eighty-four when he died in 1857.

After the Treaty of Yandaboo British forces remained in Rangoon until all its terms were fulfilled, finally leaving in November. The former governor of Syriam, Gun-lat, seized the surrounding territory for the Talien tribe and bottled up a Burmese garrison in Rangoon. King Bagyidaw assembled another army 'to catch, murder and squeeze the beggarly Taliens'. His army succeeded in driving out the usurper the following February. Bagyidaw, known as the 'Golden Foot', never forgot nor forgave the British for the humiliations they heaped on him. He continued to use intrigue and subterfuge to water down the terms he had agreed to, but was outwitted by a succession of envoys who knew that, if needs must, they could always use gunboat diplomacy. His frustrations were cited as the cause of his mental breakdown after March 1831. Four years later his brother, Tharrawaddy, seized the throne in a palace coup and renounced the 1826 treaty.

Tharrawaddy, too, became insane and was succeeded in 1846 by his eldest son, Pagan Min, who cautiously executed most of his relatives and then less cautiously arrested the captains of two British merchant ships. The Second Burma War ensued in 1852. The British commander was Sir Henry Godwin, now elevated to the rank of general. He wanted to repeat the operations of the earlier war, notwithstanding the terrible cost, saying 'nothing that was not done then can be done now – everything that was done then must be done now.' Fortunately for the men under his command he was tactfully overruled by the new Governor-General of India, Lord Dalhousie. Rangoon, Martaban and Bassein were taken easily before the rainy season and then the province of Pegu was annexed. The British now ruled the whole of Lower Burma.

Pagan Min was deposed and replaced by the greatly esteemed Mindon Min who built the great city of Mandalay as his capital, established a fleet of British-run steam vessels, introduced European technology to factories and constructed a telegraph system. When he died his younger son Thibaw resurrected many of the old despotic ways. His attempts to negotiate with France and to impose cash penalties on British timber firms led to the Third Burma War of 1885–6. A British force under General Sir Harry Prendergast took Mandalay. Thibaw and his surviving family were deported to India. The kingdom of Ava had fallen and Britain annexed the entire country. Burma's wealth in precious metals, teak, petroleum and food were fully exploited by Britain.

During the Second World War Burma suffered a brutal Japanese invasion before gaining independence on 4 January 1948. Now it trembles under another type of dictatorship.

In Britain Burma retained a vivid hold on the popular imagination for many years, not least for the poems of Rudyard Kipling. One summed up the feelings of those soldiers who did come home from its wars:

> By the old Moulmein Pagoda, lookin' lazy at the sea,
> There's a Burma girl a-setting, and I know she thinks o' me;
> For the wind is in the palm trees, and the temple bells they say:
> Come you back, you British soldier; come you back to Mandalay!

★　　★　　★

CHAPTER THREE

The Black War – Tasmania, 1824–30

'For every man they murder, hunt them down, and drop ten of them.'

Princess Lalla Rookh, known to her own people as Truganina, was born in the first decade of the nineteenth century. At that time there were at least 8,000 and possibly as many as 20,000 native aborigines living on the island of Tasmania. They were nomads, hunters, gatherers, a naked people ill-prepared for the coming of European settlers, sealers and hardened convicts. By the time Lalla Rookh was twenty there were 320 such settlers.

She was a beauty who was not shy about giving sexual favours freely. One settler wrote: 'She sadly tried the patience of several husbands. Her features, despite her bridgeless nose, were decidedly pleasing . . . when lighting up her sparkling black eyes in animated conversation.' As the young wife of a chief of the Bruni tribe she witnessed the most one-sided war in the history of British colonialism. She was repeatedly raped and saw her first intended husband shot before her eyes. Her mother was also shot by a British soldier and her sister was kidnapped by sealers for use as a sex slave. She died in May 1876, aged something over seventy. She was the last of the Tasmanians.

★   ★   ★

The history of the Tasmanians as a separate aboriginal people began twelve thousand years ago when their mountainous peninsula was cut off from mainland Australia by rising seas. A Stone Age people without the ability to build craft able to sail the dangerous 200-mile wide straits, they were cut off from the rest of humanity. And from predators.

The first European known to have landed on the large island to the south of Australia was an employee of the Dutch East India Company named Abel Jans Tasman. While on a voyage of exploration he made landfall in November 1642 and marked the unknown territory on his maps as Van Diemen's Land, in deference to one of his Company bosses. No contact with the natives was made. The aborigines were left in peace for over 150 years, although various expeditions followed Tasman's to fill in the blank spaces on their seafaring maps.

However, in 1802 the British administration at Port Jackson on the mainland become suspicious of a French scientific expedition, and decided to encourage settlement of an island nominally under the British flag. The new territory was scouted by men such as Matthew Flinders who founded the harbour in the north of the island. It was an island of rugged mountains, dense eucalyptus forests, scrubby bush, fertile valleys and impenetrable rainforests. One early visitor described 'innumerable flights of parrots, cockatoos . . . legions of black swans . . . we were disturbed by two savages who ran towards the beach, both of them shewing the most extraordinary gestures of surprise and admiration'.

Contact between the early settlers and explorers and the aboriginal inhabitants were brief, rare and largely friendly. Captain Collins, who later founded Hobart Town, recorded one meeting: 'His face was blackened, and the top of his head was plastered with red earth. His hair was either naturally short and close, or had been made so by burning . . . He was armed with two spears, very badly made and of solid wood only.' The native took no interest in the landing party's firearms, but was fascinated by the red silk handkerchiefs which the sailors wore around their necks.

Paraberi, an aboriginal Tasmanian, *c.* 1807. (Allport Library)

The Frenchman François Peron described a woman in her mid-twenties with a kind and benevolent appearance:

> She was entirely naked, with the exception of a kangaroo skin, in which she carried a little girl, which she continued to suckle. Her breasts, a little withered already, appeared otherwise to be pretty well-formed and of the pendulous type, and were sufficiently furnished with milk. Her eyes were the most expressive part [of her face], and there seemed to be even something spiritual, which surprised us.

Another early visitor remarked that Tasmanian eyes were 'dark, wild, and strongly expressive of the passions'.

The aborigines were a loose-knit confederation of tribes with up to ten distinct languages. A typical clan consisted of several extended families, with around eighty people in all. Men and women coupled for life and looked after their children and ageing relatives. The most populous regions were coastal, but there is evidence that some tribes inhabited the most inhospitable areas. Europeans described them as of average height and dark-skinned, but with facial features quite different from those of mainland Australia. The women, as described above, wore kangaroos skins around their shoulders, mainly to carry children and equipment, and little or nothing else. The men went completely naked save for decorative strips of skins and shells. Both sexes adorned themselves with charcoal and ochre.

They were a healthy people and early visitors saw no signs of starvation. The men hunted kangaroo and wallaby while the women gathered berries and roots, dived for shellfish and scooped up cockles from the beach. The eating of scaled fish was taboo. A low-alcohol cider was made from gum trees but the main drink was water. The aborigines had not learnt to use metal and all implements and weapons were made from wood, bone and stone. Canoes were made from bark and rushes and were used to hunt seal. Women served the men who, in turn, jealously guarded them from marauders. They believed in spirits, good and bad, and superstitions, and the breach of taboos led to internal conflict, retold by generations of storytellers. But there is no evidence of any sort of large-scale war between the tribes or clans.

After one peaceful encounter Peron wrote: 'The general union of the several individuals of the family, the kind of patriarchal life which we had witnessed, had strongly affected our feelings: I saw realised with inexpressible pleasure those charming descriptions of the happiness and simplicity of a state of nature, of which I had so often read, and enjoyed in idea.'

Peron was clearly influenced by Rousseau's concept of the 'Noble Savage' but, while it is easy to overstate the simplicity and harmony of such unspoilt people, European observers agreed that the natives appeared to live in peace, at one with their environment. As nomads they saw no need for permanent encampments, far less buildings. They sheltered under crude windbreaks and in caves and hollow tree trunks. The white men who landed on their shores were alien and incomprehensible to the native Tasmanians. They soon learnt to be fearful.

Settlers began to stake out their claims around the mouth of the River Derwent in the south, and the Esk in the north. Clashes with the aborigines over food supplies occurred when the early settlers faced bouts of famine. European sealers in the north kidnapped women and children for sex and servitude. But the real violence began when the London and Australian authorities realised that the remoteness of Van Diemen's Land made it ideal for convict colonies. Prisoners were steadily imported to what swiftly became one large open gaol. Other settlers were twice-convicted prisoners from Port Jackson. Many convicts simply walked out of the penal settlements and roamed the island's rugged interior, becoming bushrangers. Others were allowed to roam freely as stockmen and herders for their masters. As writer Lloyd Robson pointed out, the result was a 'bandit society' in which the roaming convicts were joined by refugees from labour gangs. They learnt the bush skills of tracking and survival and roving bands became such a threat to the settlements that Lieutenant-Governor Thomas Davey declared martial law, although that was quickly suspended by the Sydney authorities. The bushrangers were a much greater threat to the aborigine whom they considered, quite literally in many cases, to be fair game.

The bushrangers killed Tasmanian men and children for sport and raped the women (called *gins* by the whites). Males were tied to trees and used for target practice. One former bushranger recalled: 'I would as leave shoot them as so many sparrows. At the same time, I derive much amusement from this form of sport.' The murder of a husband was usually followed by the rape of his wife. A correspondent wrote of one incident: 'The Bushranger Carrots killed a black fellow, and seized his gin; then cutting off the man's head, the brute fastened it round the gin's neck, then

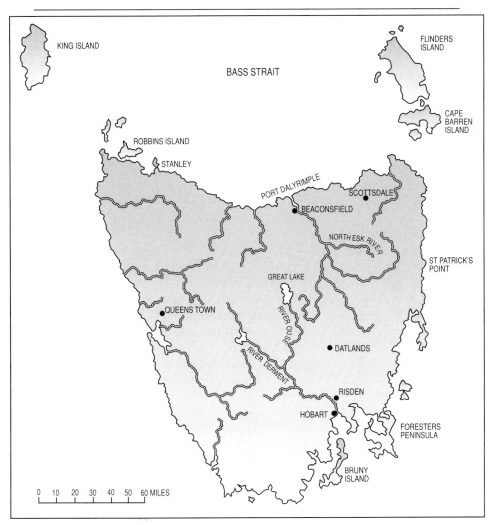

The Black War – Tasmania in the 1820s.

drove the weeping victim to his den.' In an incident that shocked even some of the most hardened murderers an aborigine baby was buried up to its neck in sand in front of its mother and its head kicked off. A sealer confessed to an officer that he 'kept a poor young creature nude and chained up like a wild beast, and whenever he wanted her for anything, applied a burning stick, a firebrand from the hearth, to her skin'.

There are many explanations for such conduct, such as the scarcity of women and the absence of all moral and social constraints which is found on any frontier. The convicts had themselves been brutalised. Many were outcasts from the Industrial Revolution who had survived journeys that killed their friends and families. Others were ruthless criminals and known murderers. All had been the victims of severe judicial cruelty including repeated floggings, starvation, routine buggery and the shadow of the rope. They thought nothing of inflicting similar cruelty on black beings whom their rough society did not recognise as humans. But nothing can excuse the sadistic delight with which they pursued and tormented their quarry.

But it was not just the lowly criminal classes who engaged in such sport. In some areas hunting aborigines was regarded as a family entertainment among gentlemen and their ladies. The white women would prepare picnics while the gentlemen and their convict servants hunted the blacks with dogs or shot them from a distance. If none were found in the bush, occasionally a previously captured woman would be paraded before the marksmen. One settler had a pickle tub in which he kept the ears of all the blacks he had shot. In that harsh frontier society it was all considered great fun. Captain Holman recorded a stockman who approached a native with a pair of pistols, only one of which was loaded. He fired the empty one at his own head and invited the aborigine to do the same with the other weapon. The black man innocently complied and blew his brains out against a tree trunk.

The aborigines fought back, often to rescue stolen womenfolk or avenge a rape. A convict stockman who flogged a black girl with a bullock whip to prepare her for the 'marriage bed' was speared to death while carrying water. Stock-keepers at Salt Pan Plains raped two black women who later escaped while the men were drunk. The women told their husbands and the tribe surrounded the hut and killed two of the three men inside. Another band, unable to kill the heavily armed rapist and bushranger Dunn in his den became so frustrated they instead murdered several of his inoffensive white neighbours. The outrages continued and all suffered. A typical Tasmanian tactic was to wound or kill isolated stock-keepers and shepherds by setting fire to the roofs of their huts and then spearing them as they emerged choking and blinded by smoke. The killing of outlaws was one thing, but the murder of settlers pushing back the frontiers of civilisation was something quite different. Bands of militia, vigilantes and soldiers struck deep into the bush in search of black miscreants. The real slaughter began.

The first organised conflict occurred in 1804, at Risdon, 5 miles from Hobart. A settler called Burke complained that large numbers of aborigines were menacing him because he had built his hut on sacred hunting grounds. A detachment of troops was sent out under Lieutenant Moore, a notorious drunkard. In the late morning a mass of aborigines was seen swarming down from the heights, driving a herd of kangaroos towards a hollow where they were slaughtered for a feast. The aborigines were unarmed except for the waddies or clubs used for killing kangaroos, and with them were their families. The soldiers of the New South Wales Corps, most of whom were as drunk as their officer, opened fire either in panic or for sport. At least fifty men, women and children were killed. A witness of the massacre, Edward White, gave evidence to the subsequent inquiry, saying that he was hoeing turnips when he saw several hundred aborigines come down the hillside in a half circle, driving the kangaroos before them. 'They looked at me with their eyes,' he said. 'I went down the creek and reported them to some soldiers, and then went back to my work. The Natives did not threaten me in any way, and I was not afraid of them. The Natives did not attack the soldiers. They could not have molested them. The firing commenced about eleven o'clock. There were many Natives slaughtered and wounded. I don't know how many. But some of their bones were sent in two casks to Port Jackson in New South Wales to be studied.' A later chronicler, Captain Holman, wrote of the incident: 'From this moment on, a deep-rooted hatred sprang up among the aborigines for any strangers, and since that time all endeavours at friendship have proved ineffective.'

For twenty years the skirmishes and bloody raids continued, dying down in one part of the island, only to flare up in another. Sometimes the disputes arose over the herding of cattle across aboriginal lands; at other times they resulted from brutal outrages committed by convicts and settlers. Every time the aborigines retaliated, retribution followed. Soldiers and vigilantes, pursuing supposed murderers, fired indiscriminately into any aboriginal encampment they encountered. One witness to such a night attack wrote: 'It was interesting to see how they fell after they were shot. One man, being shot while bending over the fire, sprang up, turned round and round and round like a whipping toy, before he fell dead.' The Wesleyan builder G.A. Robinson reported:

A party of military and constables got a number of natives cornered between two perpendicular rocks, on a sort of shelf, and in the end killed 70 of them. The women and children had pressed themselves into the crevices of the rocks, but were dragged out and their brains dashed out on the convenient rocks.

Another incident was described to Brough Smith:

A number of blacks with women and children were congregated in a gully near Hobart and the men had formed themselves into a ring around a large fire, while the women were cooking the evening meal of opossums and bandicoots. They were thus surprised by a party of soldiers, who without warning fired into them as they sat, and then rushing up to the panic-stricken natives started to go in at them with rifle butts. A little child being near its dying mother, the soldier drove his bayonet through the body of the child and pitchforked it into the flames.

Governor George Arthur, by an unknown artist.

Such savagery was applauded on the wild frontier but there was a growing backlash in the newspaper offices, courtrooms and pulpits of the mushrooming towns. One clergyman wrote: 'The wounded were brained; the infants cast into the flames; the musket driven into quivering flesh; and the social fire, around which the Natives gathered to slumber, became, before morning, their funeral pyre.'

The first Bishop of Tasmania, Dr Nixon, said:

> There are many such on record, which make us blush for humanity when we read about them, and forbid us to wonder that the maddened savage's indiscriminate fury should not only have refused to recognise the distinction between friend and foe, but have taught him to regard each white man as an intruding enemy, who must be got rid of at any cost.

An 1818 editorial in the *Hobart Gazette* said:

> The aborigines demand our protection. They are the most helpless members, and being such, have a peculiar claim upon us all, to extend every aid in our power, as well in relation to their necessities as to those enlightening means which shall at last introduce them from the chilling rigours of the forest into the same delightful temperature which we enjoy.

But the aborigines would not, could not, be civilised as servants and gardeners and for every smugly enlightened white dove there was a hawk who wanted nothing less than the extermination of the 'niggers'. A writer to the *Courier* said: 'Let them have enough of Redcoats and bullet fire. For every man they murder, hunt them down, and drop ten of them. This is our specific – try it.' That proved to be a conservative ratio of retribution as the scattered bush wars continued.

★   ★   ★

By 1820 the aborigines of Tasmania were facing extinction. Epidemics of diseases introduced by the white men swept through the tribes, killing more than marauding parties of bushrangers and soldiers could ever do. The once-plentiful game dwindled as civilisation encroached, causing starvation and further illness. Tree-felling and new cultivation squeezed them into smaller and smaller pockets of terrain, ending their nomadic way of life. And they stopped having children. No one knows the full reason. Constant pursuit and despair made the women barren, according to some sources. When tribes were being remorselessly chased, infants were an encumbrance they could not afford; according to other sources, infants were slain at birth because their parents couldn't feed them. Crude forms of contraception were employed, according to yet others. Historian David Davies reckoned there were 7,000 aborigines left in 1817; seven years later there were just 340. Whatever the reason, the remaining population aged and dwindled, with little fresh blood invigorating the tribes. Where once there were thousands, now there were hundreds. And still the carnage continued.

The whites' fear and contempt of the blacks was heightened by the activities of Mosquito, an Australian aborigine who was transported to Tasmania for the murder of a black woman. He quickly became the leader of a gang of desperate Tasmanians who hung around the townships to drink and steal. Many settlers regarded his rampage in 1824 as the start of the Black War. He was an unlikely, and unworthy, hero. His men were blacks who had lost all fear of the white man; according to his white prosecutors he dispatched them to raid and murder. The Oyster Bay region on the east coast was terrorised for a while and Mosquito's cunning helped him to elude all forces sent against him. His outrages were compounded by his henchman Black Jack, who delighted in torturing to death white captives and whose catchphrase was 'I'll kill all the white bastards.' They were finally captured by Tegg, a seventeen-year-old aborigine tracker who was hired by the constabulary with the promise of a boat as reward. Mosquito and Black Jack were tried for murder in Hobart and hanged in public. Tegg never got his boat. The writer Gilbert Robertson remarked: 'Although Mosquito has been removed, yet the lessons he afforded the aborigines of this island have not been forgotten by them; experience has taught them craft, cunning, activity and watchfulness, and at this moment they have found the means to spread terror among the Colonists residing in the interior.'

It was into this climate of fear and ferocity that a new Governor stepped in 1824. Colonel Sir George Arthur was forty and a hardened veteran of the Napoleonic Wars. He had served in Italy, was severely wounded in the attack on Rosetta during the Egypt campaign, and was again wounded in the attack on Flushing. During the latter battle he and his single company took prisoner 5 officers and 300 men. On his return to London he was awarded a sword and the Freedom of the City. After further service in Jersey and Jamaica he was made Governor of British Honduras, where he suppressed a slave revolt. But his dispatches condemning the institution of slavery influenced and aided the emancipation crusade of William Wilberforce, and by the standards of the time he was regarded as a humane man. His task in Van Diemen's Land was principally to reform and improve the system of transportation and penal servitude. His biographer wrote:

> His strong good sense and humanity indicated the possibility of a middle course between the extreme severity of the system which would make transportation simply deterrent, and the over-indulgence of the system which aimed at reforming the convict by gentle treatment. He held that it was possible to make transportation a punishment much dreaded by criminals, while offering every facility for reform to those who were not hardened by crime; but he entertained no quixotic expectations of frequent reformation. His plans were never allowed a fair trial.

His main opponents were colonists who wanted Tasmania to grow into something more than a penal settlement. That meant fewer convicts and a solution to the aboriginal problem.

Arthur's first dealings with the aborigines was benevolent. He was shocked, on his arrival, to see and hear evidence of the barbarity inflicted on the blacks by the white

Bark windbreak, an aboriginal family's only shelter, 1802. (Engraving by C.A. Leseur)

race. One tribe asked him for his personal protection, which he readily gave and helped them settle on a tongue of land at Kangaroo Point. Arthur's efforts to protect other tribes, however, proved ineffectual and hostility against them intensified as they grew bolder in their sporadic attacks on outlying farms and settlements. During a period of six years 121 attacks were recorded in the Oatlands district alone. In a typical incident Mr Miller, a farmer on the River North Esk, was returning home when he saw a number of aborigines on his property. He ran to a neighbouring farm for help but found the owner dead in his yard and his foreman dead with eleven spears in his body. He ran back to his own silent homestead where there was by now no sign of the raiders. Inside he found his wife lying on their bed, her brains bashed out by waddy blows. The aborigines had taken his meagre stocks of sugar, flour and clothing. In another attack near the town of Jerico, aborigines lay in ambush for three days before catching the farmer, Mr Hooper, unarmed. They speared him to death and went on to butcher his unprotected wife and seven children. Another band, the 'Ouse Mob', burnt down the hut of a shepherd and killed him as he emerged. His small daughter begged for mercy on her knees and was spared. The colonists and soldiers responded with their now customary ferocity. Clans were hunted down and massacred with little regard as to whether they included the guilty men.

Towards the end of 1828 the increasingly frustrated Governor Arthur issued a new proclamation placing a bounty on aborigines who would not stay within strict boundaries. Authorised hunters were employed to bring them in alive. Captured adults were worth £5 each and children £2. In addition, successful hunters were promised grants of land. Clerics and supposed champions of the aborigines persuaded many blacks to come in of their own accord, and pocketed the reward money. The policy worked for a time and there seemed to be a real prospect of peace. But the few hundred remaining blacks were outraged by the idea that they could be sold. Simmering resentment boiled over and once again panic spread throughout the white settlements as out-stations, travellers and isolated farmhouses came under attack. Arthur declared martial law in every part of the island.

Sturdy, fortified farmhouses offered some protection from marauding natives but not from a determined raid. There were several instances of aborigines clambering down chimneys to murder the families inside. White men taken alive suffered agonising deaths. They were tortured with fire and spear points until the warriors were tired of them. Those captives who were still alive were handed over to the aborigine women, who smashed their genitals to mush with sharp flints. The aborigines also became superb guerrilla fighters. They knew the terrain and could move with astonishing speed – there were some recorded instances in which raiders travelled 50 miles a day on foot. The very scarcity of the aborigines, their mobility and their cruel experiences at the hands of the whites meant that the old military tactics of surprise, night ambushes and massacre were no longer effective against them. Something drastic had to be done to solve the problem once and for all. The result was 'The Line'.

Arthur was persuaded to authorise an audacious plan to form a line of soldiers, militia and civilian volunteers right across the island, to drive the aborigines before them – like 'beating' game in a country estate shoot – towards the narrow-necked Forester's Peninsula in the south. There they could be easily rounded up. Government order 166 was issued on 27 August 1830 to 'repel and drive from the settled country those Natives who seize every occasion to perpetrate murders, and to plunder and destroy the property of the inhabitants'. Arthur asked that consignments of convicts should be of useful classes – 'not Irish' – so that they might aid the enterprise. Volunteers were offered no special reward, only the thrill of the chase.

The Australian press was sceptical from the start. One editorial said: 'It is little better than idiocy to talk of surrounding and catching a group of active, nimble-minded, naked men and women, divested of burdens of all sorts.' Another said:

We call the present warfare against a handful of poor, naked, despicable savages, a humbug in every sense of the word. Every man in the isle is in motion, from the Governor down to the meanest convict. The farmer's scythe and reaping hook are transmuted to the coat of mail and bayonet! The blacksmith, from forging shoes for the settler's nag, now forges the chains to enslave, and whets the instruments of death.

Sir George Murray wrote: 'the adoption of any line of conduct, having for its avowed or secret object the extinction of the native race, could not fail to leave an indelible stain upon the British Government'.

The Line operation started on 7 October with the Oyster Bay and Big River tribes as the principal targets. A chain of rallying posts was thrown across the island from St Patrick's Head on the east coast to Campbell Town on the west. In all, 3,000 armed men were deployed, comprising units of the 63rd, 57th and 17th Regiments, several hundred constables, volunteers and 738 convicts. The non-military parties were organised into groups of ten, each with a guide. The daily ration for each party was one and a half pounds of meat, three ounces of sugar, half an ounce of tea and two pounds of flour. Alcohol was brought by the men themselves. Supplies were organised by General Browne, who efficiently provided drays and pack-horses, although boots suitable for the rough terrain were in short supply, as were heavy duty trousers and jackets. Most units, however, were well armed. A central depot was established at Oatlands, containing 1,000 spare muskets, 30,000 cartridges and 300 handcuffs.

In fits and starts the various components of the Line began to push south. They quickly found that it would be no easy country shoot. The broken nature of the rough terrain made it impossible to maintain good order. Captain Donaldson's Launceston Corps scaled a high bluff but spent a miserable night without shelter, battered by icy wind and rain. Other units found their inadequate clothing slashed to rags by sharp-thorned bushes. A soldier gathering firewood was pierced in the leg and shoulder by spears thrown by an unseen enemy. Progress was slow and arduous and the thrill of the chase soon wore off. Free tobacco was issued to ease the discomfort of the cold, black nights.

Despite the repeated issue of new regulations which decreed the correct distance between men, campsites and fires, the Line was impossible to secure through the day and night. In the darkness shadows were glimpsed crossing the Line, evading sentries who, in the flickering light of the campfires, were uncertain as to whether they were natives, animals or ghosts. One sentry tripped over a log, only to see it stand up and melt away into the trees. Thousands of rounds were expended shooting at genuine shadows, or at branches shaken by the night breezes.

The Line plodded on, and occasionally there was some limited success. Mr Walpole recorded that on 26 October he spotted the rough camp of a small group of foraging aborigines. 'I returned for the rest of my party, and in the evening placed them within 300 yards of the Natives,' he wrote, 'where we waited until dawn of day and crept to one of the Natives, without being perceived by any of the others in the windbreak and there I caught him by the leg. The other four rushed away. One, however, was caught after he had fallen into the creek, and two others were shot.' The rest of the forty-strong tribe were alerted and rushed through the Line in a body, spearing one settler in the leg as they passed.

At the beginning of November some of the most experienced soldiers were ordered to clear aborigines out of the Three Thumbs, a chain of tree-covered hills about 300 yards apart, near Prosser's Bay. It was believed that this natural citadel held the largest remaining body of blacks. The ashes of camp fires, wood chippings and aboriginal artefacts were found but the soldiers were unable to cut their way through the dense scrub and undergrowth. They fired volley after volley into the trees while beaters created a storm of noise to drive away the game. Half-starved blacks, deprived of their food supplies, smothered the cries of their few remaining infants whenever the soldiers got too close. Governor Arthur personally led several sorties in the hope of a triumphal return to Hobart with chained captives. Finally, after criss-crossing the area he had to concede defeat – the aborigines had melted away, slipping through the Line while the soldiers blasted empty glades.

They and other clans, by now enraged, attacked farms behind the Line. Newspapers, critical of the Line from the start, questioned why the northern part of the island had been left defenceless. After four white men were speared near Launceston, a northern magistrate wrote: 'I have no person I can send after these Blacks. I have no-one that I can spare, nearly all the constables being out of the country, catching the Blacks in

Buckingham.' Such reports of endangered homes caused an upsurge in desertions along the Line.

Arthur, however, was determined to press on, heartened by reports that blacks had been seen on Forester's Peninsula. He issued an address to his scattered commanders:

A few days must now terminate this great work in the most satisfactory manner, and His Excellency earnestly hopes that the leaders will, for the remaining short period, continue to show the excellent spirit which has all along been so conspicuous in their parties, for they will perceive that the advance of the scouting parties will render redoubled vigilance necessary on the part of those who guard the Line, as the Natives, when disturbed in the interior, will undoubtedly increase their efforts to break through the positions.

He gave his men four days to advance, driving the blacks before them, to East Bay Neck, a narrow sliver of ground which connected the peninsula to the mainland. Everything went to plan and each unit met its strict timetable. The shorelines were watched to prevent aborigines escaping by canoe. At last Arthur's forces crossed the Neck and entered the peninsula. Not a single aborigine was there.

The Line operation had cost the Government £30,000 and the Colony as a whole over £70,000. It had involved, including back-up forces, reinforcements, suppliers and transporters, upward of 6,000 Europeans. And the net result was two aborigines captured by Walpole's party. The Revd John West wrote: 'The settler-soldiers returned to their homes, their shoes worn out, their garments tattered, their hair long and shaggy, with beards unshaven, their arms tarnished, but neither blood-stained, nor disgraced.'

Governor Arthur believed that, disappointments aside, the Line had achieved an important objective. In his parting order of 26 November he said that the remaining aborigines, having seen at first hand the military and numerical power of the white man, would be persuaded to surrender without more bloodshed. Events proved him partially right. The aborigines were dispersed, hungry, cut off from their traditional hunting grounds. Constant pursuit and harrying had taken their toll. A small northern tribe, about thirty souls, did indeed surrender. Individual aborigines were lured out of the bush and forests by relatives who told them that the white man's life offered comfort and glittering presents. The Line may have been a farce in strictly military terms, but it demonstrated that the nomadic way of life which had sustained the native population for centuries was over.

★ ★ ★

George Augustus Robinson was a classic nineteenth-century mixture of humbug, high-minded Christianity, personal greed and ambition mixed with compassion and an unbreakable certainty in his own infallibility. It was a lethal concoction, and it resulted in the destruction of an entire race. An Englishman with few family connections, he was Hobart Town's chief bricklayer and preacher. His Wesleyan zeal

George Augustus Robinson, bricklayer and preacher, who organised the last round-up.

was focused on the protection of a 'lesser race' from the ungodly excesses of a white society which he considered equally barbaric. He became the self-styled 'Defender of the Aborigine'. He believed that God had commanded him to save the aborigine and that meant 'civilising' him.

Before, during and after the Line operation Robinson embarked on a series of epic journeys into the hinterland, trying to gain the trust of the tribes and to persuade them to come in. He was greatly helped by 'semi-civilised' natives, women spies and go-betweens including Truganina, and by aboriginal trackers whom he converted by bribery and the promise of eternal salvation. His treks were a success and, of course, Robinson saw no reason to spurn the bounties in cash and land which were his reward on earth for his Christian endeavours. He became a very rich man. His success in bringing out of the bush small groups of half-starved natives brought him to the attention of Governor Arthur and the Hobart Aborigine Committee. There was certainly a need for new tactics. The Line operation had spurred on the few warriors left to acts of increasing, almost suicidal, savagery. John Batman, a farmer near Ben Lomond and Robinson's chief rival as a humane native-catcher, wrote:

The Natives last Thursday week murdered two more men at Oyster Bay, and the next day they beat a sawyer to death. On the Sunday after they murdered a soldier. On last Wednesday, they attacked the house of Mr Boultby, when he was absent; and if it had not been for a soldier who happened to be there, they would have murdered Mrs Boultby and all the children. On Friday last they murdered three men at a hut belonging to Major Gray, and left a fourth for dead.

Robinson, Batman and others traversed the island to persuade the aborigines that their only hope was to trust the white man, give up their lands and move to a wondrous new land teeming with game. The result was the Flinders Island Reservation, an early example of a concentration camp. The man placed in charge, at an annual salary of £100, was G.A. Robinson. In 1832 the first group of 220 aborigines were sent to their new home. They were horrified by what they found. Flinders Island is 40 miles long and 12 to 18 miles wide. As promised, it had a small population of kangaroos for hunting. It had wild and beautiful mountains. But generally it was exposed to storms and lashing rain, cold, barren and desolate. Some aborigines tried to leap overboard, others moaned and twitched convulsively in dismay. Weakened already by famine, rheumatism, consumption and sea travel, many aborigines felt they were looking at the place of their own death. They were proved right. Almost immediately scores died of the common cold – against which they had no antibodies – tuberculosis, pneumonia and cultural shock.

Robinson chose a bay on the island's south-western side for the building of his new model settlement, to be called Wybalenna. Exposed to the western winds, neither forest nor high ground offered the bay any protection, but nevertheless it was here that he decided to try out his theories on moral and social reform. Soldiers built long huts of wattle and daub to provide shelter before more permanent buildings could be erected. Sympathetic settlers donated a small flock of sheep. Conflict broke out almost immediately. Quarrels between feuding clans were daily occurrences. Soldiers clashed with white sealers over the favours of the naked black women. The black men resented the whites' attitude to their wives and daughters, who were themselves becoming uncontrollable. The men became dissipated and listless. Food was continually in short supply. A number of blacks protested and the soldiers' commander, the tough old convict-flogger Sergeant White, called it a rebellion. As a punishment he marooned fifteen aborigine men on a granite rock out to sea without food, shelter or water, save for whatever they could scoop up from rainwater puddles. They were rescued after five days by Batman, although several later died from their treatment.

The subsequent scandal led to White's replacement by the more humane Lieutenant Darling, who swiftly ordered all sealers off the island, and moved the main encampment to a more hospitable site. Robinson moved to the island two years later and claimed the credit for Darling's initial humanitarian work. The island was supplied with cows, shoes and crude furniture. Well-meaning souls sent the aborigine women petticoats and checked aprons. But still the aborigines died in alarming numbers. They died of dysentery, cholera, venereal diseases, influenza and occasional violence. Some seemed simply to give up on life and wandered into the rocky hinterland, never to return. Their spirits withered as they came to terms with what was effectively imprisonment without conviction; they were convicts with no foreseeable end to their sentences. The Revd Dr Lang of Sydney wrote to one newspaper that the blacks had been given 'the security of death . . . the happiness of leaving their unburied bones to be bleached by the sun and

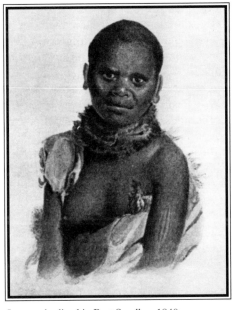

Jenny, who lived in Port Sorell, *c.* 1840.

rain in every nook and dell of that island'. In July 1837 a single epidemic claimed twenty-nine lives. By January 1838 the 220 original captives had been reduced to 93 – 39 women, 38 men, 5 adolescents and 11 children under ten.

Despite the high death rate, Robinson pressed on with the creation of a model settlement in which the surviving aborigines would embrace Christianity and the white man's ways. Robinson renamed all his charges with names of classical, literary and religious significance. Truganina, who was growing old disgracefully, was named Lalla Rookh after an Arabian princess in a popular poem. Other women were renamed Cleopatra, Queen Adelaide, Juliet, Andromache and Semiramis. Decrepit warriors he called Napoleon, Ajax, Achilles, Columbus, Nimrod and Romeo. Robinson may have been amused by his own inventiveness, but he also claimed a higher purpose: a new name allowed sinful blacks to embrace the Christian virtues of decency and chastity.

By the beginning of 1838 the forty-three whites on the island, including the garrison, were well housed. Robinson and his family lived in a fine brick mansion, while officers, storemen and others lived in cosy cottages with gardens. There was a small hospital, a store, barracks and decent accommodation for the sixteen convict labourers and their families. A brick chapel towered over the settlement. The aborigines lived in a 'terrace', also made of brick. Robinson established a school for all aborigines who could be bullied or bribed into attendance. The adults were paid four pence a week to attend night schools twice a week and Sunday attendance at chapel was compulsory. A visiting party of Quakers was very impressed. One wrote: 'A large party of aborigine women took tea with us at the Commandant's. They conducted themselves in a very orderly manner; and, after washing up the tea things, put them in their places.' In one progress report Robinson wrote: 'Some of the native youths were able to answer questions in regard to the leading events of the Scripture History, Christian Doctrine and Duty, Arithmetic, the principal facts of Geography, also on several facts of useful information. Some very fair specimens of handwriting were exhibited on such occasions.' Robinson praised an essay by a fifteen-year-old youth: 'It was expressed in simple and tolerably correct language, and breathed a warm spirit of gratitude to myself.'

But Robinson was deluding himself and few others. Between January and July 1838 another nine blacks died. It finally dawned on him that all would perish if he continued with his experiment. In any case, he had now been appointed Chief Protector of Aborigines at Port Philip on the Australian mainland. Robinson did try to persuade the authorities to allow him to take his remaining Flinders Island charges with him but was unsuccessful and, ultimately, he abandoned them in his pursuit of further fortune and spiritual enlightenment. He was a man of God – but the aborigines would have been much better off if he had never touched their lives.

The Tasmanians left behind fell into a lethargic depression which saw their numbers cut down even further. The simple cause, according to some medical opinion, was homesickness. One authority wrote:

They have been treated with uniform kindness; nevertheless the births have been few, and the deaths numerous. This may have been due in great measure to their change of living and food; but more so to their banishment from the mainland of Tasmania, which is visible from Flinders Island, and the aborigines have often pointed it out to me with the expressions of the deepest sorrow depicted on their countenances.

Eventually the new governor, Sir John Franklin, whose wife had adopted a pretty black girl as her servant and then dumped her when she found other amusements, took pity on the survivors. By now the aborigines were such a pathetic bunch that they posed no threat to the settlers. In 1847 the remaining forty-four aborigines were removed from Flinders Island to Oyster Cove. Only ten men were left.

For a time their new home revived their spirits. They were given provisions to stock their gardens with peas, beans and potatoes. The women learnt to sew their own clothes and to boil or roast their food. An official wrote: 'Their houses are comfortable and clean. They are as contented as possible.'

However, all attempts at 'improving' the sullen natives resulted in frustration. Their temperaments were not suited to a settled life and, although conditions were much better than on Flinders, the men had lost the will to live. By the end of 1854 only 3 men, 11 women and 2 boys were left. Most had died, although some children had been removed to a notorious orphanage which was a virtual death sentence, and some of the girls and women moved in with rough whites and half-castes. The writer James Bonwick described a visit to the settlement: 'I saw a miserable collection of huts and outbuildings, the ruins of the old penal establishment, profoundly dirty, and fleas were swarming everywhere, as I found to my cost.' The sleeping huts were bare and filthy. Government-issue blankets had either been stolen by white men, or sold by the blacks for liquor. Dogs shared the 'bed and board' of the natives.

Governor Arthur, who had returned to England in March 1837, was festooned with honours. His reforms of the convict system were judged a great success and the fate of the aborigines under his stewardship was rarely commented upon. He became lieutenant-governor of Upper Canada and later of Bombay where he took a great interest in the education of the natives. He died in 1854, a baronet, a knight, a lieutenant-general, a privy counsellor with an honorary doctorate from Oxford University. His biographer noted: 'He was an eminently unselfish man, imbued with a deep sense of religion, and as much respected for his unswerving integrity in private as in public life.' He left a grieving widow and ten children.

Meanwhile, the blacks of Oyster Cove made no more children and died one by one during the 1860s. The last man was William Lanney, also known as King Billy, who had been one of the few aborigines born on Flinders Island. He died of alcohol poisoning in 1869, aged thirty-four. At his burial it was discovered that his head had been removed and sent, surreptitiously, to the Royal College of Surgeons for study. A surgeon had secretly skinned his head in the mortuary and replaced it with another skull. Others cut off his hands and feet. After burial the rest of his body disappeared.

The reason for such grave-robbing was simple. The destruction of a race coincided with an upsurge of medical, scientific and amateur interest in anthropology and the origins of man. The Tasmanians had by custom cremated the bodies of their relatives. Consequently high prices were paid for Tasmanian skulls. Body-snatchers went to work in the graveyards of Flinders Island and Oyster Cove. The Royal Society obtained over twenty skulls. This collection was bombed during the London Blitz and the pathetic, charred remnants were swept out with the debris.

The last surviving true Tasmanian was Truganina, who was haunted by fears that her body would suffer the same fate as Lanney's. She had survived venereal disease contracted from a white man, a trial in which she was acquitted of the murder of two Europeans (two co-defendants were hanged) and the privations of Flinders Island. For several years she had been in the care of a white woman, Mrs Dandridge, who was paid a government allowance for her trouble. After Truganina's death on 6 May 1876 Mrs Dandridge successfully petitioned the Hobart administration to continue her payments.

Truganina's body was buried for security in the grounds of Hobart's women's penitentiary. Two years later, under the terms of a special Act of Parliament, she was dug up and her bones put on display in Hobart Museum.

In barely seventy years an entire race had been driven to extinction. It is a stain which has never been removed from the banners of the British Empire.

★   ★   ★

CHAPTER FOUR

The Opium War, 1839–42

'I am sick at heart of war.'

On 3 March 1843 five massive wagons, each hauled by four horses, arrived at the Mint in London escorted by a detachment of the 60th Regiment. The wagons were filled with wooden boxes, one of which had been broken on the journey, spilling out strange silver coins. Troopers held back a curious and avaricious crowd which gave a 'lusty cheer' when the word went around that the money was an instalment of the 'China Ransom' – payment on account of the war indemnity imposed on that far-away Celestial Empire. The Chinese war had been a popular one in Britain and the victory pumped back to the Exchequer almost £5.75 million in 'China money'. Other spoils of war included the Crown colony of Hong Kong.

At Westminster the Duke of Wellington and the high-spirited Lord Stanley moved a vote of thanks to the officers and men involved in the China operation, by whose valour and skill 'a series of brilliant and unvaried successes' was given to England. In

Canton factories, *c.* 1780. (Peabody Museum of Salem)

May the young Queen Victoria received presents from the defeated Emperor of China. They included a golden bedstead, ear-drops worth a staggering £1,000 apiece; a shawl decorated finely with portraits of 'every kind of beast known to them', rare silks and a box full of exquisite jewellery.

The Chinese Emperor was humbled, thousands of men, women and children had been lost in one-sided battles, and the defeat at the hands of western military technology resulted in the forcible opening up of China after centuries of voluntary isolation. But the British lost something too . . . the respect of civilised people at home and abroad. The war had been fought to protect the opium trade. Even by the standards of the day this was seen as a despicable ambition. MP Justin McCarthy said: 'The principle for which we fought the China War was the right of Great Britain to force a peculiar trade upon a foreign people.' Thomas Arnold, the headmaster at Rugby, called it a national sin of the greatest possible magnitude. The American missionary Howard Malcolm thundered: 'The proud escutcheon of the nation which declaims against the slave trade is made to bear a blot broader than any other in the Christian world.' Lord Ashley, on hearing that the war was won, rejoiced that 'this cruel and debasing war is terminated'. He added: 'I cannot rejoice in our successes; we have triumphed in one of the most lawless, unnecessary and unfair struggles in the records of history.' In 1843 Balzac said that while before they had been regarded as noble-hearted, the China War had demonstrated how 'the English flaunt their perfidiousness in the face of the whole world'. Britain lost its good name and, in the Far East at least, would never fully regain it.

★   ★   ★

The Quing dynasty ruled the most extensive Chinese empire in history, with boundaries encompassing the Ili Valley and Kashgar, Tibet and Nepal, with Korea and Annam as vassal states. The population had almost doubled from 200 million in the seventeenth century and food shortages and famine sparked unrest. But despite recent revolts in Formosa and Kweichow which were suppressed ruthlessly, it was an empire largely at peace. The Emperor sat at the apex of a strong central administration which controlled the judiciary, education and the arts. He was patron to a classic period of painting, literature and the production of superb porcelain. His Summer Palace and the Forbidden City in Peking, while not quite so grand as in previous generations, were warrens of sumptuous halls, audience rooms and private chambers, beautifully carved, tiled and painted. Lord Macartney, on an abortive mission to the Summer Residence in 1793, marvelled at the ornamental buildings: 'They have not the air of being crowded or disproportionate; they never intrude upon the eye but wherever they appear they always show themselves to advantage, and aid, improve and enliven the prospect.' The people largely practised differing blends of Confucianism, Taoism and Buddhism under the broad umbrella of ancestor worship. The cornerstone of every community was the sanctity of the family.

It was a cultured world but one that was closed to virtually all foreigners. Trade with the outside world was permitted and thrived as the west craved tea, but from 1757 foreign ships were confined to the single port of Canton to keep at arm's length the pernicious influence of the 'Ocean Devils'. British, French, Dutch and

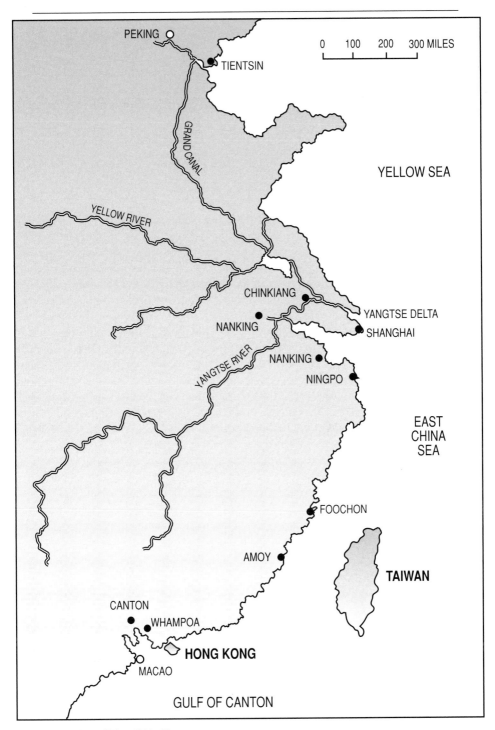

The Opium War – China 1839–42.

American ships would sail from Macao harbour up the Hsi Chiang river to sell opium from India for silver which would then be used to buy tea and silk. Western traders had to deal solely with the Co-hong, a designated group of merchants.

To undiscerning westerners China was a strange land, so populous that 'multitudes are compelled to live in boats, floating about to pick up dead dogs for food'. It was tyrannised by a Tartar government which regarded all Europeans as 'barbarians', and believed that 'their sole endeavour in regard of foreigners is to insult and mock them'. In fact, Harriet Martineau reported, merchants of any nation who had lived long enough in the neighbourhood gave a very different account: 'They declare that the government is on the whole favourable to the industry and comfort of the people; that the rights of property are respected; that the Chinese possess a greater body of literature than Europe can show.' It was difficult to assess the importance of that literature, she admitted, because 'nothing is known among us of its quality'.

Despite Martineau's over-rosy portrait of commerce, the balance of trade was heavily in China's favour in opium-for-tea transactions, and disputes often flared up. They were exacerbated by the absence of fixed tariff charges, the corruption of some officials and the refusal of the Chinese authorities to treat foreigners as equals. But the real problem was the nature of the trade itself. Opium had been used as a pain-killer in China for at least a thousand years and initially the British felt little sense of guilt in stepping up its export to feed a growing addiction among the Chinese people. In India and Britain it was drunk as a stimulant and was used both to alleviate dysentery and as a vital aid to surgery. It was generally regarded as a more exotic form of alcoholic spirit. The East India Company had, however, long understood its dangers when taken by the rich for relaxation. Warren Hastings said it was 'pernicious'. The Chinese had banned its importation in 1729 and again in 1796, by which time annual imports had risen from a thousand chests, each weighing 140 lb, to four thousand. The trade remained stable until 1830, when it doubled, and by 1836 it stood at 30,000 chests. Uniquely, the Chinese smoked opium by mixing it with tobacco, which greatly increased the risks of addiction and overdose.

The East India Company, which had limited opium production, was forced into a price war by private growers. Prices fell to a level where mass consumption became possible in the huge Chinese market. By the 1820s one-seventh of the Company's revenues in India were derived from opium. Its exchequer in Canton received eighteen million Mexican dollars a year from opium sales. One-twelfth of British revenues at home came from duties on tea, which could only be purchased through the opium trade. Opium was crucial to British trade in the East, and therefore vital to an economy free to expand after the ravages of the Napoleonic Wars.

The opium was bought by British and Parsee merchants and shipped to China, commission agents in Canton handling the next transaction. As the trade was nominally illegal the cargo was taken ashore by Chinese boats crewed by outcast Tanka sailors. An 'unofficial' tax was levied by the controller of customs in Canton, who in turn paid up to a million dollars annually into the emperor's private coffers. The Chinese opium merchants were backed by the huge Shanxi banks who also acted on behalf of the Chinese Government. Distribution inland was generally handled by the Triad secret societies. Official duplicity could not, however, hide the increasing cost of addiction suffered by the ordinary Chinese populace and in 1821 the Chinese Government tried for the first time to enforce their anti-opium legislation.

The edict came from the very top, the Emperor Daoguang (or Ch'ing Tao-kuang), who had taken the Dragon Throne the year before. He was a well-meaning but ineffectual man who wanted to boost the imperial prestige which had been weakened by westerners who had ignored earlier crackdowns with impudence and impunity. The emperor, whose name meant 'Glorious Rectitude', was politically naive but later historians agreed that he really tried to help his people. Morality was not his only concern. Economic instability was being caused by the quantity of silver draining into the foreign pockets of opium importers. Opium ships were ordered out of the river and the traders were forced to use Lintin Island as their distribution centre.

By then the East India Company's monopoly on the opium trade had been broken and private traders were less willing to put up with the restrictions and bureaucracy imposed by the Chinese. The opium ban did not halt the trade, but only increased the bribes necessary to do business. The Hongs prospered in Canton through smuggling not just opium but also saltpetre and salt. Trading expeditions along the coast broke Chinese laws which were impossible to enforce. The British traders, crammed into their 'factories' on Lintin, complained bitterly that the Hongs were cheating them and welshing on debts.

Canton Governor-General Lu Kun, anxious to avoid more tension, and aware of the dwindling influence of the Company whose Charter was due to end shortly, urged the British to appoint an official to represent the British merchants. The merchants in turn wanted just such an emissary to break the stranglehold enjoyed by the Hongs. In 1834 Lord Napier was appointed 'Superintendent of Trade' and dispatched to Canton on a misguided mission which would only heighten the tension, increase the misunderstandings between two cultures, and eventually spark bloody warfare.

William John, the eighth Baron Napier, was a 47-year-old sea captain who had seen action at Trafalgar. He had also fought bravely in the attack on the French fleet in Aix Roads. With that war over he settled comfortably in Selkirkshire to a life of sheep-farming and road building. His 1822 book *A Treatise on Practical Store-farming as applicable to the Mountainous Region of Etterick Forest and the Pastoral District of Scotland in general* was well received. On succeeding to his peerage he commanded the frigate *Diamond* on the South American station for two years from 1824. None of his experiences or his diverse talents qualified him for his new post.

Napier's instructions were clear. He was to aid the lawful pursuits of British merchants, ensure they conformed to Chinese laws 'so long as these were fairly and equally administered', and investigate the possibility of extending trade. He was not to enter negotiations on behalf of the Crown, nor use menacing language, nor appeal for help to British warships forbidden to enter the Canton River at Bocca Tigris, 'the Tiger's Mouth'. He was, in short, to raise as little fuss as possible and employ diplomatic skills not usually associated with Scottish sheep-farmers and sea captains. He broke just about every instruction.

Napier arrived at Macao on July 15 and was outraged to discover he was expected to stay there until the necessary permits had been arranged for him to travel up to

Canton. Governor-General Lu had asked for a simple merchant to act on behalf of the British traders, yet he had been sent a government representative. He argued, quite reasonably, that permission should have been asked in advance. Napier was also not carrying any credentials from the Palmerston Government which Lu could forward to Peking. Napier simply ignored all the protocol and, dodging the Chinese officials sent to intercept him, arrived in Canton on 25 July. He announced his arrival in a letter which did not conform to any of the Chinese diplomatic niceties, and Lu promptly returned it. An interview between Napier and Canton officials broke down because the seating arrangements would have put the proud Scot in a position lower than the Chinese. Napier also took offence when he discovered that the Chinese interpretation of his name, when written down, was 'laboriously vile'. No offence was intended by this, but Napier failed to understand that the Chinese expressed names new to them by the words in their language which came closest phonetically. Mr Morrison, for example, was written as 'a polite horse'. Napier, like many westerners after him, bitterly resented being called a 'barbarian' or 'barbarian eyes' by the Chinese. Again, no insult was intended. The literal translation is 'head of the southern people' or 'foreigners from the south' – the direction from which the ships came. Westerners often complained about the 'childish arrogance' of the language used by Chinese officials. Again this was not intended to be insulting, only to underline the importance of the emperor. Historian Brian Inglis pointed out:

> The Emperor had to rule over a vast population, with the additional handicap that his dynasty were usurpers; and this had led to an exaggerated insistence upon respect and reverence for the Dragon Throne. His subjects, it was felt, must perpetually be reminded that their country was the centre of the civilised world, the Middle Kingdom, to which all others were tributary; and that their emperor was *the* Emperor, the representative on earth of the divinity.

Such considerations did not occur to Napier who lost both his composure and any chance of promoting a peaceful mission. He described Lu as a 'presumptuous savage' and told London that trade could be extended to the whole of China by the use of a force smaller than that needed to take a 'paltry West Indian island'. Lu ordered Napier back to Macao. Napier refused to go and summoned two men-of-war into the river. Alarmed and perplexed, the Chinese authorities suspended all trade. Napier's household servants were withdrawn and he was forced to suffer 'many petty annoyances'. He sent orders to the British frigates to attack. The ships fired on shore installations and lost three men when batteries fired back. The stress and climate made Napier seriously ill and his surgeon told him he must leave Canton. He arrived back at Macao at the end of September and died two weeks later. He left two sons, five daughters and a legacy of distrust and disdain which irretrievably soured relations between two mutually incomprehending empires.

Lu expressed sympathy for his death but proclaimed:

> The Chinese nation has its laws. It is so everywhere. England has its laws; and how much more so the Celestial Empire. The said foreign minister having

crossed a sea of many thousand miles to inquire into, and take the superintendence of commercial affairs, ought to be a person acquainted with the principles of government, and with the forms essential to its dignity.

Napier's death, and Lu's good sense, had prevented a clash of etiquette escalating into war, and tensions eased for two years.

Charles Elliot, a 35-year-old naval captain who had impressed Lord Palmerston with his ideas on China, was appointed the new Superintendent of Trade in Canton in June 1836, having already spent two years there as secretary to the trade commissioners. As a junior naval officer he had served in the East Indies, off the African coast and Jamaica, where he was commander of the hospital ship at Port Royal. This was the peak of his naval career. Since 1828 he had held diplomatic or colonial posts, including working as the protector of slaves in Guyana. A nephew of former Governor-General Lord Minto, he had good contacts in the Colonial Office and boasted of friends in high places. A political rival complained he 'has now in his writing desk a copious expression of their sentiments, views, decisions and plans for the future' which he kept secret. Elliot believed that Chinese protocol should be accepted and wrote: 'Practically speaking, the aggregate of our trade with China is less burdened than it is in any country with which we have commerce.' British dignity, however, was affronted by the requirement to negotiate with the Chinese through petition, and Palmerston ordered Elliot to halt that practice, offending Chinese sensibilities. The Hongs were instructed to open and read all letters from foreigners.

Meanwhile the volume of opium trade increased and the Chinese authorities began seriously to consider bringing it under control by legalisation. Lu and several powerful friends at the Imperial Court advocated it, as did many smaller British traders. For several months legalisation seemed inevitable, but opponents fought back. They were led by the bigger opium-runners who could afford the risks and reaped the rewards of prices kept high by illegality. Officials from inland regions pointed to the 'moral degradation' that opium had inflicted on the soldier classes – an 1832 campaign against Yao aborigines had been aborted because the fighting men were weakened by addiction. One estimate suggested that by the mid-1830s between ten and twelve million Chinese were incurably addicted. The emperor, also aware of the drain on silver which threatened his economy, agreed that urgent action was vital and a serious effort to suppress the opium trade was launched late in 1836.

In Canton the new Governor-General Deng Tingzhen ordered all foreign opium ships out of the river. The trade was brought to a standstill and even the biggest trader, Jardine & Matheson, warned shareholders that this time the Chinese meant business. In London the government officially backed the crackdown and Palmerston acknowledged China's right to halt imports, saying that any losses would have to be suffered by the traders themselves. Captain Elliot described the opium trade as 'a traffic which every friend to humanity must deplore'. The opium merchants took violent action to evade the ban. British ships crewed by lascars landed their cargoes on to the Canton wharves from where heavily armed vessels spread their poison along the Chinese coast. There were one-sided clashes with unwieldy Chinese junks. The violent anarchy outraged both Chinese and British

Chinese 'rebels'. (Illustrated London News)

officials. The American firm Russell & Co. withdrew from the opium trade in February 1839. Deng and Elliot were both prepared to cooperate to stamp out the smuggling, but were hampered by the diplomatic stand-off which prevented proper communication. Their efforts to prevent disaster effectively ended when a hard-liner from Peking arrived on 10 March 1839.

Imperial Commissioner Lin Zexu was one of the richest men in China, a renowned scholar and a leading member of the reform party. He was born in Foochow, had studied Manchu at the Hanlin Academy and had risen rapidly through the ranks of the civil service where he was regarded as a highly able administrator. Then in his mid-fifties, he was a large man, running to fat, with a heavy black moustache and a long beard. He walked with dignity and a 'rather harsh or firm expression', according to one English witness. His own journal suggests that he was a humane and learned, if calculating, man. His scholarship was tempered with ruthlessness. As Governor-General of Hunan and Hubei he had suppressed home-grown opium addiction by executing all known dealers. Addicts were given eighteen months, with medical help, to break their habit. If they failed they, too, were executed. Such draconian actions had worked, but the 54-year-old commissioner knew that the immediate execution of foreign importers was not an option. He was convinced, however, that the opium merchants had no support at home and believed, wrongly, that the import of opium to Britain was illegal. He also mistakenly believed that British ships involved in the trade must be unlicensed pirates. But his biggest mistake was to regard Elliot, a potential ally in ending the trade, as a renegade opium merchant rather than as a British official. Lin ignored Elliot's assurances, despite the captain's stated view that 'the Chinese government had just grounds for harsh measures'. As a signal of intent, just before Lin's arrival a native opium smuggler was publicly strangled with military pomp.

Lin issued proclamations to the Chinese population ordering all smokers to hand over their opium and pipes within two months. Students were organised into five-man teams pledged to ensure that none of their number smoked. In a special assembly 600 students of the Confucian classics were asked to name opium dealers as part of their examinations. Within a few months over 1,600 Chinese had been arrested and about 50,000 pounds of opium and over 70,000 pipes had been confiscated.

Lin turned his attention to the British, urging them to stick to their legitimate trade in tea, silk and, bizarrely, rhubarb which he believed was essential to the good health of all foreigners. In a letter to Queen Victoria Lin appealed to her personal morality to end the opium trade at source, in the poppy fields of India. He wrote:

> It appears that this form of poison is illegally prepared by scoundrels in the tributary tribes of your honourable country and the devil-regions under your jurisdiction, but of course is neither prepared nor sold by your sovereign orders. . . . Not to smoke yourselves, but yet to dare to prepare and sell to and beguile the foolish masses of the Inner Land – this is to protect one's own life while leading others to death, to gather profits for oneself while bringing injury upon others. Such behaviour is repugnant to the feelings of human beings, and is not tolerated by the ways of God.

It is doubtful whether Queen Victoria even saw that appeal. There was, in any case, no reply.

Lin ordered the surrender of all foreign opium supplies stored at Lintin, so that it could be burnt. His edict also required a bond that ships should land no more opium and those crews that did so would forfeit their cargoes and their lives. Lin had already demanded the surrender of opium in the hands of Chinese dealers, saying he would spare them the death penalty if they complied within an agreed time. The British merchants argued that the opium in their stores did not belong to them, as they were merely agents of companies in India, and they had no legal mandate to give it up. Lin responded by demanding that the senior British merchant in Lintin, Mr Dent, be handed over to a Chinese court. When the traders refused Lin moved troops to surround the island factories. The British community as a whole, rather than one man, had been taken hostage.

The blockade lasted six weeks. Any Chinese who worked in the factories, as servants, dockers or labourers, were ordered to stay away. Heavily armed soldiers manned barricades blocking the entrances. A mixed fleet of junks and other craft patrolled the river. Lin warned that if any attempts were made to breach it he would obtain imperial permission to close the harbour forever. Moreover he would enforce Chines law, including the death penalty for opium smuggling, on all foreigners.

Eventually Elliot persuaded the traders to hand over the drugs, even though he had no legal powers to insist, by promising that the British Government would compensate them. He had no authority to make such a promise, either, although the traders did not know that. For them, ironically, it promised an end to their worries. If the opium had remained in their Chinese depots the price would plummet when the next year's shipment arrived from India. Instead they had the promise of indemnity at market prices backed, they believed, by the British Government. They did, however, fear that Lin or other, perhaps corrupt, officials would not destroy the confiscated opium, but sell it on, drastically affecting the prices of subsequent crops. Such fears were groundless.

A total of 20,283 chests were surrendered, close to three million pounds of raw opium. Lin ordered the digging of three trenches, each 7 feet deep and 150 feet long, into which the balls of opium were hurled. Five hundred labourers broke up the balls and mixed their contents with water, salt and lime until dissolved. The resulting sludge was flushed into the Pearl River. The British were free to leave. Sixteen traders were detained at the factories but permitted to leave later, under injunction never to return. For the Chinese the action had been a success. But Lin's tactics changed the entire nature of the tussle. Most British officials and ministers had previously sympathised with the suppression of the trade, but the confinement of British subjects, many of them unconnected with the opium trade, and the destruction of British property, however disreputable, was quite another matter. In a dispatch to Palmerston Elliot said that for 'the first time, in our intercourse with this Empire, its government has taken the unprovoked initiative in aggressive measures against British life, liberty and property, and against the dignity of the Crown'. From now on there could be no peace.

★ ★ ★

Reports of the imprisonment of the British in their factories reached London on 21 September 1839; they were soon followed by news of the surrender of the opium. There was widespread outrage, especially among businessmen, those involved in the China trade and chambers of commerce. Canton's wealthiest trader, Dr William Jardine, who had returned to Britain earlier that year, headed a merchant delegation with a $20,000 war chest. Through pamphlets they portrayed the siege of the factories as another Black Hole of Calcutta, although the Lintin hostages had suffered little deprivation. The confinement of the traders, officials and families was a deadly insult to Her Majesty's flag. Jardine had been given enough money to 'secure, at a high price, the services of some leading newspaper to advocate the cause'. The public, which before then had barely known of the opium trade, were told that Englishmen were in danger in a foreign country and that they were being harshly treated and recklessly imprisoned. Jardine avoided the issue of morality, arguing that the government owed the merchants a responsibility for permitting the growing of opium in India for the China market. One observer unconnected to the trade said that while the crisis may have begun with opium, the issue now was how to restore trade without 'the most cringing and humiliating concessions'. Captain Elliott had written urgently to Lord Auckland, the Governor-General of India, asking for as many warships and armed vessels as could be spared 'for the defence of life and property'.

Meanwhile Lin withdrew Chinese servants from the British factories following the death of a peasant, Lin Weihi, in a drunken brawl. He demanded that the murderer should face Chinese justice but the British refused, saying they did not know which of a gang of sailors was responsible for the crime. Elliot held an official inquiry, which was inconclusive, and refused to hand over a symbolic culprit to the Chinese executioner. The British, fearing a repeat imprisonment, left Canton and sailed to the island of Hong Kong, which already had a rapidly growing British community. The opium ships which Elliot had ordered out of the Canton River provided them with some defence. Local Chinese poisoned wells on the rocky outcrop and refused to sell food to the foreigners.

On 3 November Chinese war junks approached the 28-gun British frigate *Volage* and the sloop *Hyacinth* in the Kowloon estuary and again demanded the execution of the sailor who had murdered the peasant. At noon Captain Smith of *Volage* gave the signal to engage the imposing force of twenty-eight war junks and fire-ships. The *Annual Register* reported:

> The ships then lying hove to at the extreme end of the Chinese line, bore away ahead in close order, having the wind on the starboard beam. In this way, and under easy sail, they ran down the Chinese line, pouring in a destructive fire. The lateral direction of the wind enabled the ships to perform the same evolution from the other extreme of the line, running up again with their larboard broadsides bearing.

The Chinese 'answered with much spirit' but the impact of a British broadside was devastating. One war junk blew up after a pistol shot from *Volage*, three were sunk, and several others became water-logged. In his dispatches Captain Smith paid tribute 'to the gallantry of the Chinese admiral, who in a junk mounting 12 guns bore down upon the ships, and sustained for some time a very heavy fire; he was at last compelled to turn, his vessel evidently being in a sinking state'. The remaining vessels limped back to their anchorage and Captain Smith let them go. His clemency, and the fact that he soon rejoined the main fleet at Hong Kong, allowed the Chinese Admiral Kwan to claim victory in the sea battle. One man on *Hyacinth* was slightly wounded and that ship, the captain reported, which 'was for some time surrounded by junks, has got her main-yard so much damaged that I fear it will be necessary to get a new one'.

Palmerston, urged on by Jardine, sent Elliot word that an expeditionary force would reach China by the following March to blockade Canton and the River Peiho below Peking. The decision to declare war was reached at a Cabinet meeting in which the only issue raised was the question of compensation. It was agreed that with the Melbourne administration already in deficit, Parliament would never accept extra taxes to compensate the merchants. Therefore the Chinese would have to pay, not only for the destroyed opium but also to cover the costs of the expedition to be mounted to chastise them. Palmerston acceded to Jardine's demands that to the reparations would be added a commercial treaty, the opening of four new China ports, and the formal occupation of several islands, including Hong Kong.

In February 1840 Elliot and his cousin, Admiral George Elliot, who had sailed from the Cape, were appointed heads of the expeditionary force. Their orders were to blockade China's major ports and capture the island of Chusan, which was to be held as surety for reparations.

In Britain the impending war was broadly, but not universally, popular. During a Commons debate on a Tory motion of censure the young minister Thomas Macaulay said that the Canton merchants 'belonged to a country unaccustomed to defeat, to submission or to shame; to a country which had exacted such reparation for the wrongs of her children as had made the ears of all who heard it to tingle; to a country which had made the Bey of Algeria humble himself in the dust before her insulted consul; to a country which had avenged the victims of the Black Hole on the field of Plassey. . . . They knew that, surrounded as they were by enemies, and separated by great oceans and continents from all help, not a hair of their heads would be harmed with impunity.' But the young William Ewart Gladstone replied:

> A war more unjust in its origin, a war more calculated to cover this country with permanent disgrace, I do not know. The right honourable gentleman opposite spoke of the British flag waving in glory at Canton. That flag is hoisted to protect an infamous contraband traffic; and if it were never hoisted except as it is now hoisted on the coast of China, we should recoil from its sight with horror.

The Tory anti-war motion was narrowly defeated after Palmerston declared that the paramount point was that Great Britain and her citizens had been insulted. The war was on.

* * *

By June 1840, 16 British warships carrying 540 guns, 4 armed steamers and 28 transport ships carrying 4,000 soldiers had assembled off Macao. Their cargo included 3,000 tons of coal for the steamers and 16,000 gallons of rum for the men. Already in the Canton River were the frigates *Volage*, *Druid* and *Hyacinth*.

The Chinese army numbered about a million men. Its nucleus was the Bannermen, mainly cavalrymen, a hereditary army of Manchu Tartars organised in eight divisions known as the 'Eight Banners'. Their weapons were obsolete matchlocks and bows, but they were adroit at using them from horseback. These were the troops the British were generally to face in the open field. The defenders of forts and cities were largely Chinese levies who had acquired the knack of gunnery. Most ordinary infantrymen carried spears, poleaxes and swords. Some still wore chain armour. Captain Granville Loch wrote:

> If drilled under English officers, they would prove equal, if not superior, to the Sepoys. The matchlock man carries the charges for his piece in bamboo tubes,

contained in a cotton belt fastened about his waist. He loads without a ramrod, by striking the butt against the ground after inserting the ball; the consequence is that he can charge and fire faster than one of us with a common musket. The best marksmen are stationed in front and supplied by people whose only duty is to load [for] them.

The British accused the Cantonese of sending a boatload of poisoned tea to be sold to the English sailors. In fact, the consignment was stolen by pirates and sold to Chinese civilians, many of whom died. A Chinese proclamation was issued offering rewards to those who destroyed the English. Anyone who captured a man-of-war carrying eighty great guns and delivered it to the mandarins would receive 20,000 Spanish dollars. The bounty for taking alive a foreigner peaked at 5,000 dollars for a warship's chief officer, sliding down a scale linked to other ranks. The reward for killing officers was one-third that for capture, on the production of evidence that the dead man held the alleged rank.

As more British ships assembled the Chinese let loose eighteen fire-rafts 'constructed of old fishing-boats and some cargo boats chained together two and two, and filled with combustible matter of all descriptions'; the alarm was raised among the British as their flames lit up the darkness. The *Canton Register* reported:

The appearance was very beautiful. The wind and the tide were then favourable for their course. As they approached they blew up like some (fire) works, what in

Chinese rifleman with matchlock. (Illustrated London News)

English pyrotechnical science would be called a flower pot. The beauties of the sight, however, did not dissipate the alarm felt on board the ships, who were also fearful there might be other crafty schemes in progress, and that they might be attacked from other quarters; consequently, most of the ships slipped their cables and moved out of danger, each more anxious than his neighbour to get into the rear. The scene and danger caused great excitement; the night was very dark.

Some British ships collided, but escaped serious damage. When light came some of the wreckage of the fire-rafts was collected: enough to supply the fleet with firewood for a month.

Unaware of this action, Palmerston hoped that the minimum use of force would be enough to force the Chinese to seek peace with suitable reparations and the legalisation of the opium trade. He issued orders to Elliot to bypass Canton, sail to the mouth of the Peiho and present a note to the Chinese Emperor dictating terms. Captain Elliot disagreed, knowing that a mere blockade would be ineffectual, but he dared not disobey such direct orders. A small force was left to blockade Canton, while the rest of the fleet headed north.

Admiral Elliot had meanwhile fallen ill – he was invalided out of the navy later that year – and was effectively replaced as an interim measure by 54-year-old Commodore Sir James John Gordon Bremer who had served assiduously but without special distinction during the later Napoleonic Wars. During a chequered career he had been shipwrecked on Newfoundland, founded a colony on Australia's Melville Island and took part in the first Burma War. A series of timely deaths of superior officers had seen him briefly hold the senior officership in India.

The Cantonese believed that the English had been frightened off by their shore batteries but on 5 July the fleet launched an attack on Chusan Island in Hangzhou Bay, intending to use it as a temporary base. Chusan officials at first thought they had come to trade but naval commander Bremer quickly demanded the surrender of the city-port Ting-hai. The Chinese officials prevaricated and Bremer gave them notice that hostilities were about to begin. His look-outs reported that the hills, shores and walls of the town were packed with large numbers of troops. Twenty-four small-calibre cannon were positioned along the town's wharf and on a nearby round tower. War-junks were also preparing for battle. Two divisions of British troops under Major-General George Burrell landed about a mile from the town on 5 July, and Bremer's ships bombarded the town for exactly nine minutes. Casualties in the city were severe, although Bremer used round shot instead of grape or canisters to minimise the carnage. Burrell, commanding men of the 14th Royal Irish Regiment, Royal Marines and Madras Sappers reported: 'I pushed forward advanced posts to within 500 yards of the city [walls] which, although in a dilapidated state, are extremely formidable and difficult of access, being surrounded on three sides with a deep canal of about twenty-five feet wide, and a continued flat of inundated patty land.' Musket fire from troops stationed on a nearby hill poured fire into the city's disorganised defenders all through the day and evening.

Early next morning the town was silent. A couple of unarmed Chinese hung a placard from the shot-scarred walls which read 'Save us for the sake of our wives and children.' A company of the 49th took the main gate and hoisted the British flag. Those defenders who survived the bombardment had fled during the night. Troops looted shattered buildings, picking their way among numerous bodies. The army commander, however, declined to billet his men in the town, to avoid causing more resentment within the civilian population. Instead they camped under canvas in a malarial swamp where fever and dysentery soon kept the burial parties busy. The troops drank copious amounts of a rice spirit. Salt provisions from India were bad, and little fresh food could be found. Within a short time more than one-third of the soldiers were rendered unfit for duty. After a month twelve or more coffins a day were needed to cope with the death toll. By the end of the year 450 men were dead, out of the 3,000-strong garrison. The heaviest casualties were suffered by the Cameronians, who had relied almost entirely on food supplies from India; packed in old bags or insanitary boxes, these quickly proved inadequate. That regiment started with 930 officers and men. They lost 240 dead through sickness, while only 110 men were fit enough for active duty.

The British had expected the capture of Chusan to shock the Chinese into surrender. The Chinese believed, however, that the British could not fight on dry land and since Chusan had been taken by naval bombardment, its fall did not destroy that belief. Their confidence was shaken when the fleet moved up towards the Peiho and imperial advisors warned that the invaders were planning to take Peking itself. As the British prepared to battle their way past the Taku forts guarding the mouth of the river, a court envoy was sent to negotiate with them.

A letter from Palmerston was dispatched to the imperial court, which mistakenly gained the impression that the British would be satisfied if Lin Zexu, the architect of opium suppression, was removed from office. Lin had his enemies at court and they prevailed – he was stripped of his rank and exiled to Ili near the border with Russia. Quishan, the Governor-General of the Zhili territory, off which the British fleet lay, conveyed the news to Elliot and persuaded him to pull back the fleet so that the Canton difficulty could be sorted out without further violence. Quishan's ploy, endorsed by the emperor, was to exhaust and weaken the enemy by protracted negotiation. While the English talked to Quishan, sufficient forces were being assembled to annihilate the invaders. Elliot fell for it, withdrew his increasingly sick forces south, and negotiated for five weeks off Canton.

Even his patience eventually snapped and he authorised a salutary attack on the outer Bogue forts guarding the Pearl River. On 7 January 1841 *Nemesis*, the navy's first iron steamer, used its shallow five-feet draught to float towards the shore, under the angle of the Chinese battery's embrasures, spreading carnage and panic. Some 1,500 troops outflanked the forts after an amphibious landing commanded by Major J.L. Pratt of the 26th Foot and launched a direct attack. Pratt reported in dispatches:

> After advancing a mile and a half, on reaching the ridge of hill, we came in sight of the upper fort, and of a very strong intrenchment, having a deep ditch outside, and a breastwork round it which was prolonged upwards, connecting it with the upper fort; it was also flanked by field batteries. . . . The whole was strongly lined

with Chinese soldiers, who immediately on seeing us cheered, waved their flags in defiance, and opened a fire from their batteries; our guns were promptly placed on the crest of the ridge, and commenced firing; this was duly returned by the Chinese for about 20 minutes, and indeed in this, as well as our other encounters with them, it is but justice to say they behaved with courage.

The British troops, made up of men from the 26th and 49th Regiments, the Royal Marines, the 37th Madras Infantry and the Bengal volunteers, forced back 'considerable numbers' of the enemy from neighbouring hills and woods to the front of the fort. Pratt took a detachment 'into the intrenchment and proceeded up inside the breastwork to the upper fort, in which there were still a number of men; these were speedily dislodged by the two marines who first reached it; the fort was entered, and the British ensign hoisted by a Royal Marine'. Pratt continued:

> The lower fort, which had sixteen guns facing the sea, and was surrounded by a high wall, and a small battery between [were now] completely exposed, but the fire of these had been silenced by the ships attacking on the sea face. They were still in considerable numbers in the lower part of the fort, and had locked the gate; a fire was therefore kept up from the hill, and the advance coming round the lower side to the gate, fed it by musketry. On entering they met with considerable resistance which was speedily subdued; some men then entering an embrasure on the flank, the fort was taken and our flag hoisted.

Such laconic dispatches do little but suggest the carnage inflicted on the defenders by naval and field artillery, musket fire and the bayonet. The defenders fought bravely and almost all were killed. Pratt reckoned that between 300 and 400 were slain. The British suffered thirty-eight men wounded but not a single man killed. Up to 200 more Chinese died when *Nemesis* and boatloads of marines from other vessels attacked eleven large war-junks anchored in shoal water to the east of the forts. They were all set on fire and blown up; one exploded with the loss of her entire crew when a lucky rocket found the magazine. The magazines in the forts were also blown up and the surrounding barracks and houses were levelled by fire. About 100 prisoners were taken but released at nightfall.

Elliot, anxious to prevent further slaughter, withdrew to let his lesson sink in. Again, this gave the Chinese the chance to present the action as a victory for them. Elliot then ordered an attack on the inner Bogue forts. Captain Sir H. Fleming Senhouse of *Blenheim* led a small naval force, including four rocket boats, and opened fire on Anunghoy fort. Its batteries were destroyed after less than an hour's bombardment. Other ships flattened the shore batteries at Wantong. Senhouse and a detachment of marines went ashore and drove the surviving gunners and their soldier escorts from battery to battery until the whole chain was taken at a cost of five men slightly wounded. Again the Chinese suffered heavy losses including Admiral Kwan and several other high-ranking mandarins.

On the 27th a light squadron went further up-river under the command of *Calliope's* Captain Herbert. They found the enemy strongly fortified on the left bank of the river, with over forty war-junks and a former East Indiaman. Several vessels had been scuttled to block the passage. The Chinese opened fire but their cannon were no match for the British salvoes. Marines and small-arms men stormed adjacent batteries, driving out over 2,000 Chinese troops and killing nearly 300.

Again Elliot withdrew and awaited a positive response. None came, so he reluctantly ordered the fleet up-river to Canton itself. A Chinese fleet of thirteen war-junks proved little obstacle. Ten were captured and the admiral's flagship was destroyed by a rocket fired from HMS *Calliope*. *Nemesis* found a passage for the warships through the mudbanks and the force anchored 5 miles from the city. The Chinese launched a useless fire-raft attack, provoking the British into moving on to the Canton factories, over which the British flag once again flew.

The commander of the British troops, Major-General Sir Hugh Gough, took the heights around Canton itself and confronted four strong forts and the city walls. Gough reported that his rocket battery, with two mortars, two 12-pounder howitzers and two 9-pounder guns, kept up well-directed fire on the two western forts 'which had much annoyed us with heavy fire'. His mainly Indian troops cut off the two eastern forts. He recorded: 'At about half-past nine o'clock the advance was sounded, and it has seldom fallen to my lot to witness a more soldier-like and steady advance or a more animated attack. Every individual, native as well as European, steadily and gallantly did his duty.' The first two forts were captured with 'comparatively small loss' and a little over thirty minutes after the advance was sounded British troops were within 100 paces of Canton's walls.

Gough was about to attack the last obstacle, the Hill of the Five-Storeyed Pagoda, when Elliot ordered a halt. Gough obeyed, but his inaction was interpreted by the Chinese as a sign of weakness. They organised a militia and, in a typhoon downpour, 700 British and Indian troops were attacked by up to 10,000 irregulars. The rain-soaked British muskets were initially useless. An officer of the 37th Madras Native Infantry later wrote:

> At this time not a musket would go off, and little resistance could be offered against the enemy's long spears. The men, after remaining in this position for a short time, were enabled to advance to a more defensible one, where they were soon surrounded by thousands of the enemy, who, had they possessed the slightest determination, could have at once annihilated them. The rain ceasing to fall for a time, enabled a few of the men to discharge their muskets. The enemy was not removed above fifteen yards and every shot told as a matter of course.

The British forces retreated in good order with no losses and a few flesh wounds.

The next morning Gough warned that if the Chinese militia was not recalled they would be devastated by firepower. The Canton authorities obeyed and pulled back their men. At about the same time Elliot informed Gough that a peace deal had been reached and he should return to the main force. The sight of Gough's forces heading back down-river created another myth – that the British could be defeated by irregular troops. The bigger myth, that the foreigners were not much good on

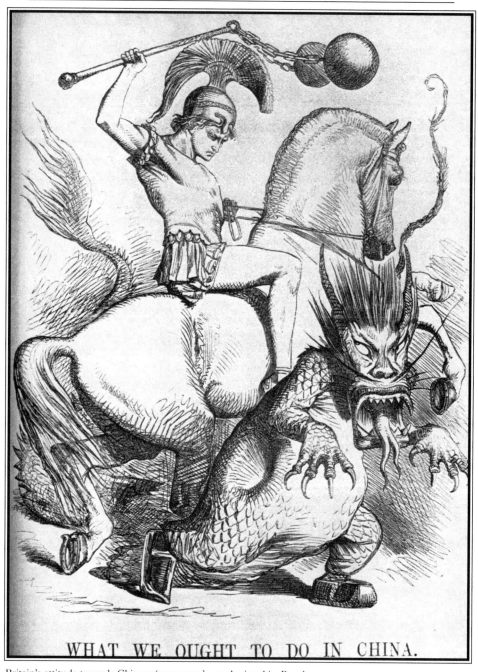

WHAT WE OUGHT TO DO IN CHINA.

Britain's attitude towards Chinese 'arrogance' – as depicted in *Punch*.

land, was reinforced. From then on any official who tried to reach terms with the British was denounced as a coward.

British losses that day were 15 dead and 112 wounded. To that toll was later added the gallant Senhouse who fell ill with a fever 'brought on by his great exertions and exposure to the sun during the operations against Canton' and died aboard HMS *Blenheim*. The *Annual Register* also reported with some astonishment: 'The soldiers of the 49th, finding a quantity of a spirit called sham-shu in the village they had taken, without order or previous knowledge of their officers, brought the jars containing this pernicious liquor and broke them in front of their corps, without the occurrence of a single case of intoxication.'

*   *   *

The peace deal which Elliot and Quishan signed at Chumpi on 20 January reflected both men's desire to avoid further massacre. Its terms called for the secession of Hong Kong, a $6 million indemnity paid by the Chinese, official communications on an equal basis, and the widening of Canton trade on terms beneficial to the British. In return the British agreed to lift the siege of Canton and hand back Chusan and the Bogue forts. Both governments, in Peking and London, rejected it.

The emperor, who now felt that the English were 'outrageous and not amenable to reason', would not countenance the surrender of Hong Kong. To put Chinese citizens, even the scattering of fishermen and farmers on the island, under such barbarian jurisdiction was repugnant to him. Even before the Chumpi Convention was signed he had ordered 4,000 reinforcements to march to Canton from neighbouring provinces. By the end of January he had appointed his cousin, I-shan, to lead an 'Army of Extermination' to destroy the foreigners. Rumours circulated in Canton that Quishan had accepted a huge bribe in return for Hong Kong. The emperor was thrown into a fury. He wrote: 'In governing the country as the Emperor I look upon every inch of our territory and every subject as belonging to the empire.' The treaty was disavowed and Quishan, his vast properties confiscated, was led out of Canton in chains on 13 March.

The reaction of Lord Palmerston when he received the Convention was equally scathing. In a savage dispatch he castigated Elliot for giving up the important naval base of Chusan for the inhospitable rocks of Hong Kong. He said that the indemnity was not only too small but had been agreed in terms which allowed even that to be recouped in taxes on British trade. The young Victoria wrote to a relative: 'The Chinese business vexes us much, and Palmerston is deeply mortified of it. All we wanted might have been got, if it had not been for the unaccountably strange conduct of Charles Elliot . . . who completely disobeyed his instructions and tried to get the lowest terms he could.' Elliot was to be recalled home.

Unaware of his impending disgrace, Elliot was kept busy facing the build-up of imperial forces at Canton. I-shan was now in command alongside the Manchu noble Lung-wen and the seventy-year-old general Yang Fang, a stone-deaf veteran of Jehangir. During February they strengthened their forces, recruited a local patriotic militia, rebuilt redoubts and dammed waterways. All this activity convinced

Elliot, unaware of developments in the two capitals, that the Convention was about to be breached. He moved his fleet back up-river, blowing up several forts as he went, and again threatened Canton with naval guns. Yang Fang, well aware that the city was in no fit state to withstand a bombardment – new, 5-ton cannon fresh from local foundries as yet had no mountings – agreed to a truce. This was quickly overruled by I-shan.

On 21 May flaming rafts were sent down-river to engulf the British fleet anchored at Whampoa. As before, the attack failed dismally and in the following battle seventy-one war-junks were destroyed and sixty shore batteries seized. Bremer described one part of the action in dispatches: 'On arriving at Whampoa, I found . . . that the enemy were in considerable force at the end of "Junk Reach", having as usual sunk several large junks in the river, and further protected themselves by a strong double line of stakes across it, and large bamboos and branches of trees between them.' He ordered the ship *Sulphur* up-river to reconnoitre, towed behind three boats commanded by Lieutenant Symonds, an officer of *Wellesley*. Bremer continued:

On rounding a point on the right bank, they came in front of a low battery of twenty-five guns, masked by thick branches of trees, which opened a heavy fire on them. Lieutenant Symonds instantly cut the tow-rope, and gallantly dashed into the battery, driving the enemy before him, and killing several of their number. The *Sulphur* anchored and some shot from her completely drove them from the thick underwood in the vicinity of which they had taken shelter. The guns were destroyed, and the magazines and other combustible material set on fire. The number of troops was probably 250, and they were the chosen Tartars; their loss was about fifteen or twenty killed; ours was one seaman of the *Wellesley* mortally wounded (since dead), and the boats were repeatedly struck by grapeshot.

Troopships protected by *Nemesis* landed forces which occupied the northern heights above the city's crumbling walls. Gough urged a pulverising onslaught but Elliot held back once more, not wishing to inflict slaughter on the 'unoffending populace'. Instead another truce was agreed under which the three Chinese commanders were required to pay a ransom of six million dollars and to leave the city, taking with them all troops from outside the province. Their departure was followed by looting and civil disorder as local pirates and robbers went on the rampage.

The ransom of Canton was seen in Peking as weakness. The emperor wrote: 'The English barbarians . . . are like dogs and sheep in their disposition – a dog in forehead, but in heart a deer – they are not worth an argument. Moreover they had already been chastised and repressed, and the terrific majesty of my soldiers has already been manifested.' He added:

It is impossible to fathom the disposition of the barbarians; and it is right to prepare secret means of defence, nor should there be the least degree of negligence or remissness. Wait until after the barbarian ships have retired, then quickly resume possession of the forts, and guard and maintain the important passes and such-like places. Build new and strong forts and put the old in the best poss-ible state of defence. If the English barbarians evince any disposition to be proud or domi-neering, then the troops should be led on to exterminate them.

Elliot's replacement, Sir Henry Pottinger, was appointed in May 1841 but did not reach Hong Kong until August. He was a workmanlike, 52-year-old Irishman with long experi-ence as a political agent in Sind. His instructions from Palmerston were simple: to retake Chusan and force the Chinese into humiliating terms. These included the retention of Hong Kong, the opening up of four more ports and compensation of almost $12 million covering the cost of the destroyed opium, Hong debts and the expenses of the expeditionary force itself. Palmerston also wanted the abolition

Major-General Sir Hugh, later Viscount, Gough. (Engraving by G. Stodart)

of the Hong monopoly and the legalisation of opium 'for the interest of the Chinese government itself'.

Pottinger arrived in Hong Kong just as his new expeditionary force was gathering from ports across the Indian Ocean and Singapore. Eventually it would consist of 25 warships, 14 steamers, numerous support vessels and 10,000 infantry in troopships. Its commander-in-chief was 59-year-old Admiral Sir William Parker, a former captain of *Volage*. As a young officer he had sailed and fought in the West Indies, off Cuba and Mexico. He was highly commended for his part in the action which led to the capture of the French warship *Belle Poule*. After the war with the French he lived the life of a country gentleman near Lichfield before returning to the navy where, after commanding the royal yacht *Prince Regent*, he became an Admiralty Lord. He was regarded as a skilful campaigner and tactful negotiator but is largely remembered as a naval disciplinarian who pursued his duty with religious zeal. He had a hatred of tobacco and no officer who smoked remained long aboard his flagship. He drilled his crews relentlessly and it was later reckoned that no subsequent commander ever achieved such drill perfection. He required all around him to wear a sloping peaked cap, a type that was later adopted as part of the regulation uniform.

Gough remained troop commander and Parker was well aware of his fine reputation. Aged sixty-two then, by the end of his career Gough had taken part in more general engagements than any other officer in that century. He was popular with men and officers because of his proven personal courage, his racy language, delivered with a Limerick accent, and his sense of chivalry. Sir Charles Napier wrote: 'Every one who knows Gough must love the brave old warrior, who is all honour and nobleness of heart.' Others were not too sure of his military judgement, and Lord Ellenborough wrote later that Gough 'despite his many excellent qualities, had not the grasp of mind and the prudence essential to conduct great military operations'. A descendent of a Bishop of Limerick, Gough had fought with the 78th Highlanders at the recapture of the Cape of Good Hope, and with the Prince of Wales's Irish in St Lucia, Trinidad, Puerto Rico and Surinam. He was severely wounded at the battle of Talavera in Portugal and became the first British officer ever to receive brevet promotion for battle service at the head of a regiment. At the battle of Barossa he led a famous charge against the French 8th Light Infantry at which the first French 'eagle' was captured. At Tarifa the dying French commander, Laval, surrendered his sword to Gough through the bars of a portcullis. Gough suffered another disabling wound at the battle of Nivelle and spent several years on his Tipperary estate. In 1837 he was appointed to command the Mysore division of the Madras Army, and it was from there that he had sailed to China.

The first task facing Parker and Gough was the capture of the important port of Amoy in the north. Some 2,000 British troops, the first to arrive, faced 9,000 Chinese infantry, over fifty junks and three recently improved forts which were deemed 'impregnable'. A long battery of seventy-six cannon stretched for a distance of over half a mile. The fleet anchored offshore on 26 August and engaged in a duel with the shore gunners at point-blank range. The granite ramparts of the defences deflected the British shellfire with little damage but the Chinese gunners were unable to concentrate their fire on the landing parties of the Royal Irish who overran their artillery emplacements. One mandarin, who was second-in-command, ran into the sea and drowned himself. Another was seen to cut his own throat and fall in front of the advancing soldiers. The Chinese commander, Yen, had been so sure of his outer defences that he had not bothered to fortify the narrow pass between them and the city. The British marched through and took the city of 70,000 inhabitants at a cost of just 2 dead and 15 wounded.

The city's citadel was found to contain five arsenals holding 'a large quantity of powder, gingals, war-pieces, matchlocks, and a variety of fire-arms of singular construction . . . military clothing, swords of all descriptions, shields, bows and arrows, and spears'. Within the sea defences there was also a foundry with moulds and materials for casting heavy ordnance.

Amoy was garrisoned and the fleet moved on through bad weather to Chusan, which had been re-fortified after the Chinese reoccupation. The town of Tinghai proved hard to crack, and the Chinese defenders held out for three days. Gough was shot in the shoulder during the attack but finally the island fell. There were only two British fatalities. One was Ensign Richard Duel of the Westmorlands, a veteran of thirty-two years' service, who was killed while carrying the regimental colour into action. Only the day before he had been promoted from sergeant-major. Marines

Capture of Tinghai, Chusan, from a sketch by Lieutenant White, Royal Marines.

dodged the fire from Chinese howitzers but the defenders broke and ran after suffering the heavy offshore barrage from ships and steam vessels covering the landing party. Several Chinese, including one who was waving a banner, were hit by a single cannon-shot fired from 700 yards. Admiral Parker wrote:

> We had the gratification of seeing the British colours planted by the troops in one of the batteries on the opposite shore; and in a few minutes the others on that side were all carried, and the Chinese [were] observed flying in all directions before our gallant soldiers on the heights . . . the wall of the citadel was breached by the fire from the ships, and the defences being reduced to a ruinous state, the Chinese abandoned their guns.

The next target was the nearby port of Ningpo, the fall of which would allow the British to control much of the Chekiang coast. The river-mouth fort of Chen-hai was swiftly overrun. On 13 October the main city's troops ran away after their cannon overheated. Gough reported:

> No enemy appeared, and it was evident that no ambuscade was intended, as the inhabitants densely thronged the bridge of boats, and collected in clusters along both banks. The troops landed on and near the bridge and advanced to the city gate, which was found barricaded; but the walls were soon escaladed and the Chinese assisted in removing the obstructions and opening the gate. The little force of soldiers, seamen and marines drew up on the ramparts, the band of the 18th playing God Save the Queen. The second city of the province of Che-

Sir Henry Pottinger.

keang, the walls of which are nearly five miles in circumference, with a population of 300,000 souls, has thus fallen into our hands. The people all appear desirous of throwing themselves under British protection, saying publicly that their mandarins had deserted them, and their own soldiers are unable to protect them.

Ningpo served as the expeditionary force's rest and refitting base over the winter. Pottinger's forces were now largely spread among the occupied cities and reinforcements would take some time to arrive. He decided to wait until the late spring or early summer before embarking on the next phase of his plan – to sail up the great Yangtse, effectively cutting China in two, and prevent grain moving up the Grand Canal, thus blockading Peking itself. The delay, however, allowed the Chinese to prepare a spring counter-offensive.

The preparations were entrusted to the emperor's cousin I-ching, director of the Imperial Gardens and Hunting Parks and commander of the Forbidden City's police force. An excellent planner, he agreed with the emperor that the foreigners were now committed to land warfare and could thus be swallowed up by China's teeming population. At Soochow he organised 12,000 regular troops and 33,000 militia. They made an impressive spectacle, with their bright uniforms and fluttering pennants. A month before they clashed with the British, a noted artist painted their victory in traditional style. Tea parties, feasts and poetry readings entertained the commanders, and I-ching held a contest for scribes to come up with the best-written proclamation for the coming victory. Such confidence was misplaced. The army was officered largely by young scholars who had read about the glory of combat but had no experience of it. Regular units refused to take orders from other provincial officers, and there was no clear chain of command. Supply lines broke down. The troops reached Ningpo exhausted and starving, having had no food for several rain-sodden days.

I-ching's overall plan involved his main force seizing Ningpo, with 15,000 more men taking Chen-hai and 10,000 marines snatching back Chusan. In reality only a fraction of these numbers would be in the vanguard of any attack. I-ching kept his own personal guard of 3,000 men close to his headquarters in the wine-producing town of Shaohsing and 60 per cent of the whole army actually served as bodyguards for the general staff. Only around 4,000 men attacked each British garrison. An oracle told I-ching the best time to attack – between 3 a.m. and 5 a.m. on 10 March 1842: a tiger-hour on a tiger-day in a tiger-month during a tiger-year.

The frontal assault on Ningpo was launched by 700 Szechwan aborigines. It was a disaster. Their commanders had mistranslated a Mandarin order to hold fire until close to the enemy, thinking it directed them to leave their muskets behind. Armed only with long knives the soldiers were slaughtered by British howitzers and mines. Other inexperienced Chinese troops were pushed forward on to the piles of bodies, only to be cut down in turn. So many corpses were piled up outside the city's West Gate that blood flowed down the gutter channels. Some of the attackers were allowed to climb over the city walls and were lured by the British into the central market-place. There they were massacred by disciplined volleys. Those who retreated in confusion were pulverised by field guns drawn by ponies, which discharged grape and canister into the dense, panic-stricken mass at a range of less than 100 yards. Around 250 bodies were counted within the city walls. Veterans said they had not seen so many dead in the street since the siege of Badajoz during the Peninsular War. About twenty Chinese wounded were treated in a British hospital station but some died on the crude operating tables.

The Chinese forces besieging Chen-hai were better disciplined and the coordinated attack might have succeeded if their reserves had backed them up. But the reserve commander lay in a litter at Camel Bridge, puffing opium until he fell into a stupor. It was the ultimate irony of the war.

It was during the Chinese attack on Chen-hai that the British first encountered a form of booby-trap which claimed several lives. Boats were floated down-river carrying large red boxes of the sort Chinese women used to contain their furs and silks. If an unwary British sailor opened the lid of a box it immediately exploded. A mine of another sort exploded in a nearby river battery, killing one sailor. Rear-Admiral Parker reported: 'Considering the number of our men which were assembled at this time, it is most providential that the consequences were not more disastrous.'

I'ching had intended that the marines attacking Chusan should be ferried to the island on war-junks and fishing boats. Most had never been to sea and on leaving port they were horribly seasick. Their cowardly commander sailed up and down the coast for twenty days, sending in false reports of doing splendid battle with the English.

The Chinese forces were reduced to harrying British supply lines and Gough decided to attack a camp of around 4,000 soldiers at Tse-kee, 11 miles to the west of Ningpo. A force of 1,100 men in transports was towed up-river behind the steamers *Nemesis* and *Phlegethon*, and scaled the walls of the town without any resistance. When the British went out to attack the troop encampments, however, the Chinese fought back strongly with gingalls and matchlocks. The Chinese included 500 elite members of the imperial bodyguard and Kansich troops from the Turkestan frontier whom Gough described as 'a strong and muscular race' and whom the Chinese regarded as invincible in battle. But a three-pronged attack by the better-armed British forced them into retreat and the troops 'then did execution on the flying mass'. Estimates of the Chinese dead varied from 400 to 900 compared to British losses of 3 dead and 20 wounded. The British burnt the camp and several suburban houses before returning to Ningpo.

For several months the war degenerated into a sordid affair of small-scale atrocities and reprisals which did not reflect well on either side. The Chinese picked up stragglers on marches, and British and Indian troops were captured drunk in ale-houses and brothels. They were taken away for execution. A British sea captain, Stead, wandered into the wrong harbour and was tied to a post and publicly flayed alive. When the British forces left Ningpo the town was burnt behind them in retaliation. That did not prevent Gough reporting to London that the evacuation of the city left among the Chinese inhabitants of Chekiang province 'a deep feeling of respect and gratitude for the orderly and forbearing conduct of the British soldiers'. It proved, he said, that 'while pressing on the [Peking] Government, and overthrowing every opposing display of military force, it has been our object to protect the Chinese population of every class and grade as much as lay in our power.'

Pottinger launched his Yangtse campaign on 7 May 1842. The first city to fall to the river-borne troops was Chapu, despite stiff resistance put up by its 1,700 Manchu bannermen. About 300 Tartar troops, finding escape impossible, mounted a desperate last stand in a joss-house which they defended with 'wonderful obstinacy'. Rockets and powderbags were hurled at them by the Royal Irish, whose Colonel Tomlinson was killed making a frontal charge at the door. The Chinese continued fighting until the blazing building fell in on them. Only 53 were taken alive and those were almost all wounded. An elderly Chinese officer, skewered by British bayonets, refused to surrender, despite promises of good treatment. He said he could neither give nor accept mercy, but added, 'If you wish to gain my gratitude and can be generous, write to my reverend sovereign and say I fell in the front fighting to the last.' Total Chinese losses were estimated at over 1,200 for just 9 British dead and 55 wounded.

At Chapu and elsewhere the British were shocked by the ferocity of the defenders and their actions once reconciled to defeat: they killed their own wives and children, slitting their throats to save them from rape and shame, before hanging themselves from rafters. After capturing a temple the 18th Royal Irish found a 'butcher's shop' inside. An English officer explained in a letter home that it was impossible to report accurately Chinese battle losses, 'for when they found they could stand no longer against us, they cut the throats of their wives and children, or drove them into wells or ponds, and then destroyed themselves'. The officer added: 'In many houses there were from eight to twelve dead bodies, and I myself saw a dozen women and children drowning themselves in a small pond, the day after the fight.' Gough wrote: 'I am sick at heart of war.'

The British forces certainly did rape and loot their way across China, despite the harsh punishments, erratically enforced, for such offences. Gough admitted that there had been misconduct but claimed instances were few 'when it is considered that they were in the midst of temptation, many of the houses being open, with valuable property strewed about, and many shops in every street deserted, but full of sham-shu'. Worse were the Chinese camp-followers, described as 'hoodlums of the delta',

Battle of Chapu: the body of Colonel Tomlinson of the Royal Irish being carried away after the attack on a joss-house. (Illustrated London News)

who plundered homes in captured towns and villages. Many Chinese townspeople fled before the barbarian advance, leaving the defending garrisons with no provisions.

Another factor accounting for the collapse of Chinese resistance in some areas was the widespread belief that the British were employing nei-ying, 'inner allies', or traitors. Local commanders spent more time searching out supposed fifth columnists from among the Han minorities, salt smugglers and market hooligans than on preparing their defences. Manchu soldiers murdered suspects, and civilians feared local commanders more than the invaders. Rumour and suspicion spread to further undermine morale.

British forces marched unopposed into an abandoned Shanghai. But at Jinjiang bannermen disputed every alley, house and street of the city. Those not killed by the British died by their own hands. Lieutenant Alexander Murray of the Royal Irish was appalled when he saved a Chinese soldier from being killed out of hand and 'the ungrateful fellow, instead of being pleased at his escape, deliberately began to cut his throat with a short sword'. However, Murray was not one to mock the tremendous casualties the Chinese suffered against massively one-sided firepower. He wrote: 'Far from their great losses being proof of the cowardice of the Chinese, I take it to be a strong proof of their courage; for if cowards they would have taken very good care that we should never have got within reach of them.'

The British squadron moved into the Yangtse, much to the alarm of the Chinese generals, and engaged in a running duel with shore batteries. In all 364 guns, 76 of them brass, were captured. Some of the brass cannon were very new and were inscribed with Chinese characters signifying 'the tamer and subduer of the

Chinese soldiers carrying a wounded comrade. (Illustrated London News)

barbarians'. Most of them were of heavy calibre, over 11 feet long, and mounted on pivot carriages 'of new and efficient construction'. They were fitted with bamboo sights. This naval expedition cost 2 dead and 25 wounded; it is astonishing casualties were not higher. All the warships engaged were hit by cannon fire: the frigate *Blonde* took fourteen cannonballs through her hull, and the steamer *Sesostris* eleven.

The hardest fight of the war was the taking of the garrison town of Chinkiang, the chief military depot of the province, on 21 July. The main body of British troops charged the walled city's south gate which they blew open with powder bags. The men rushed through but found themselves in a labyrinth of alleys leading to outworks. A smaller party had meantime clambered over the north walls and taken the inner gateway after vicious hand-to-hand combat. Gough recorded:

> I have seldom witnessed a more animated combined attack: the Chinese cheering until we got close to them, now poured in a very heavy but ill-directed fire, and displayed in various instances acts of individual bravery that merited a better fate; but nothing could withstand the steady but rapid advance of the gallant little force that assailed them; field-work after field-work was cleared, and the colours of the 49th were displayed on the principal redoubt above the sea and river batteries.

At the same time the 18th Foot charged up a steep gorge into the central military encampment. Gough added: 'From 1,200 to 1,500 of the enemy, that had stood longest, were driven down the heights into the river, their retreat being cut off by the flank movement of the 55th; many were drowned in attempting to swim across; others sought concealment on a rock in the stream, and were afterwards picked up by the boats of the Queen.' Parker reported: 'A body of Tartars was driven into one division of the western outwork, without a possibility of retreat; and as they would not surrender, most of them were either shot or destroyed in the burning houses, several of which had been set on fire by the Tartar troops themselves, or by our guns.' Another report said:

> The Tartars fought desperately, and the heat of the sun was so overpowering that several of our soldiers dropped down dead from its effects. This prevented the advance of the troops into the town until about 6 o'clock in the evening, when they pushed forward into the streets. Dead bodies of Tartars were found in every house that was entered, principally women and children, thrown into wells or otherwise murdered by their own people. A vast number of Tartars who escaped the fires of our soldiers committed suicide after destroying their families. The city was nearly deserted before we had fully taken possession of it . . .

The Chinese commander, Hai-lin, realising that defeat was certain, returned to his sumptuous home, sat down in his favourite chair and ordered his servants to torch the building around him. British troops shot dead one Tartar soldier as he cut his wife's throat with a rusty sword. They bound up her wound and pulled her children, alive, from the garden well into which they had been thrown, but the newly made widow cursed them all the same. Parker said: 'A great number of those who escaped our fire committed suicide, after destroying their families; the loss of life has been, therefore, appalling, as it may be said that the Mantchoo race in this city is extinct.' Gough described it as a 'frightening scene of destruction' and kept his troops away from the human abattoirs. British casualties totalled 34 dead (16 from sunstroke), 107 wounded and three missing.

The following morning the British destroyed all arms and ammunition found in the city and confiscated 60,000 dollars worth of Syce silver. However, Gough claimed in his dispatches that the city was looted not by the British but by plunderers who flocked in from the surrounding countryside. 'Such is their systematic mode of proceeding,' Gough wrote, 'that in one instance which came to my knowledge they set fire to both ends of the street in the western suburb, where there was a large pawnbroker's shop (uniformly the first object of pillage) in order to check all interruption while they carried off their booty by the side lanes.' He was anxious to stop such 'scenes of devastation' but decided that it was not practicable to deploy his troops in the maze of streets and alleys during the hottest season of the year, especially given the number of Tartar corpses. He said: 'From the decomposed and scattered state of these bodies, it would have been impractical to bury them without much risk to the health of the troops employed.' Cholera also appeared and the first to die was Ensign Weir of the 49th Regiment.

The capture of Chinkiang achieved Pottinger's main aim of blocking the Grand Canal. Nanking, the former southern capital of the Ming Empire, was exposed and vulnerable to the remorseless British advance. The city of a million people was guarded by a Tartar garrison of 6,000, swelled by several thousand fugitives from Chinkiang who, Gough reported, 'are all trained to arms, and perhaps the most formidable opponents, as they fight for their families and their homes'. The city walls varied from 28 to 70 feet high. *Cornwallis*, *Blonde* and the heavy steamers were brought into position 100 yards from a main gate, ready to start the bombardment. Gough deployed 4,500 'effective fighting men', most of whom had fought with him through the entire campaign. Sappers and engineers prepared to destroy outworks.

In the event, they were not needed. The Governor-General of Nanking reported to the Emperor that the city simply could not be defended. The Celestial Son was forced to accept the inevitability of defeat. He appointed two princes, Yilibu and Qiying, to negotiate the best terms possible. They first sent a domestic slave, Zhang Xi, dressed as a mandarin, to spy on the foreigners. He convinced them that the British were more interested in trade than in war. The two princes boarded Pottinger's flagship, HMS *Cornwallis*, where they bowed to a portrait of Queen Victoria as an indication that they were prepared to negotiate with the British on equal terms.

This simple gesture sliced through the tangle of courtly etiquette and diplomatic posturing which might otherwise have tripped up the peace process. The Treaty of Nanking was speedily concluded and with it the war came to an end.

The opium ships had followed Pottinger's fleet up the Yangtse. As soon as the treaty was signed notices were nailed up in occupied territories proclaiming: 'Opium is on sale very cheap – an opportunity not to be missed.'

★　★　★

The treaty was signed aboard *Cornwallis* on 29 August 1842. Given the scale of the Chinese defeat the terms could have been much sterner. The main British objectives were achieved: compensation of $21 million to be paid in instalments; the opening up of the trade ports of Canton, Amoy, Foochow, Ningpo and Shanghai, with British consuls at each port; diplomatic relations on equal terms; the abolition of the Hong monopoly; uniform tariffs on both imports and exports; and the secession of Hong Kong island as a British territory. The Chinese negotiators played down or omitted until later details of the biggest concessions in their dispatches to the emperor. The strict interpretation of the draft treaty kept negotiators and diplomats busy for a long time. It was a decade before Foochow began foreign trade and rights of foreign entry to Canton were not secured until 1858. The British could have demanded a much greater degree of free trade and annexed far richer territories. Instead they insisted only on the bare minimum to guarantee reasonable conditions for trade. The British Government had serious qualms about developing Hong Kong as a British territory, but as traders and builders poured in they were left with no other option.

Opium was not even mentioned in the Treaty of Nanking. The new Hong Kong administration briefly outlawed the drug and consuls were instructed to help stamp out smuggling, in the expectation that the Chinese trade ports would do the same. Instead the Chinese authorities at first did nothing and then actively encouraged the trade in order to obtain tax revenues from it.

Such official duplicity did not, however, stem world-wide dismay over a war in which the might of the British Empire was harnessed on behalf of drug-dealers. The Dutch ambassador to London told an English MP 'that Palmerston had contrived to alienate all nations from us by his insolence and violence, so that we had not now a friend in the world, while from the vast complication of our interests and affairs we were now exposed to perpetual danger'. That was an exaggeration but the humbling of a mighty empire by a small seaborne force brought little glory. The *United Service Journal* reported: 'The poor Chinese – with their painted pasteboard boats – must submit to be poisoned, or must be massacred by the thousand, for supporting their own laws in their own land.'

Not all overseas judgements were so harsh. Some people then, and revisionist historians now, blamed the Chinese for their refusal to embark on trade as equals and their insistence on such degrading practices as the kow-tow, whereby visiting dignitaries were obliged to display their supposed inferiority. The US President John Quincy Adams wrote that the seizure of chests of opium had no more caused this war than the throwing overboard of chests of tea in Boston harbour had caused the American War of Independence. He went on: 'The cause of the war was the kow-tow! – the arrogant and insupportable pretensions of China, that she will hold commercial intercourse with mankind not upon terms of equal reciprocity, but upon insulting and degrading forms of relation between lord and vassal.'

The morality of the war may have been in doubt from beginning to end, but the courage of the participants was not. General Gough wrote in dispatches: 'It is now my pleasing duty to bring to your Lordships' notice those gallant officers and troops who, throughout the active operations in China, in a warfare new to the British arms, exposed in various instances to temptations of no ordinary kind, assailed by sickness which in some cases left but few effective men in strong corps, and often subjected to great fatigue, under a burning sun, have never in any instance met a check.' This, he said, 'was not because their foes were few in number, devoid of courage, or slow to hazard life in personal contact, but because their own science, discipline, and devotion, made them irresistible'.

Elliot's career continued despite the circumstances in which he had been recalled home. He was appointed chargé d'affaires in Texas as the Opium War ended and from 1846 held governorships of Bermuda, Trinidad and St Helena, one of the empire's most remote outposts. He was knighted in 1856 and held honorary rank in the navy's retired list, becoming a paper admiral in 1865. He died ten years later at Witteycombe, Exeter. His cousin, Admiral Sir George Elliot, continued to be prone to ill-health and died in London in 1863 after a protracted sickness.

Sir Gordon Bremer received the thanks of Parliament and was later appointed commodore-superintendent of Woolwich Dockyard before his death in 1850. Admiral Parker was awarded a baronetcy and an annual good service pension of £3,000. He commanded the Channel Fleet and later the Mediterranean Squadron. He chaired a committee which recommended far-reaching reforms in naval manning. He died of a bronchial attack a few weeks short of his 85th birthday and a monument to his memory still stands in Lichfield Cathedral.

Gough was also made a baronet and continued his remarkable military career as Commander-in-Chief in India. He led the forces that routed the Maharatta army and defeated Sikh invaders at the battles of Mudki, Ferozshah and Sobraon. In the Second Sikh War he again beat them at Ramnuggar and Chillianwallah, although the second battle was not decisive. He re-established his reputation with the crushing defeat of the Sikh armies at Gujerat. He was made a viscount, was granted a pension of £2,000 a year for himself and the next two heirs to his title, was voted the thanks of Parliament and the East India Company, and was awarded the freedom of the city of London. In 1862 he became a field marshal and died peacefully at home near Booterstown in 1869, aged almost ninety.

The East India Company enjoyed a boom time with the legalisation of the opium trade, while Jardine & Matheson flourished in Hong Kong. But opium damaged other British merchants because of the squeeze it put on the market for manufactured goods. Two hundred merchants, in a petition to the British Government, had warned that it would 'operate for evil . . . by enervating and impoverishing the consumers of the drug' and prevent them buying British goods. They were proved right.

Emperor Daoguang died in 1850, by which time further western incursions had undermined China's wall of isolation. In Britain public attention switched elsewhere but for years a popular exhibit at Madame Tussaud's waxworks was entitled: 'Commissioner Lin and his Favourite Consort, Modelled from life, by the Celebrated Lamb-Qua, of Canton, with Magnificent Dresses actually worn by them.'

★   ★   ★

CHAPTER FIVE

The Persian War, 1856–7

'They drew their swords in triumph . . . all smeared with blood.'

To the Victorian public, not yet weary of imperial glories, the short war on Persian soil had everything. There was an epic march in foul conditions, a tremendous cavalry charge and a swift victory; best of all, few British sons were left buried under foreign soil. In addition, this British success helped to wipe away the awful memories of the muddy trenches of the Crimea and restore the reputation of British generalship. It also helped to maintain the delicate balance of interests which in turn kept the Russians out of India. British force of arms again seemed irresistible. Yet the gunfire had barely faded when British soldiers and civilians were caught up in the horrors of the Indian Mutiny, and the Persian expedition became just another forgotten war.

★　　★　　★

During the first half of the nineteenth century Britain, France and Russia, each intent on dominating the crumbling empires of the Middle East, competed for influence over the ancient land of Persia. Its strategic importance at the crossroads of East and West was obvious. British officers aided the Persians in their war against Russia in 1812 and many stayed on as private soldiers of fortune and advisors. After a series of Persian defeats and the 1828 Treaty of Turkmanchai which ended hostilities, Russian influence over Persian policy increased. Russian, rather than British, officers organised and disciplined the Persian army along European lines. Anglo-Persian relations became increasingly strained, and the flashpoint came on a dusty city-state road to India.

When Tamerlane conquered Khorassan in the fourteenth century, the city of Herat within the Douranee empire of Afghanistan, fell under the dominion of Persia. On the death of Nadir Shah it ousted its Persian rulers and took as its sovereign General Ahmet Khan, who assumed the crown at Khandahar. In 1829 Herat was governed as an independent state by the Afghan Prince Khamran-Mirza; in order to gain protection from his neighbour, the king of Kabul, the prince acknowledged the sovereignty of Persia and agreed to pay an annual tribute to the Shah. That tribute was not paid and in 1836 Mohammed Shah, using the capture and enslavement of a number of Persians as a convenient excuse, marched against Herat. A long and obstinate siege followed, with the Shah deploying a battalion of Russian mercenaries led by the Polish General Berowski. The city held out, helped by Lieutenant Eldred Pottinger, and Berowski was killed. After more than nine months the Persians withdrew when Britain threatened military intervention.

Britain had good reason to demand Herat's continued independence. It had huge strategic importance, being described as the 'Gate of India', and its security was vital to prevent Russian encroachments on the Raj. Within the limits of the city-state's territory converged all the main roads leading to India. The contemporary historian J. Kaye wrote:

> At other points, between Herat and Cabul, a body of troops unencumbered with guns, or having only a light field artillery, might make good its passage, if not actively opposed, across the stupendous mountain ranges of the Hindoo-Koosh; but it is only by the Herat route that a really formidable, well-equipped army could make its way upon the Indian frontier from the regions of the north-west. Both the nature and the resources of the country are such as to favour the success of the invader.

Mohammed Shah died in 1848 after ruling for just fourteen years. His son, Nasir ud-Din succeeded him and was faced with an empire crippled by internal strife. He took two years to suppress an insurrection in Mashhad, during which time three Babi revolts broke out. In 1852 an assassination attempt by Babis led to savage reprisals. Russian influence on the Shah continued to increase, although a British mission in Tehran also convinced him of the need not to antagonise Queen Victoria.

Meanwhile Herat's new ruler, Sa'id Mahommed, allowed Persian troops into the city to help quell discontent. Britain protested and in January 1853 a convention was agreed between the Persian Government and the British envoy. Under its terms the Shah undertook not to send troops to Herat, unless that territory was invaded by a foreign army. In that case, if troops were sent, they must be withdrawn as soon as the foreigners were expelled. The Shah pledged not to interfere in the internal affairs of

Gateway at Bushire. (Illustrated London News)

A Persian ambassador. (Illustrated London News)

General Sir James Outram. (Illustrated London News)

Herat, while the British promised to use their influence to induce foreign powers to leave Herat alone. The convention was never formally ratified by the British Government.

Diplomatic relations froze late in 1854 when the new British envoy to Tehran, Mr Murray, took offence at some alleged insult and withdrew his mission beyond Persia's borders. Russian diplomats happily filled the void.

In September 1855 Mahommed Yusuf Sadozai, a member of the old, deposed royal family, led a revolt in Herat, executed Sa'id Mahommed and seized power. At the same time Afghanistan was in uproar, with Dost Mahomed, the king of Kabul, capturing Kandahar. The Shah used both events to annexe Herat formally and a Persian force again besieged the city. Following the failure of diplomatic efforts, war was declared on 1 November 1856. The proclamation, issued by the Governor-General of India, said in part:

The siege of Herat has now been carried out by the Persian army for many months. Before its commencement, and during its progress, the unfriendly sentiments of Persia towards the British Government have been scarcely veiled; and recently the movement of troops in different parts of Persia have indicated a determination to persist in an aggression which is as unprovoked as it is contrary to good faith.

★   ★   ★

The British fleet and transport ships rendezvoused at the port of Bunda Abbas at the mouth of the Persian Gulf, under the command of Rear-Admiral Sir Henry Leeke, the 67-year-old commander-in-chief of the Indian Navy. As a young midshipman Leeke had served during the later years of the Napoleonic War and once, waving a cutlass, had single-handedly halted a rush of escaping French prisoners. But his reputation was built mainly on patrolling the west coast of Africa, 'reducing the native kings to order and obedience'. He and his fleet came together on 23 November. They sailed on three days later and on the 29th the first four vessels of the fleet, the corvette *Falkland* and the steam-frigate *Feroze*, towing two merchant ships, appeared off Bushire. The governor of that town sent a message to the British Resident of the Gulf, Commander Felix Jones, 'begging to be apprised of the object of their visit'. Jones, who had left Bushire to join the squadron, responded by enclosing the proclamation of war.

The squadron took, unhindered, Karrak Island to the north of Bushire for use as a military depot. More ships arrived and Leeke decided to land his force in Hallila Bay, 12 miles south of the town. The operation began on 7 December. Persian troops posted themselves in a date grove 200 yards from the beach and fired a few ineffectual shots at the approaching boats. They were soon driven out by fire from the ships and well-directed shot from the steam-frigate *Ajdaha*. Over two days the troops were landed without any casualties, although there were difficulties in bringing ashore the horses and cannon owing to a lack of available native boats.

On 9 December the army, commanded by Major-General Stalker, advanced on the village and old Dutch fort of Reshire, about 4 miles south of Bushire. This time the enemy were strongly entrenched among the ruins of old houses, garden walls and steep ravines. Shells fired from the fleet burst among the defenders, causing considerable losses. The remainder were driven out after a short but savage skirmish in which the British and Indian troops made extensive use of the bayonet. The defenders, members of the Dashti and Tungestoon tribes, were regarded as among the bravest and most skilful irregulars on the Persian side. In the confused hand-to-hand fighting Brigadier Stopford of the 64th Regiment and the popular Lieutenant-Colonel Malet of the 3rd Bombay Light Cavalry were killed. The army camped outside the ruins for the night but Leeke pushed on with the fleet and the following morning took position off Bushire.

Commander Jones, aboard the small steamer *Assyria* which was carrying a flag of truce, proceeded to summon the garrison to surrender on honourable terms. As the craft passed through the narrow channel two shore batteries opened fire. Jones reported: 'Deeming it might be a mistake, I caused the vessel to stop, but a second and third shot passing close to us, I was compelled to retrace my steps, and even then two more guns were discharged. I could scarcely account for this conduct, having taken some pains to explain the meaning of a flag of truce before quitting the town.' Shortly afterwards a Persian vessel bearing its own flag of truce approached the fleet, bearing a written apology from the governor. He explained that he had been outside the town walls inspecting its defences, and blamed the unfortunate incident on the ignorance of his artillerymen. Leeke and Fox accepted the apology for themselves but added that 'the act itself, in whatever way originating, must stigmatize the Persian Government and its officers in the eyes of all civilized States'.

Stalker was poised to attack the town from land while Leeke disposed his fleet in order of battle, aiming first to dismantle the newly erected outworks and then to breach the south wall. The following morning a second flag of truce was waved out as the governor asked for a 24-hour delay but this was refused. At 8 a.m. the signal was hoisted to engage. Shot and shell were aimed at the redoubts thrown up to the south of Bushire. The bombardment at first appeared to have little effect, owing to the great range, but eventually the Persian troops manning the redoubts had had enough and retreated with their guns to the town.

Persian troops, 1856–7, including camel-borne light artillery and a fusilier (third from right) of the Shah's Guard. (Illustrated London News)

The ships moved closer but captains and crew were over-eager to close in and every vessel ran aground at the turn of high water. For almost four hours they continued to cannonade the defences while stuck fast. The Persians fired back. Most of their guns were not large enough to reach the stranded flotilla but Jones recalled 'the perseverance of the Persian gunners in firing from the more heavy pieces was admired by every one'. Shot repeatedly hit the hulls of *Victoria, Falkland, Semiramis* and *Feroze.* Jones said: 'Although the hulls, masts and rigging of the ships were frequently struck by the enemy's shot, not a single casualty to life or limb occurred.' Finally the Persian batteries were silenced both by the fleet's stationary cannon and by Stalker's vanguard, now approaching the town. The Persian flag was cut down in token of submission.

After the surrender the governor and garrison, some 2,000 men, hesitated to come out of the town. The British commanders sent them a reassuring note, coupled with the threat of a resumed attack within half an hour. This created panic among some of the garrison. Many escaped by back routes while others drowned as they tried to scramble down the cliffs to the sea. When the remaining Persians finally agreed to the terms, the town gates were opened and the garrison laid down their arms. They were later escorted inland by British cavalry and ordered to disband. The British colours were hoisted at 4.30 p.m. on the Residency flagstaff by Lieutenant Clarkson of the Indian Navy. The troops ordered to take control of the town moved in at sunset. The *Annual Register* said:

> Nothing could have exceeded the vigour and efficiency of all the arrangements, both by land and sea, which led to the success of the expedition, and both

services vied with each other in the gallantry and skill with which they carried out the separate duties which each had to perform.

The town of Bushire was declared a military post under British rule, and subject to martial law. Among other regulations it was proclaimed that the traffic in slaves was abolished, and that newly imported Negroes of every age and sex would be seized and set free. Stocks of coal were stored and arrangements were made to obtain cattle and grain from the surrounding area. The damaged ships were patched up and all floated free on the next tide. The expeditionary force settled down to await orders and reinforcements, but it was no cosy billet, despite the lack of any apparent threat from the Persian army. The Paymaster, Major Barr, wrote to a friend:

Such a coast along which we have been sailing, and that which surrounds us, I never saw before – barren and burnt up is no term for it. Except in the vicinity of Aden and of Suez, I never remember to have seen such a wild scene as the hills around us present. The nearest approach both in structure and character are the hills on the Cosseer Desert. The town of Bushire is dirty and filthy in every direction; and to look at the streets one would imagine the place was uninhabited, as the houses are built with a courtyard to the centre, and all the windows open on this court; so that, except the door that leads from the street into the court, there are nothing but long rows of blank walls visible. The streets are rarely more than five or six feet wide. A few miles from the town flocks of gazelles and rock partridges are seen.

A book newly published by a jaded traveller was equally disparaging:

Bushire looks a miserable place . . . it can never look otherwise than a poor apology for a great commercial seaport town. Ships of any large size are obliged to lie off in a roadstead, three miles from the town, in consequence of the sandbanks which prevent any but small craft from entering the harbour. It stands on the end of a peninsula ten miles or more in length and three in breadth. The extremity on which the town is built consists of a crumbling, stony formation; and the further portion, joining with the mainland, is low and swampy, being often over-flowed by the sea. The town possesses no claim to antiquity. It was originally a small fishing village and rose to importance during the last two centuries. With the exception of the Residency there is not really a good or comfortable building in Bushire. Most of the dwellings are built of a soft, friable mud full of shells, like indurated marl; and some of brick plastered with mud, or imperfectly whitewashed. The habitations of the poorer classes consist of *kappars*, or mere hovels, covered with mats made by the date-leaf, called *peezur*, which grows in swampy soil. The largest is so low that one cannot stand upright in it, except in the centre.

Another contemporary account described the unhealthiness of the region:

It is a peninsula surrounded on the land side by marshy swamps, from which deadly exhalations arise in the heat of summer. And the access to the interior is so blocked up by a chain of lofty mountains as to be almost impracticable for an army. The paths which lead across these mountains wind through defiles where a single false step precipitates the traveller into an abyss, and where a few marksmen could easily arrest the advance of an invading force. And if an attempt were made to turn the barrier which nature has imposed by marching either to Darabgherd, on the east, or to Bebahan, on the west, difficulties of the same kind must be encountered, for the rocky chain extends in both directions.

*   *   *

A stronger force was needed to impress on the Persians the seriousness of Britain's intentions. The man picked to lead it was 54-year-old General Sir James Outram, a renowned big-game hunter.

Outram, the son of a Derbyshire engineer, secured an East India cadetship when he was sixteen. His legendary hunting exploits won him the affection of his Indian troops. During the ten years from 1825 he shot and killed 191 tigers, 25 bears, 12 buffalo and 15 leopards. His military adventures were also bloody. He seized the hill-fort of Malair from rebels in 1825 with much slaughter. He suppressed insurrection in the Yawal and Sauda districts. He captured a standard in the First Afghan War and was made major in 1839. After his defence of the Residency at

Brigadier-General Sir Henry Havelock.
(Engraving by C. Holl)

Hyderabad he was nicknamed 'The Bayard of India'. As a political agent he exposed corruption within the Bombay Government and in 1854 was appointed Resident at Lucknow. He carried out the annexation of Oudh and became chief commissioner of that province. He chain-smoked cigars and was generous in sharing his supplies. He was small and had rather a hesitant manner but seems to have been universally liked by officers and men.

He sailed from Bombay on 15 January 1857 and landed at Bushire on the 27th. His force comprised two divisions, one commanded by Stalker, the other by the renowned Christian soldier Sir Henry Havelock, a veteran of campaigns against the Afghans and the Sikhs. On his arrival Outram sent officers to reconnoitre the town of Mohammerah to investigate reports that Persian troops were erecting new fortifications there. They discovered a large Persian force assembling at the village of Burazjoon, 46 miles inland from Bushire. Outram decided to strike first rather than await attack. A garrison of 1,800 infantry and 14 guns were left at Bushire. His strike force consisted of over 4,650 infantry and cavalry, a company of European artillery and 18 guns. Units included the Poonah Horse, 2nd Europeans, 3rd Cavalry, 64th Foot, 78th Highlanders, 20th and 26th Native Infantry, 4th Rifles and 3rd Troop Horse Artillery.

It was acknowledged that the enemy was much more than a disorganised rabble. The veterans in the Persian infantry and cavalry had, after all, been trained in modern warfare by both the British and the Russians. The army facing Outram included a 900-strong battalion of the Kashkai Regiment – the Shah's guard, who wore British-style uniforms of red jackets and white trousers – four Sabriz regiments, two from Karragoozloo and one from Shiraz, an Arab regiment, and 500 regular cavalry. In all, these totalled 4,200 fully trained and experienced soldiers. Units of irregular cavalry, mobilized only in wartime, brought the strength up to almost 7,000. By common consent the Persian artillery was the most efficient in their army, although the gunners were hampered by the wide variety of ordnance and ammunition.

The British set out from Bushire on the evening of 3 February. Each man carried his great-coat, blanket and two days' provisions. No tents were taken nor any other equipment. Ahead of them lay a 41-hour forced march in deluging storms of rain and bitterly cold nights. The drenched troops reached the enemy's entrenched positions on the afternoon of the 5th but the Persians had abandoned their positions on hearing the army's approach, leaving behind their camp equipment and large quantities of stores and ammunition. Local plunderers were attempting to carry off stores, but fled when the British column arrived.

Outram said in his dispatch:

> The enemy having succeeded in withdrawing their guns to the strong passes, where I did not deem it prudent to follow them, and being satisfied with the moral effect of our occupying their position . . . I decided upon moving the troops. The return march was accordingly commenced on the night of the 7th, first destroying their magazines, found to contain about 40,000 lbs of powder, with small-arm ammunition and a vast quantity of shot and shell, and carrying away large stores of flour, rice and grain, which the Persian Government had been collecting for a long time past for their army, thereby effectively crippling their future operations. Some of their guns were supposed to have been cast into wells, and as their wheels and axles fell into our hands, it will be impossible that they can be used again for the present

The destruction of the magazine almost ended in tragedy. An infantryman and an artilleryman fired two rifle shells into the stacked ammunition from a range of only 70 yards. The concussion sent them and their rifles 'flying in the air' but they landed unharmed, if first dazed and then deeply embarrassed.

Meanwhile the Persian Commander, General Soojah-ool-Moolk, had only retired to the Shiraz road and now planned to attack the British in the camp with up to

Punjab battery preparing to enter the Durwanzal Pass. (Illustrated London News)

7,000 men, including the Eilkhanee cavalry. The explosive destruction of the powder and ammunition gave him notice of the British departure and he hurriedly gave chase. At midnight advance cavalry units of the Persian army attacked the British rearguard and threatened the line of march on all sides. The troops halted and formed a protective ring around the baggage train. Four enemy guns opened up on the column unhindered, as the darkness prevented any bid to capture them. The British and Indian soldiers kept the Persian Horse in check until daybreak.

At dawn the entire Persian army was drawn up ready for action to the rear left of the British column, near a place called Khoosh-ab. Outram's artillery and cavalry moved rapidly to the attack, supported by two lines of infantry. (The third line was left protecting the baggage.) The cannon slashed bloody gaps in the enemy's massed ranks and the cavalry brigade charged twice 'with great gallantry and success'. The Poonah Horse captured a standard of the Kashkai regular infantry regiment. The pole was topped by a 900-year-old silver hand, engraved with the inscription 'The Hand of God is above all things'. But it was the charge of the 3rd Bombay Light Cavalry against a disciplined Persian square which won the greatest glory.

An anonymous officer writing in the *Bombay Telegraph* gave a first-hand account of the action:

When Forbes, who commanded this regiment, gave the order to charge, he and his Adjutant, young Moore, placed themselves in the front of the 6th troop, which was the one directly opposite the nearest face of the square. The other Moore, Malcolmson and Spens came the least thing behind, riding knee to knee, with spurs in their horses' flanks, as if racing after a hog. In the rear of them rushed the dark troopers of the 3rd, mad to avenge the death of poor Malet at Bushire. In spite of steel, fire and bullets, they tore down upon the nearest face of the devoted square. As they approached Forbes was shot through the thigh and Spens' horse was wounded; but, unheeding, they swept onward. Daunted by the flashes and the fire and the noise and crackle of the musketry, the younger Moore's horse swerved as they came up. Dropping his sword from his hand and letting it hang by the knot at his wrist, he caught up the rein in both hands, screwed his horse's head straight, and then coolly, as if riding at a fence, leaped him at the square. If, therefore, any man can be said to have been first, the younger Moore is the man. Of course the horse fell stone dead upon the bayonets; as did his brother's, ridden with equal courage and determination. The elder Moore – 18 stone in weight and 6 ft 7 in, or thereabouts, in height – cut his way out on foot. Malcolmson took one foot out of his stirrups when he saw his brother officer down and unarmed (for his sword had been broken to

Officers in the camp of the Persian Force. (Illustrated London News)

The charge of the 3rd Bombay Light Cavalry against Persian squares at Khoosh-ab. (Illustrated London News)

pieces in the fall) and, holding on to [the empty stirrup], the younger Moore escaped. The barrier once broken, and the entrance once made, in and through it poured the avenging troopers. On and over everything they rode, till getting clear out, they re-formed on the other side, wheeled and swept back – a second wave of ruin. Out of 500 Persian soldiers of the 1st Regular Regiment of Fars, who composed that fatal square, only twenty escaped to tell the tale of its destruction. Thus the 3rd Light Cavalry, to use their own phrase, gave our enemies a *jewab* (answer) for the death of Malet Sahib Bahadur.

An artilleryman, whose account was published in the same newspaper, wrote:

All say that the cavalry charge was one of the most splendid ever witnessed . . . Next morning I went out to meet the force coming in, the rearguard of the army; and as the cavalry came in by two and threes, and salaamed to us, they drew their swords in triumph, crying out 'Dekho Sahib', and there they were, sure enough, blades and hilts, all smeared with blood, and their white belts bespattered all over; they must have made a glorious charge. Poor Frankland, of the 2nd Europeans, was made Brigade-Major of Cavalry, to go out with them, only the day before they started, and in the charge he cut down three men, but the fourth shot him dead, right in the bridge of the nose, the ball penetrating into the head.

The artillery and cavalry bore the whole brunt of the battle as the Persians moved away too rapidly for the British infantry to overtake them. By 10 a.m. the Persian defeat was complete. Two 9-pounder brass cannon were captured, along with gun ammunition loaded on mules, and at least 700 men lay dead. Outram said: 'The number of wounded could not be ascertained, but it must have been very large. The remainder fled in a disorganised state, generally throwing away their arms, which strewed the field in vast numbers, and nothing but the paucity of our cavalry prevented their total destruction and the capture of the remaining guns.' British and Indian losses were 16 men killed, including Lieutenant Frankland, and 16 wounded. Outram said: 'The loss on our side is, I am happy to say, comparatively small, attributable, I am inclined to believe, to the rapid advance of our artillery and cavalry, and the well-directed fire of the former, which almost paralysed the Persians from the commencement.'

Outram was himself out of action for most of the battle. He took a nasty fall from his horse at the first cannonades, and lay insensible in his tent for two hours, as he acknowledged in his dispatch: 'I myself had very little to do with the action, being stunned by my horse falling with me at the commencement of the contest, and recovering only in time to resume my place at the head of the army shortly before the close of this action.'

The anonymous artilleryman wrote:

They spoke very well on the whole of the Persian troops, and especially of their artillery. Certainly, the two guns that were captured were as good as any of ours – horses, harness, limbers, and all in very fine order. They have got 25 prisoners, two of whom they say are Russians. The Sukh-el-Mulk, who commanded the Persian army, narrowly escaped being taken himself, escaping without his hat. And going back with a bare head in this country, I suppose you are well aware, is disgrace.

The troops bivouacked close to the battlefield and the day was marked by further alarms as stragglers and wounded from both sides came into camp. The artilleryman and two others went out, armed, to find more stragglers:

One wounded man was bundled out of his *dhooly*, the bearers running away, leaving the poor fellow on the ground with the calf of his leg shot off by a round-shot. I returned and took him back in a *dhooly*, but he died just after he came in. We were out until two in the morning, having picked up ten unfortunate devils who would not move, some of them asking us to let them die.

That night the troops marched 20 miles over countryside made almost impassable by the incessant heavy rain. After a six-hour rest most of the infantry continued their march to Bushire which they reached before midnight, thus completing 44 miles, including rest and fighting a battle, in fifty hours. Some had passed through a notorious swamp and were 'masses of mud, dropping with fatigue'. The cavalry and artillery followed on. In his dispatch, Outram wrote:

The greatest praise is due to the troops of all arms for their steadiness and gallantry in the field, their extraordinary exertions on the march, and their cheerful endurance of fatigue and privation under circumstances rendered doubly severe by the inclemency of the weather, to which they were exposed without shelter of any kind; and I cannot too strongly express the obligation I feel to all under my command for the almost incredible exertions they have undergone and the gallantry they have displayed on this occasion.

Two senior officers did not share his sense of glory. On 14 March, in the rain-sodden camp at Bushire, General Stalker committed suicide. Commander Ethersay followed suit three days later. No explanation was given in dispatches for what were then considered shameful acts, other than they were both 'labouring under aberration of mind'.

The Persians had for several months been fortifying their position at Mohammerah. Batteries were erected of solid earth, 20 feet and 18 feet high, with casement embrasures, on the northern and southern points of the Karoon and Shat-ool-Arab, where the two rivers join. They and other earthworks armed with heavy guns were so skilfully and scientifically placed as to command an immense sweep of the river approaching the town. An intelligence report said:

Everything that science could suggest and labour accomplish in the time appeared to have been done by the enemy to effectively prevent any vessel passing up the river above their position; the banks, for many miles, were covered by dense date groves, affording the most perfect cover for riflemen; and the opposite shore, being neutral territory [Turkish], was not available for the erection of counter batteries.

The Persian army of 13,000 men, with 30 guns, was commanded in person by the Shahzada, Prince Khauler Mirza. Outram decided to attack, sailing up the Euphrates delta with 4,886 men in steamers and transports and assisted by sloops of war. His expedition was delayed by the non-arrival of reinforcements owing to 'tempestuous' weather in the Gulf and he was not able to leave Bushire until 18 March.

The flotilla began to move up-river a week later and at daybreak on the 26th the warships opened fire on the shore batteries. Outram also positioned four mortars under the command of Captain Rennie on a raft towed by the steamer *Comet*. The combined fire was swiftly effective, 'bursting immediately over the inside of the enemy's works, while, from the position of the raft, but few of the Persian guns could be brought to bear upon the mortars'. Within two hours of constant bombardment from ships and raft the northern and southern batteries were silenced, with an estimated 200 defenders dead, including a well-respected enemy officer, Brigadier Agha Jan Khan.

At 9 a.m. the infantry was able to land above the ruins of the northern battery without any casualties among the troops, although they had to run the gauntlet of musket fire from the shores on both sides. An officer noted in passing: 'Two or three native followers only were killed in consequence of their unnecessarily exposing themselves.' The troops formed into ranks and advanced relentlessly through the date groves and across a plain to the enemy's entrenched camp. The Persians, after blowing up their largest magazine, turned and fled without waiting to be attacked, leaving behind seventeen guns and all their camp equipment. The abandoned artillery included five brass 12-pounders, one of them Russian, three 9-pounders and two whose calibre was unknown because they were buried in mud. Only five guns and the Shahzada's personal property were carried away in the panicked retreat. The town itself was taken without any opposition.

Outram said:

> With the exception of the artillery, with the mortar battery, no portion of the military force was actively engaged with the enemy, beyond some European riflemen sent on their war vessels; but I am not the less indebted to all for their exertions and zeal, and especially for the greater order and despatch with which the landing of the troops was effected under Brigadier-General Havelock.

Lack of cavalry prevented Outram pursuing the foe but he sent a party of Scind irregular horsemen under Captain Malcolm Green to follow for some distance. He reported that he came upon the Persian rearguard retiring in good order but that the road was in many places strewn with property and equipment. Outram next sent an armed flotilla of three small steamers, with a hundred European infantrymen in each, on a reconnaissance under Captain Rennie of the Indian Navy up the Karoon River to Ahwaz. Rennie's mission was to ascertain the movements of the Persian army and, if possible, destroy the magazines in the town. The expedition set off on 29 March.

Near Ahwaz a Persian force of around 7,000 men with cavalry and some artillery was spotted occupying a low range of hills at right angles to the river on the right bank. Rennie decided to attack the town, having reason to believe it was either abandoned or weakly guarded. He landed his 300 troops, deploying them in formations which gave the appearance of many more men than he actually had, while the gunboats took up a position within range of the enemy's camp and opened fire. As the tiny British force advanced to occupy the town the Persians were seen in full retreat towards Dizful. After buying supplies from the townspeople, who were grateful for the business, Rennie's force returned to Mohammerah.

This was the last action, if it can be called that, of the war. Soon after Rennie's return the news arrived that peace had been concluded between Great Britain and Persia.

★   ★   ★

The Treaty of Peace between Her Majesty the Queen and the Shah of Persia was signed at Paris on 4 March, and the ratifications were exchanged at Baghdad on 2 May. It provided for 'perpetual peace and friendship' between the two nations. The Shah agreed to withdraw his forces from the territory and city of Herat and from every other part of Afghanistan within three months. Persia agreed to relinquish all claims to sovereignty over those territories and never to demand any tribute from them, or interfere with the independence of those states. It added: 'In case of differences arising between the Government of Persia and the countries of Herat and Afghanistan, the Persian Government must engage to refer them for adjustment to the friendly offices of the British Government, and not to take up arms unless those friendly offices fail of effect.' The Persians also agreed to allow the thin-skinned Mr Murray back into Tehran and that he 'on approaching the capital, shall be received by persons of high rank deputed to escort him to his residence'.

The British Government, for its part, agreed to remove its troops from Persian lands within three months and free all prisoners of war. Persia would be allowed to take action against Afghan tribes who crossed her border but any military incursions must be recalled as soon as the culprits were caught and punished. 'The British Government engage at all times to exert their influence with the States of Afghanistan to prevent any causes of umbrage being given by them, or by any of them, to the Persian Government; and the British Government, in the event of difficulties arising, will use their best endeavours to compose such differences in a manner just and honourable to Persia.'

Britain was by now much more concerned with India. The Great Mutiny, which started on 24 April 1857 when eighty-five men of the 3rd Bengal Cavalry refused to accept new cartridges rumoured to be greased with cow and pig fat, sent shock waves across the Empire, especially when Sepoy mutineers began to massacre Europeans. The Bombay Cavalry's heroic charge at Khoosh-ab was quickly forgotten.

Outram was recalled to India along with Havelock. He was given command of two divisions and the commissionership of Oudh. He joined his force with Havelock's and unselfishly conceded command to his brother-officer, saying he wished only to serve as a volunteer. Together they achieved the relief of Lucknow after first defeating a large enemy force at Fatehpur without the loss of a single soldier. Havelock said that the victory was due to 'the blessing of Almighty God on a most righteous cause, the cause of justice, humanity, truth and good government'. He conceded, however, that the British artillery, the Enfield rifle and British 'pluck' had also played their part. Aged sixty-two and worn out by the march, Havelock died in the besieged town on 27 November. Outram commanded the Lucknow garrison until the second relief. He was created a baronet in November 1858 and remained as commissioner of Oudh, where he advocated leniency in the vicious aftermath of the Mutiny. He returned to Europe in 1860, his health broken by hard campaigning, and he died at Pau in March 1863. He is buried in Westminster Abbey. Leeke missed the Mutiny, returning to Britain at the end of five years' service heading the Indian Navy. He was made an admiral in 1860 but died less than four years later.

Both sides honoured the Treaty of Paris. The British army was withdrawn, apart from a small force under General John Jacob, which was left at Bushire for three months. Anglo-Persian relations became cordial and in 1862 an agreement was concluded for a telegraph line to connect India with England via Persia. Shah Nasir ud-Din visited Britain amid great pomp in 1873 and 1899 and was received by Queen Victoria herself. The Shah also kept up his ties with Russia and in 1882 the Persian Cossack Brigade was formed, officered by Russians but subject to the Persian minister of war. In 1888 the Karoon (Karun) River was opened to international navigation, while European sciences began to be taught in Persian schools. A naturalised Briton was involved in setting up the first Persian state bank while in 1889 the Russians were granted concessions covering Persian railways. In

1891 a tobacco concession was granted to a British subject but it was withdrawn after strikes and riots broke out.

Throughout these years Nasur ud-Din served Persian interests by balancing those of Britain and Russia. The wily Shah sat on the Peacock Throne for forty-eight years but during his latter years poverty, corruption and misgovernment increased. In 1896 he was assassinated by a follower of the revolutionary and anarchist Kemalu'd-Din. The Shah's son, Muzaffar ud-Din, succeeded him and in 1903 he was invested with Britain's highest award of chivalry, the Order of the Garter.

Anglo-Russian rivalry over Persia continued but British interests became dominant after the Russian Revolution, to the enrichment of her oil companies. With supreme irony, a joint British-Soviet force invaded Persia during the Second World War to protect the oil supply lines to Russia.

★   ★   ★

CHAPTER SIX

The Arrow or Second China War, 1856–60

'This mode of warfare is hard to deal with . . .'

Present at the signing of the Treaty of Nanking, which ended the Opium War, was fourteen-year-old Harry Parkes. A year earlier Harry, an orphan from a Staffordshire iron-making family, sailed to China to join his two sisters who were already settled with the family of the explorer and clergyman Charles Gutzlaff. In Macao Harry learnt Chinese and made himself useful as an interpreter to Sir Henry Pottinger, then still Governor of Hong Kong. In the last months of the war he impressed military men and diplomats alike with his 'manner and energy of character'. Two years later, barely sixteen, he took delivery of three million dollars of Chinese war indemnity.

Subsequent years saw him prosper as a diplomatic agent, and in 1845 he was transferred as interpreter to the consul of Foochow, where a Tartar garrison was established. He suffered insults and stoning from drunken Tartar soldiers. Later, while he was serving in Shanghai, the husband of his elder sister was among three missionaries beaten and almost murdered by a gang of junkmen. Parkes was heavily involved in encouraging a blockade by a single British gunboat until the attackers were caught and punished.

Duties followed in Amoy, Formosa and the interior at Hinghwa which helped him better understand and exploit the intricacies of Chinese diplomacy. A successful mission with Sir John Bowring to help negotiate the first European treaty with Siam resulted in Parkes being received by Queen Victoria. In June 1856, aged only twenty-eight, he was appointed acting consul at Canton.

Parkes was short and slight, with a fair complexion and bright, alert blue eyes. He was earnest, religious and zealously devoted to his country. His absorbing passion was how best to serve the interests of the British Empire, and he had a short fuse when anything or anyone tried to block those interests. He was not an evil man, but his youthful stubbornness and first-hand experience of barbarity led directly to a war which claimed thousands of lives and was perhaps the greatest piece of vandalism ever inflicted by the West on the Orient.

★   ★   ★

The Treaty of Nanking had created little more than a troubled truce. Other western powers, notably France and America, scrambled to take advantage of the emperor's

Harry Smith Parkes, British Commissioner at Canton. (Illustrated London News)

humiliation in order to win trade concessions of their own. The deals struck by all satisfied no one. The Chinese believed that, as the terms had been imposed by brutish force by the 'barbarians', they had no moral worth and should not be adhered to in any great detail. The foreigners discovered that they still could not trade in the interior, nor settle and trade anywhere except the five open ports which included Hong Kong. A supplementary treaty was signed in 1844 guaranteeing protection to British seafarers from arrest while conducting legitimate trade. But clashes continued along a thousand miles of coast, infested with smugglers, pirates and adventurers on all sides. On the mainland the new emperor, Hien-feng, who succeeded to the imperial throne in 1850, was at first preoccupied with fighting Tai-ping rebels in genocidal clashes which saw whole cities destroyed. But another major confrontation with Britain was inevitable, and it was a relatively minor incident that lit the fuse.

In October 1856 Chinese police seized a *lorcha*, or merchant vessel, near the Dutch Folly Fort off Canton, after hearing claims that a crew member was a pirate. *Arrow* had been trading for two years in Chinese waters under a British flag. Owned by a Chinese Hong merchant in Canton, it was Chinese-built and Chinese-crewed. But it had been registered in Hong Kong and therefore, by the British interpretation of the 1844 treaty, it came under Crown protection, even though the annual registration had technically expired. All but two of the fourteen-man crew were arrested and taken on board a Chinese war-boat which anchored close to *Arrow*.

Commissioner Yeh.

Consul Harry Parkes was outraged on hearing reports that the British flag had been disregarded. He was rowed out to the war-boat, where he demanded that the arrested men should be taken to his Consulate where the charges against them might be investigated. The Chinese officers refused on the grounds that as they had already reported the matter to their own superiors they must await orders. To break the deadlock, Parkes appealed to the Governor of Canton, Commissioner Yeh Ming-ch'en, demanding both the release of the crew and an apology to the British Crown. He must have known that his appeal would be rejected. Commissioner Yeh was an 'arrogant' official with a well-known hatred of foreigners, who had used every bureaucratic trick to block the interests of European merchants.

His rejection, however, was couched in reasonable terms. He stated that

Arrow was not the property of a British firm, that the British flag was not flying at the time of the seizure and that no foreigner had been on board. He added: 'Hereafter Chinese officers will on no account without reason seize and take into custody the people belonging to foreign *lorcha*s, but when Chinese subjects build for themselves vessels, foreigners should not sell registers to them, for if this be done it will occasion confusion between native and foreign ships, and render it difficult to distinguish between them.'

Parkes would not back down. Even before receiving Yeh's reply he sent a message to the Governor of Hong Kong, Sir John Bowring, calling for support. Bowring gave it gladly, despite admitting in his return message that the British case was fundamentally flawed: 'It appears, on examination, that the *Arrow* had no right to hoist the British flag; the licence to do so expired on the 27th of September.' Bowring believed, however, that the Chinese had broken the spirit of the treaty because they 'had no knowledge of the expiry of the licence'. The Chinese were therefore guilty of an act of provocation. He told Parkes: 'You will inform the Imperial Commissioner that I require an apology for what has taken place, and an assurance that the British flag shall in future be respected; that forty-eight hours are allowed for this communication, which being passed, you are instructed to call on the naval authorities to assist you in forcing redress.'

Parkes now had the authorisation he needed to bring Yeh, who had previously obstructed his work as Consul and whom he personally detested, to heel. He told Yeh that he had 'clear and satisfactory' proof that *Arrow* had been flying the British ensign and that a hired English master had been on board – neither was true – at the time of the seizure. Threatened with British naval might, Yeh signalled he might relent and release the prisoners. This was not enough for Parkes, as no formal apology was forthcoming. He thus called on Rear-Admiral Sir Michael Seymour, commander-in-chief of the British fleet on the China station, to restore the honour of the flag.

A Chinese junk was seized by the tender *Coromandel* and brought down to Whampoa. This action produced no further reply and on 23 October Seymour, with a fleet of gun-boats, bombarded and captured the forts guarding the Pearl River approaches to Canton. After burning several buildings Seymour's force captured the Dutch Folly, a fort of fifty guns on an island opposite Canton. The British blockade of the Canton River had begun. Both sides paused to allow further negotiations before they resorted to further hostilities.

Yeh offered to surrender ten of the twelve prisoners. When this was rejected he sent all of them to Parkes, with a demand that two be sent back to face trial for piracy in the Chinese courts. There was still no apology, so Parkes refused to accept the prisoners and the men were once more taken away by the Chinese. Bowring, meantime, wrote to Yeh saying: 'There is no doubt that the lorcha Arrow lawfully bore the British flag under a register granted by me.' That was a flat contradiction of the earlier statement sent by the Governor to Parkes. He must have known it was a lie but by then British resentment at being treated as second-class by an Oriental was so acute that honesty seemed no longer relevant.

Bowring's behaviour, to modern eyes, makes him appear a dishonest, pompous and racist example of the British colonial administrator. But that is too simple. He was one of the most extraordinary men of his age. Born in 1792 to an ancient Devonshire family, he had become a Radical; still in his twenties, he was imprisoned by the French Bourbons, accused of spying and conspiring to free men sentenced to death for singing revolutionary songs. He helped to found, and then ran, the *Westminster Review* to offer a philosophical platform to Radicals. As an MP for the Clyde burghs, and later Bolton, he helped to found the Anti-Corn Law League and championed the causes of hand-loom weavers, Irish students and the arts. He successfully pushed through legislation to free the Manxmen from feudal tyranny, and advocated the abolition of flogging in the army. During extensive travels he became fluent in Spanish, Portuguese, German and Dutch, translated Swedish, Danish, Russian, Serbian, Polish and Bohemian, studied Magyar and Arabic, and later made good progress with Chinese languages. In the 1840s he invested most of his fortune in ironworks in Glamorganshire which failed owing to a general depression in prices. He won the job of Consul at Canton thanks to his friendship with Lord Palmerston, and immediately clashed with the mandarins over their refusal to allow any foreign dignitary access to the city. He got on well, however, with the Chinese merchants and ordinary people of the area, with whom he mixed a great deal. He saw parallels with the Manxmen and other modern victims of feudal rule. From 1852 he was acting governor of Hong Kong, and that appointment was made permanent in 1854. As well as governor, he was also commander-in-chief and vice-admiral of Hong Kong, Britain's plenipotentiary to China and chief superintendent of trade. He had been Parkes's superior on the mission to Siam, and their success there had helped to forge a close friendship.

Sir John Bowring, Governor of Hong Kong. (Illustrated London News)

Bowring decided to make still further demands on the Chinese while British guns threatened Canton. He instructed Parkes to write to Yeh, demanding that he allow all foreign representatives the same free access to Canton as applied to the other four free ports. The legality of this demand was dubious. When no reply was received, on the 27th Seymour opened fire on government buildings in Canton, including Yeh's own residence; a body of Chinese troops who had taken up positions on high ground behind the city was also shelled. Yeh's response was to issue a proclamation offering a reward of 30 dollars for the head of every Englishman.

The bombardment continued and the city walls were breached. On the 29th a force of seamen and Marines landed, climbed the broken parapet and blew the city gate to pieces. Three Britons were killed and eleven wounded as the attacking force entered the city and took possession of Yeh's house. Chinese troops regrouped, keeping up a steady sniper fire, and at sunset the British were recalled to their vessels.

After a further exchange of correspondence with Yeh the attack was resumed on 3 November but the cannon fire was concentrated to destroy Chinese government buildings and property. A large group of war-junks at anchor below the Dutch Folly came under attack by British steamers and gunboats. After a spirited firefight which lasted thirty minutes the Chinese were driven off the stationary junks and the vessels were burnt. At the same time the nearby French Folly fort was taken in a 'smart fight' by Marines with the loss of one dead and four wounded.

A week later Admiral Seymour sent a summons to the commander of the Bogue Forts, scene of much bloodshed in the previous war, demanding that they be surrendered, on the understanding that they would be kept intact and given back if there was a satisfactory conclusion to the dispute which had already claimed numerous lives. The commander replied that if he agreed to such terms he would lose his head. Seymour's squadron first attacked two of the forts on Wantung Island, which the Marines took in an hour in the face of 'considerable, though ill-directed resistance'. Seymour added:

These forts were fully manned, had upwards of 200 guns mounted, and were found stronger than when captured in 1841. The Chinese troops stood to their guns up to the moment our men entered the embrasures. The Mandarins had boats in readiness to facilitate their own escape, leaving their unfortunate followers, who rushed into the water until they were assured of their safety by the efforts made to save them.

British boatmen ferried many to shore and let them go. The attackers lost one boy killed and four men wounded from *Nankin*. The following day the Annunghoy Forts, on the opposite side of the Bogue entrance, were taken without casualty after only token resistance from their 210 guns.

Chinese gunners in another fort mistakenly fired at an American warship which was keeping an eye on proceedings. The American captain fired a few salvoes in retaliation but 'as what had happened was evidently an accident, and no outrage upon the United States flag was intended, the Americans took no further part in the action'.

Admiral Seymour was by now as determined as Bowring to humble Yeh and force him to allow British authorities free access to the city. Parkes made this clear to a delegation of Canton merchants, telling them that if 'simple reparation for outrage in the *Arrow* case had been all we required, the Admiral would doubtless have been long ago satisfied with what had been done; but a principle was at stake which could not be abandoned'. Seymour had the firepower necessary to level outlying forts but not the manpower to take the city. He was obliged to wait for reinforcements while a rioting mob, encouraged by Yeh, ransacked foreign factories on the outskirts of Canton and burnt them down.

As 1856 drew to a close the small steamer *Thistle*, used to carry mail from the

Canton factories to Hong Kong, took on board a party of Chinese soldiers disguised as passengers. As the ship steamed down-river they killed all eleven Europeans on board, ran the vessel aground and set it on fire before making their escape. Two weeks later, on 12 January 1857, Seymour landed raiding parties of troops in Canton's western suburbs carrying fire-balls and lighted torches. The raid left the suburb blazing for two days. But Seymour's forces were too spread out for comfort and he abandoned several forts, including the Dutch Folly. His steamers were withdrawn from the upper part of the river and his troops took up new positions in the Teatotum fort near the Macao passage. Another full-blown war was now inevitable.

★　　★　　★

Commissioner Yeh issued another proclamation promising a set tariff of rewards for anyone who succeeded in killing or capturing any of the 'red-haired foreign dogs'. Capture of an English or French 'rebel chief' was worth 5,000 dollars, the head of a barbarian 50 dollars, exposure of a traitor 20 dollars, destruction or seizure of a shallow-water steamer 2,000 dollars, and the burning or capture of a large war steamer 10,000 dollars. In addition all those Chinese employed by the English or French were given a month to return to their home villages – or suffer beheading.

The proclamation had an immediate effect, which almost wiped out the European population of Hong Kong. The large bakeries on the island supplied all the bread to the foreigners. On the morning of 15 January large quantities of arsenic were mixed in with the dough and delivered to breakfast tables in the new-baked loaves. Several hundred Europeans were poisoned and became violently ill, including Sir John Bowring and his family. Fortunately the arsenic had been mixed in such heavy proportions that it acted as an emetic and was vomited too quickly to be absorbed through the stomach in any great quantity. Analysis of samples later sent to Berlin laboratories found that each pound of bread contained between 38 and 42 grains of arsenic, spread so evenly that it must have been kneaded with the dough. No one died, although the arsenic affected Lady Bowrigg's lungs. For several days she, her husband, daughters, guests and servants suffered racking headaches, bowel pains and other complaints. Bowring wrote home: 'This mode of warfare is hard to deal with, and will, I am sure, excite a general sympathy and indignation.' Lady Bowrigg, his wife of forty years, was never well after the attack. The following year, for health reasons, she returned to England where she died shortly after her landing.

The bakery owner, a Chinese speculator called A-lum and several of his employees escaped from Hong Kong aboard a steamer but were pursued and arrested. They were put on trial before the colony's Supreme Court. The prosecution provided evidence that A-lum had been present when the poisoned dough was kneaded and baked. Commissioner Yeh's reward scheme was cited as his motive. His defence claimed that he too had eaten the bread and had been ill. His flight from Hong Kong was explained by an official requirement to present himself at Canton. No witnesses could prove conclusively that he or his men had added the arsenic to the dough. All were acquitted.

Bowring appealed to London for an expeditionary force to take and hold Canton for Britain. Lord Palmerston, the Prime Minister, was eager to oblige. He told an election rally at Tiverton: 'An insolent barbarian, wielding authority at Canton, has violated the British flag, broken the engagements of treaties, offered rewards for the heads of British subjects in that part of China, and planned their destruction by murder, assassination and poison.'

The opposition, recalling the international contempt piled on Britain during and after the Opium War, did not agree. Votes of censure against Bowring's actions and the government's support of him, were moved in both Houses of Parliament. The Earl of Derby moved the hostile resolution in the Upper

The Emperor of China, Hien-feng.
(Illustrated London News)

Chamber but after a long and loud debate his motion was rejected by a majority of thirty-six. In the Commons Cobden led the attack, claiming that Bowrigg had violated international law and acted against his orders in the matter of the unregistered *Arrow*. Cobden's motion was carried by a majority of sixteen. Palmerston appealed to the country and in the subsequent election many of Cobden's supporters lost their seats while Palmerston's administration was strengthened.

The Earl of Elgin, a former Governor-General of Canada, was sent to China as envoy to the emperor. He had full powers to negotiate a peace treaty or, if satisfactory terms were not available, to 'prosecute the contest with vigour'. An expeditionary force was prepared, supported by the French who had become involved to avenge the murder of a missionary.

Regardless of the political debates raging at home, Admiral Seymour was not idle. Born in 1802 to the son of an admiral, he was eleven when he first went to sea. His naval career saw him shipwrecked on the desolate shores of Chile, court-martialled for the wreck that put him there (he was acquitted), and a flag-captain on the North America and West Indies station. During service in the Baltic a small sea-mine he was inspecting blew up in his face, destroying the sight of one eye. Despite such narrow scrapes he had generally been a peacetime commander and was eager to see real action in China before he was pensioned off. His target now was the fleet of war-junks in the Canton waters.

On 25 May 1857 he sent Commodore Charles Elliot with a squadron of gunboats steaming up Escape Creek, the most northerly of four inlets which ran eastwards up the Canton river. Elliot soon reached a large number of heavily armed junks moored across the stream. The two sides exchanged vigorous gunfire which saw sixteen junks taken and destroyed. The shallow-draught junks retreated into waters where the British vessels could not follow. The next day Elliot pursued them via a deeper channel. When shallow water again denied further progress bluejackets and Marines took to the ships' boats and rowed 12 miles upstream. On rounding a point they were suddenly faced with the enemy fleet anchored under the protection of shore batteries in front of the large town of Tang-koon. The Chinese, startled by the arrival of the British in river waters, abandoned their junks and took refuge in a nearby fort. From there they opened a heavy fire with *jingals* (matchlocks) on bluejackets who had boarded the junks and were busy destroying them. Under constant fire the British succeeded in blowing up twelve junks before returning down-river.

Meanwhile Seymour led a flotilla comprising the steamer *Coromandel* and four gunships to Fatshan Creek where he found seventy-two junks moored under the protection of nineteen large guns on the ramparts of a hilltop fort on Hyacinth Island and a six-gun battery on the opposite shore. A correspondent wrote: 'The Chinese believe they are here impregnable. They know you cannot get at the junks without first taking the fort, and they believe no man can go up that hill in the face of their guns. Several vessels have from time to time gone in and exchanged shots with the fort and come back again. This confirms their confidence.' *Coromandel* ran aground, exposed to fire both from shore and the nearest junks. Again, ships' boats manned by sailors and marines won the day. They landed on the island and charged up the hill, and the Chinese defenders, after only brief resistance, abandoned the fort. The marines then stormed the stationary junks, destroying almost all of them with powder and shot.

At the same time a small squadron of ships' boats under Commodore Keppel took the shore battery and pressed on up the creek until they were halted by 'tremendous fire' at an island shaped like a leg of mutton. The channels on either side were narrow and exposed to the concentrated fire of twenty junks lying moored or aground alongside. Three British boats became stuck while two more dashed for the nearest channel. The correspondent reported: 'No sooner did the boats appear in the narrow passage, than 20 32-pounders sent 20 round shot, and a hundred smaller guns sent their full charges of grape and canister at a range of 500 yards right among them. The effect was terrible.'

Keppel retired but resumed the chase when the tide flowed to his advantage. The Chinese junks fled towards the town of Fatshan through narrow channels but one by one they became stuck and were deserted. During the 6 mile pursuit all but three of the junks were taken and destroyed. The ships' boats reached the walls of the town. A volley from the Marines drove back a body of Chinese soldiers but the British, their task completed, returned to join Seymour.

The general stalemate continued and was extended by other events in another part of the East. Elgin, stopping off at Singapore, was met by letters from Lord Canning telling him of the spread of the Indian Mutiny. The crisis on the sub-continent was more pressing than events in China, and Elgin's force was diverted to Calcutta. Elgin continued to Hong Kong, expecting that the revolt in India would quickly be suppressed and that his force would speedily follow on. He reached Hong Kong at the beginning of July but quickly realised his error and set sail westward for Calcutta with a force of Hong Kong troops on board HMS *Shannon*. He and his men were deployed to protect that city from the insurgents. The China War would have to wait.

★　　★　　★

James Bruce, 8th Earl of Elgin and 12th Earl of Kincardine, was a product of the aristocracy, Eton and Oxford. Now aged forty-six, he had been an able governor of Jamaica, but his later governorship of Canada was soured by rebellion and disturbances. During one riot his coach was stoned and he was accused of timidity in dealing with the rioters. Others praised 'the thoroughly practical manner in which he habitually dealt with public questions, his readiness to assume responsibility, and the strong sense of duty which enabled him to suppress personal considerations whenever they appeared to conflict with the public interest'.

It was not until late autumn that Elgin, his Indian duties done, arrived at Hong Kong. He was joined by a French squadron and that nation's envoy, Baron Gros. At the beginning of December they sent a letter to Commissioner Yeh stating that the English and French governments were united in their determination to seek 'by vigorous and decisive action' reparation for past misdeeds, including the *Arrow* incident and attacks on French missionaries. War would be prosecuted unless British subjects were given free access to Canton and compensation was paid for loss of property during the 'disturbances'. If these demands were met within ten days the blockade of the Canton River would be raised, although any captured forts would be kept until any peace treaty was ratified.

French public opinion had turned in favour of war after the 'judicial murder' two years before of the Roman Catholic priest Auguste Chapdelaine. Despite imperial edicts to tolerate Christian missionaries, a local magistrate embarked on a virulent purge of Christians in which twenty-five Chinese converts were imprisoned and tortured, two of them dying. Chapdelaine himself was arrested and put on trial, charged with preaching the Christian gospel. He was flogged and put in a *cangue* – a heavy wooden cage clamped around the neck like a portable pillory. When he unexpectedly failed to die of this mistreatment his head was chopped off and thrown to the dogs. The French Government demanded reparations.

Yeh conceded nothing to Britain or France but sent Elgin an evasive reply: 'Our two nations regard themselves as on friendly terms with each other. This being the case, there can be nothing which makes it impossible for us to consult together . . .'. Yeh's letter was dated Christmas Day 1857. By then active operations had already commenced, with the British forces under the command of Major-General Charles von Straubenzee and the French naval brigade under Rear-Admiral Rigault de Genouilly. A squadron of war steamers advanced up the Canton River and troops were landed to construct batteries on Dutch Folly island and the peninsula known as French Folly. The crews of the Chinese shore batteries watched them avidly but did not fire a shot. Groups of British and French troops made reconnaissance sorties closer to Canton. The city was given forty-eight hours to surrender before the attack began.

On the morning of 28 December the fleet opened up a heavy bombardment, while joint Anglo-French forces stormed the outlying Linn fort. The cannonade continued all day and throughout the following night until Canton 'was engirdled on the south and east sides with a wall of fire'. The next morning the battered walls were scaled and the Chinese defenders were driven from the parapets. The British troops under Colonels Holloway and Graham, with their French allies, raced along the walls, pouring fire down into the enemy as they fled into the city streets. A battery on

The gunboat *Starling* engaging a battery at Fatshan Creek on the Canton River. (Illustrated London News)

Magazine Hill at the wall's northern extremity was soon captured, and its guns turned against the enemy, while a courageous sortie by Tartar troops who threatened to outflank the attackers was beaten back. Gough Fort, further to the north, was also taken and blown up with gunpowder. Casualties were 13 British dead and 83 wounded, 2 French dead and 30 wounded. Canton was effectively taken and the firing stopped, but the allied forces remained on the parapets while a strange calm hung over the city streets below. For several days the city inhabitants appeared to go about their normal business, studiously ignoring the foreign devils above them.

On 5 January several parties descended into the labyrinth of streets. The troops captured Canton's governor, Peh-kwei, in his residence within a walled enclosure. The Tartar General Tseang-keun was also taken without a struggle. It took a few hours more to snatch the real prize. Commissioner Yeh, dressed as a coolie, was found hiding in the small mansion (or *yamun*) of a senior official and was captured by a party under Captain (later Sir) Astley Cooper Key with Parkes as interpreter. A correspondent wrote a gloating account of the capture in *The Times*:

> The place was full of hastily-packed baggage. Mandarins were running about, yes, *running* about; and at last one came forward and delivered himself up as Yeh. But he was not fat enough. Parkes pushed him aside, and, hurrying on, they at last spied a very fat man contemplating the achievement of getting over the wall at the extreme rear of the *yamun*. Captain Key and Commodore

Elliot's coxswain rushed forward. Key took the fat gentleman around the waist and the coxswain twisted the august tail of the Imperial Commissioner round his fist. Instinctively the bluejackets felt it must be Yeh, and they tossed up their hats and gave three rousing cheers.

The writer described Yeh as around 5 feet 11 inches tall, very stout, with a remarkably receding forehead, a large protruding mouth, rotten teeth and eyes which 'glared with terror and with fury'. He added: 'No habit of looking at Yeh deadens the feeling of repulsion which the expression of his huge face inspires.'

Yeh and the other captives were marched under guard to a joss-house on Magazine Hill, which had become the British headquarters. Lord Elgin decided that Yeh should be put on board HMS *Inflexible* and sent to Calcutta as a state prisoner. However, Tseang-keun was allowed to return to the city on condition that he disband his troops. Peh-kwei was reinstated as a governor, but his real powers were usurped by a European tribunal under Parkes. The puppet governor was told by Elgin that any attempt, 'whether by force or fraud, by treachery or violence', to harm the occupying force would be met with severe punishment. Elgin in turn promised that when the current dispute was settled the foreign troops would withdraw from the city and restore it to the Chinese authorities.

The emperor immediately degraded the prisoner Yeh from his office as commissioner, accusing him of reckless obstinacy in his dealings with the barbarians. Elgin and Baron Gros determined to go to Peking for an audience with the emperor to conclude a peace treaty. Their envoys were at first courteously received but the negotiations, unsurprisingly, soon became bogged down. The two western commanders quickly lost patience and the allied squadron sailed from Canton waters; heading towards Peking, the fleet reached the mouth of the Peiho River on 19 May. The Chinese had lost no time in rebuilding and strengthening the Taku forts guarding the approaches. Earthworks, sandbag batteries and parapets stretched for almost a mile on both sides of the river. The muzzles of eighty-seven big guns were visible, while forty-nine more poked out from strong mud batteries further up-river. Entrenched camps behind the batteries showed that troop reinforcements had been sent from Peking.

The forts were summoned to surrender but instead the Chinese batteries fired on the advancing gunboats. The artillery duel lasted ninety minutes and left the shore batteries silent and ruined and the forts abandoned. Further up the Peiho a barrier of fire-ships was also deserted and the Chinese troops were nowhere to be seen. The squadron continued up to the city of Tien-tsin at the entrance to the Grand Canal and on 29 May landed under a flag of truce. Dispatches noted: 'Not the slightest hostility was displayed by the Chinese either there or during the passage up the river after the capture of the forts at the mouth.' A telegram to the Foreign Office said: 'The Chinese continue to consider the proceeding as something between peace and war, but not exactly one or the other.'

High-ranking Chinese commissioners were sent by the emperor and, after several weeks of often frustrating diplomatic negotiations and ruffled feathers on both sides, the Treaty of Tien-tsin was signed on 26 June 1858. The terms included Chinese reparations for the recent war, the opening of ten more ports to European trade in future, freedom of movement for European merchants and missionaries, the right to trial under British law for any British subjects caught committing a crime in Chinese territory, the legalisation of the opium trade, consuls to be allowed to live in any open port, and foreign diplomatic missions to be opened in Peking. British and French honour was satisfied but it is difficult to see how, as was reported at the time, the dignity of the emperor was not damaged by such an unequal treaty.

Elgin and Admiral Seymour now set off for another adventure – delivering a steam-yacht to Japan as a gift from Queen Victoria to that nation's emperor. Their real agenda, however, was to negotiate another treaty to throw open Japan's closed ports to British commerce and break the monopoly then jealously guarded by the Dutch. British priorities switched elsewhere while public attention was still on the horrors of the Indian Mutiny. Peace with China, however, did not last long.

⋆   ⋆   ⋆

The Earl of Elgin's brother Frederick Bruce was appointed Her Majesty's Envoy Extraordinary to China and the Celestial Court. He reached Hong Kong in May 1859 and superseded Sir John Bowring as governor of that colony. Born in 1814, Bruce was the youngest of three siblings and had held senior diplomatic posts in Hong Kong, Newfoundland and Bolivia. His orders demonstrate clearly that the British Government expected the Chinese to prevaricate further, despite the Treaty of Tien-tsin, over Bruce's access to Peking and the establishment of a permanent mission there. They said: 'All the arts at which the Chinese are such adepts will be put in practice to dissuade you from repairing to the capital, even for the purpose of exchanging the ratifications of the Treaty; but it will be your duty firmly, but temperately, to resist any propositions to that effect, and to admit of no excuses . . .' A naval force was placed at his disposal to see that the Treaty was enforced.

Accompanied by the French ambassador M. de Bourboulon, Bruce sailed on to Shanghai. British and French suspicions were quickly proven well-founded. Chinese officials proposed that the Treaty should be ratified there rather than in Peking. The two envoys refused and headed for the Peiho River with a squadron of gunboats and other vessels under the overall command of Rear-Admiral Sir James Hope, who had succeeded Seymour as commander-in-chief on the China station. The 51-year-old Hope came from a distinguished naval family and had served in North America, the West Indies and the Baltic, but had seen comparatively little action.

At the mouth of the Peiho the squadron found their way barred. The Taku forts had again been rebuilt after the hammering they had taken the previous year. Their earthworks had been improved and strengthened with additional ditches and *abattis*. Furthermore, the river was blocked with several large booms, a series of bulky timber rafts, chains and rows of stakes and iron piles. Chinese officials at first promised to clear the obstructions, but after several days nothing had been done, so the British gave notice that they would do it themselves, using force if necessary. On 24 June several parties cut the cables of one boom, and blew two others away with gunpowder, but the following day the British saw that two had been repaired during the night. Bruce told Hope he must force a passage through.

The morning of the 25th was occupied in putting the gunboats into position. At 2 p.m., during high water, *Opossum*, under Captain Willes, was ordered to push her way through the first barrier. The ship succeeded in bursting through a line of iron stakes lashed together and proceeded towards the second obstruction followed by Hope's flagship *Plover* and other gunboats. At that moment a 'tremendous fire' was opened from the Taku forts, where large-calibre guns were concealed behind matting. This time the Chinese gunners' fire was accurate and the results were devastating. *Plover* quickly sank, and Rear-Admiral Hope was severely wounded in the right leg. Refusing to be taken out of the action, Hope and his flag were carried aboard *Cormorant*, but it too was quickly disabled. *Kestrel* fell victim next, and *Lee* was forced aground. Despite his country's declared neutrality, the American commodore Josiah Tattnall came to Hope's aid in his steamship,

Lord Elgin. (Radio Times Hulton Picture Library)

crying 'Blood is thicker than water'. It was almost certainly the first time that British and American servicemen saw action side by side, albeit only on a rescue mission. As a young midshipman Tattnall had fought the British in the 1812 War but felt that he could not stand by as a neutral observer. His launch rescued Hope and other British wounded. At the end of their efforts his crew were black with powder smoke. The battered remnants of the British squadron fell back to slightly safer positions and began pounding the forts in return. The British fire was effective and by 6.30 all but one gun in the North and South forts were silenced.

Admiral Hope later justified his subsequent decision to attack, taken while his wounds were tended. 'In these circumstances,' he wrote, 'it was clear that no other mode of attack was open to me, except that on the front of the works . . .'. Another commentator put it differently: 'Unfortunately our contempt for our cowardly enemy was carried too far, and the Admiral thought that the forts might be taken by a *coup de main* if a body of men were landed from the vessels.' It was to be a costly mistake.

The landing force selected for the assault included a detachment of sappers and miners, a brigade of Marines, and a division of British and French seamen. The British were commanded by Captain C.F.A. Shadwell of the gunboat *Highflyer* and the sixty Frenchmen by Captain Tricault. In all around a thousand men set off in landing boats at 7 p.m. An eye-witness recorded the disaster:

Interior of the North Fort at Peiho after its capture. (Illustrated London News)

Just as the first boat touched the shore, bang went a gun again from the fort, immediately followed by a perfect hurricane of shot, shell, gingal balls and rockets, from all the southern batteries, which mowed down our men by tens as they landed. Nevertheless, out of the boats they all leaped with undiminished ardour (many into water so deep that they had to swim to the shore), and dashed forward through the mud, while the ships threw in as heavy a covering fire as they possibly could.

The enemy's fire, however, continued to be deadly, and the mud proved so deep – in most places up to the men's knees at least, often up to their waists – that out of the men who landed, barely 100 reached the first of the three deep and wide ditches, which, after some 500 yards of wading through the mud, presented themselves before the gallant few who got so far, and out of that small number scarcely 20 had been able to keep their rifles or their ammunition dry. Nevertheless, they boldly faced these new difficulties, and some 50 of them, with a crowd of officers, succeeded in getting as far as the furthest bank of the third ditch, from which they would certainly have made a good attempt to scale the walls had ladders been forthcoming; but, out of the number that were landed, all but one had either been broken by shot or had stuck in the mud. With the remaining one, however, ten devoted men sprung forward, three of whom were immediately shot dead, and five wounded severely.

A vertical fire of arrows, as well as a constant fusillade, was kept up on the select band, who now crouched in the ditch, waiting, but in vain, for reinforcements; and that any of them afterwards escaped alive is miraculous. Seeing what insurmountable difficulties presented themselves, the order was at last given to retire . . .

Midshipman John Fisher, later Admiral of the Fleet Lord Fisher of Kilverstone, wrote to his mother: 'We had a hard fight for it, but what could we do against such a fearful number of guns, and us poor little gunboats enclosed in such a small place, not much broader across than the length of our ship?' He described wading back through the mud:

> I had to fling all my arms away coming back from the forts, and was nearly smothered once, only one of our bluejackets was kind enough to heave me out. You sank up to your knees at least every step, and just fancy the slaughter going 500 yards in the face of about thirty pieces of artillery right in front of you and on each flank. It was dreadful, horrible work, but thank God I came out all right.

Captain Shadwell had been shot in the foot shortly after the landing but had struggled forward to the last ditch. Captain Vansittart of *Magicienne* had a leg shot off, while Colonel Thomas Lemon of the Royal Marines was also wounded as he took what little shelter he could find. Hundreds more officers and men huddled behind banks and inside the outer ditches. Dragging the wounded, the survivors used darkness to cloak their mud-drenched retreat. The Chinese used blue lights and rockets to pinpoint the exhausted men, and more died in the mud. On arriving at the water's edge the survivors were horrified to find that so many boats had been smashed by roundshot that there were simply not enough to take off all of them. Several men were drowned trying to reach the overburdened craft which remained. Others remained up to their necks in water for up to an hour before they could get a place on a boat. Even then their nightmare was not over. Several boats full of wounded men were hit by continuing fire from the forts and were swamped on the return trip to the ships. The last survivors were brought off at 1.30 the following morning. *Coromandel* was turned into a temporary hospital ship and 'the scene on her upper deck was truly horrible'.

In all, the British force lost 89 men killed, including 4 officers, with 252 wounded. A further 25 men were killed and 93 wounded on the stricken gunboats. Two men, one English, the other claiming to be an American, were taken prisoner. The tiny French force lost 4 dead and 10 wounded. Hope reported on the fighting of his forces ashore: 'Had the opposition they experienced been that usual in Chinese warfare, there is little doubt that the place would have been successfully carried at the point of the bayonet.' The *Annual Register* reported:

> Our losses were out of all proportion to the numbers engaged, and we sustained a mortifying repulse from a people with whom our only chance of ultimate success is the conviction forced upon their minds that we are invincible. Such a defeat is likely to do away with the effect of previous victories, and to involve us in another war with the barbarian empire of China.

A Chinese description of the battle, by General San-ko-lin-son, proved such fears correct. In his dispatch he claimed that the British had fired first on the forts and shore batteries. He wrote:

Our soldiers, pent in as their fury had been for a long time, could no longer be restrained; the guns of every division, large and small, opened upon all sides, and at evening the firing had not ceased . . .

More than 20 boats now came alongside the bank of the southern Fort, and the barbarians, having landed in a body, formed outside the trench; our gingal and matchlock divisions were then brought up to oppose them, and fired several volleys. The barbarians did not venture to cross the ditch, but threw themselves down among the rushes, and fired on us from their ambush. Such murderous ferocity was, indeed, calculated to make one's hair stand up with rage; and to vindicate the honour of the State, and fulfil at the same time the expectations of the Government, your slaves were obliged to bring forward their troops to oppose them with their utmost strength . . .

As we could not tell how far these were off, our soldiers kept them back by projecting fireballs through bamboo tubes; and, as these blazed up, our guns and cannon . . . fired into them at point-blank range; till, their skill and strength alike exhausted, they dared no longer to continue the engagement, but slunk back to their ships. The barbarian dead lay piled in heaps . . .

Bloodied and dispirited, the British squadron limped back to Shanghai, having first managed to refloat the grounded *Kestrel*. British firepower had, for the first time, been defeated by the Chinese and further warfare was indeed certain.

★   ★   ★

As Hope nursed his wounds at Ningpo, reaction in Britain was intense. Military rivals criticised his tactics, questioning the wisdom of attacking the Chinese in the same manner and in the same place as Seymour had successfully done a year earlier. The Chinese were bound to have strengthened their defences in the meantime. Such comments were, however, overshadowed by the gallantry of Hope and his men. The enormity of the setback gave rise to several myths, including the totally unsubstantiated claim that the shore guns were manned by Russians or Americans. The 'treachery' of the Chinese in opening fire was also underlined, even though Hope had attacked first by trying to force a passage through the river barrier. The Chinese had openly manned the forts and barricades. Several officers under Hope's command repudiated the idea of any treachery, saying that they had known for days that the forts would resist any British attempt to force a way up-river. A later commentator said:

A man who, when he sees you approaching his hall-door, closes and bars it against you, and holds a rifle pointed at your head while he parleys with you from an upper window, may be a very inhospitable and discourteous person; but if when you attempt to dash in his door he fires at you with his rifle, you can hardly call him treacherous, or say that you had no expectation of what was going to happen.

At the time such views were in a minority, and war fever gripped both Britain and France. During an acrimonious debate in Parliament, Hope and Bruce were heavily criticised. Lord Elgin staunchly defended his brother and urged further diplomacy. He said that negotiations with Peking were necessary 'if we intend to maintain permanent pacific relations with some 400,000,000 of the human race, scattered over a country 1,500 miles long by as many broad'. Karl Marx, in a dispatch to the *New York Daily Tribune*, reported: 'The whole debate in both Houses on the Chinese war evaporated in grotesque compliments showered by both factions on the head of Admiral Hope for having so gloriously buried the British forces in the mud.'

The following year Britain and France fitted out an expeditionary force to avenge the defeat, win reparations and enforce the Treaty of Tien-tsin. The British forces consisted of around 11,000 men, including several Sikh regiments who had volunteered for the task, under Lieutenant-General Sir James Hope Grant. This 52-year-old Scot had served in the Opium War and had built a fearsome military reputation. He took part in the hard-fought battle of Sobraon, commanded the 9th Lancers in the Punjab War and saw the most ferocious action during the Indian Mutiny. His experience of hand-to-hand fighting was legendary among the rank and file, while senior officers relished his performances on the violoncello. Wolseley described him as 'a tall man of muscle and bone and no unnecessary flesh about him. He had all the best instincts of a soldier, and was a brave daring man that no amount of work could tire. He was liked by every good man who knew him.' Despite his excellent reputation for soldiering, Grant was no text-book soldier. He was ill-educated, read nothing but the Bible, could not sketch maps, never learnt to read anyone else's maps, and was so prone to issuing confusing, badly expressed orders that some of his officers called him 'puzzle-headed'. His courage, however, was never doubted. He once explained: 'To die is nothing; it's only going from one room to another.' Grant divided his command into two brigades under Major-Generals Sir Robert Napier and Sir John Michel. The fleet amounted to around 200 frigates, gunboats and transport ships. The French had 6,000 men under General Charles Montauban.

Lord Elgin and Baron Gros, again appointed plenipotentiaries in China for the two western powers, set sail in the English frigate *Malabar*. Stopping on the way at Point de Galle in Ceylon, their vessel was totally wrecked on a rocky reef in the harbour. The two ambassadors had a lucky escape and emerged unscathed, but were chagrined to lose many important papers. They were delayed in Ceylon until another ship, aptly named *Pekin*, arrived to collect them.

Meanwhile, on 8 March 1860, an ultimatum was sent by Bruce from Shanghai to the Chinese Government requiring an 'ample and satisfactory apology . . . for the act of troops who fired on the ships of Her Britannic Majesty from the forts of Taku in June last, and that all guns and material, as well as the ships abandoned on that occasion, be restored'. Bruce also demanded that the river by Taku should be cleared, Britain's envoys should be admitted to Peking with due honour, and the Chinese Government pay war indemnity of four million taels. The French made similar demands.

Peking's Great Council replied that the ultimatum caused them great astonishment, while the demand for restitution was 'yet more against decorum', especially as China's own war expenses had been enormous. The demand for a British Residence in Peking was rejected outright. The reply concluded that the ultimatum was couched in 'insubordinate and extravagant' language and warned that if Bruce continued on his obstinate course 'he will give cause to much trouble hereafter'.

Harry Parkes, meantime, was temporarily recalled from his service in Canton, where he had been busy rebuilding the destroyed British settlement and organising an emigration house for the despised Chinese coolies. Parkes's first suggestion was to lease the peninsula of Kowloon, opposite Hong Kong, as a convenient camping ground for the allied army. Astonishingly, in return for hard cash, the Chinese Governor-General agreed to lease a portion of the Celestial Empire to be used as a depot for hostile troops.

Lord Elgin and Baron Gros arrived in Hong Kong on 21 June and proceeded to Shanghai to meet up with General Grant and Admiral Hope, who remained in command of the British fleet. The British and French forces moved towards Taku, the British anchoring in the Bay of Tah-lieu-hwan, the French at Chefow on the north side of the promontory of Shantung. The troops disembarked at Pehtang, 12 miles north of the Peiho River, where they made camp. A soldier described the area as 'a wilderness of mud and water, destitute of tree, plant, shrub or grass, amidst a scene of utter misery and desolation'. Heavy rain kept them in that grim spot until the allied forces were able to march out on 12 August.

With the troops was the special correspondent for *The Times*, 43-year-old Thomas William Bowlby. The son of an artillery officer raised in Sunderland, he was a not-too-successful lawyer before turning to journalism in Berlin. He married the sister of his father's second wife and through her inherited a sizeable fortune which he spent. His debts forced him abroad and he was involved in building a railway to Smyrna when he got the call from *The Times* to accompany Elgin to China. He left behind his wife and five small children.

Napier's column of infantry, the Madras Sappers, the Cavalry Brigade, a rocket battery and three six-pounders struck off to the right of the road leading from Pehtang to Sinho, intending to turn the left flank of the Chinese defendants, but got bogged down in heavy ground. This delayed the departure of Michel's main column and the following French force. Tartar cavalry moved rapidly to attack Napier's smaller force but luckily Michel's artillery managed to bring their guns and rockets to bear in time to avert a possible massacre. So heavy was the fire that the enemy cavalry, about 4,000 strong, was forced into retreat and two lines of Chinese entrenchments were abandoned. Chinese losses were estimated at around 100, mainly horsemen who had been 'cut up' by Sikh cavalry.

The following day Grant ordered the bridging of creeks and ditches intersecting the ground between the allies and Chinese defences at Tangku. On the 14th the allies moved up-river to within a mile of the town. Two Armstrong guns and two nine-pounders swiftly silenced a Chinese battery, while a party of sailors slipped across the river and burnt a number of junks. The whole of the artillery was moved to within 600 yards of the enemy earthworks and opened a heavy fire on the walls, supported by two French batteries. The Chinese replied with twelve guns and a brisk fire of gingals and matchlocks. Grant reported:

The artillery gradually advanced to within 350 yards, and, the enemy's guns being silenced, a breach was commenced . . . by the 60th Rifles and an entrance was effected, the Chinese retiring with great precipitancy. At the same time the French advanced with great gallantry, and entered by the main gate, which had been partially broken in by artillery fire. I am happy to say that our losses in these two engagements were very slight, owing to the enemy being completely paralysed by the superior fire of our artillery.

The Chinese garrison retreated, leaving behind forty-five cannon. The Chinese had been commanded by General San-ko-lin-son. A mishearing of his name sparked the widespread rumour that he was a maverick Irishman called Sam Collinson.

The allies then moved on to attack the Taku Forts by land and river. The land force, predominantly British, hauled cannon along hastily improved tracks to within 800 yards of the inner North Fort on the left bank of the Peiho. At night batteries were built for the heavy guns, mortars and field pieces. Gunboats steamed to engage the outer North and South Forts. The Chinese forts were all constructed on the same plan: massive redoubts with thick ramparts strongly defended with heavy cannon. They were protected by two unfordable wet ditches, between which and the parapet sharp bamboo stakes were thickly planted, forming two belts, each about 15 feet wide. Any advance could be made only on a narrow front. The French commander, Montauban, believed the forts to be impregnable and, in a formal written protest, refused to commit his forces to what he believed would be almost certain slaughter. At the last minute he partially relented and dispatched 400 infantry and two batteries to 'put in an appearance'. At 5 a.m. on 21 August the Chinese opened up with every gun that could be ranged upon the attackers, forcing the allies to begin their onslaught an hour earlier than planned.

A British storming party formed up while the French contingent pushed on through wet ditches to assault the salient of the inner fort. They failed to scale the walls owing to the vigorous resistance of the defenders. The Chinese fire was so effective that fifteen Sappers carrying a pontoon bridge were knocked down by a single discharge. Fifteen-year-old Hospital Apprentice Arthur Fitzgibbon of the Indian Medical Establishment broke cover to bind the wounds of a dhoolie-bearer, and then ran further under intense fire to tend other injured men before he too was severely wounded.

Napier ordered two howitzers to within 50 yards of the fort's main gate. A small breach, big enough only for one man at a time, was made and the storming party headed for it, some of them swimming across water-filled ditches. Bowlby recorded the action:

All this time the fire of the enemy continued incessant. Cold shot, hand grenades, stinkpots, and vases of lime were showered on the crowd of besiegers . . . The ladders placed against the wall were pulled into the fort, or thrown over, and in vain did man after man attempt to swarm through the embrasures. If the defence was desperate, nothing could exceed the gallantry of the assailants. Between English and French there was nothing to choose. A Frenchman climbed to the top of the parapet, where for some time he stood alone. One rifle after another was handed up to him, which he fired against the enemy. But his courage was unavailing, and he fell back, speared through the eye. Another, pickaxe in hand, attempted to cut away the top of the wall. He was shot, and Lieutenant Burslem, of the 67th, caught hold of his pick and continued the work. Lieutenant Rogers attempted to force his way through an embrasure, but was driven back. He ran to another, but it was too high for him. Lieutenant Lenon came to his assistance, forced the point of his sword into the wall, and placing one foot on the sword, Lieutenant Rogers leaped through the embrasure . . .

Rogers was the first Briton into the fort, followed by Private John McDougall of the 44th. They were seconds behind the first Frenchman, Drummer Jean Fanchard of the 102nd who had scaled an angle wall. Ensign John Worthy Chaplin of the 67th planted the Queen's colours in the breach before being badly wounded. He was assisted by Private Thomas Lane, who had also helped Lieutenant Burslem to widen the hole in the wall. Both men were also wounded. The troops plunged through the breach and embrasures, forcing the Chinese back step by step until the defenders fled over the fort's opposite walls.

For their outstanding courage in this action Apprentice Fitzgibbon, Lieutenant Robert Montresor Rogers, Private McDougall, Lieutenant Edmund Henry Lenon, Lieutenant Nathaniel Burslem, Private Lane and Ensign John Chaplin were all awarded the Victoria Cross – Britain's foremost honour for valour – the highest number to be awarded in a single action, a record only later surpassed at Rorke's Drift. At fifteen years and three months old, Fitzgibbon was the youngest person to wear the Victoria Cross, before or since.

The outer North Fort was then attacked but its commander offered no resistance. The allied infantry scaled the walls without a shot being fired and took 2,000 prisoners. That evening the garrison of the South Forts were abandoning them, and the allies took possession of empty buildings. The Chinese army melted away. In all 400 Chinese guns were captured. The allies lost 17 men killed in the attack on the first position, and 183 wounded. It had been no pushover.

Lt Robert Montresor Rogers VC.

Lt Nathaniel Burslem VC.

Ensign John Worthy Chaplin VC.

Private Thomas Lane VC.

Lt Edmund Henry Lenon VC.

The emperor appointed Kweiliang, who had negotiated the 1858 treaty, and Hang Fuh, Governor-General of Chi Li province, as imperial commissioners charged with reaching a peace with the foreign invaders. Admiral Hope was sent up the Peiho in *Coromandel*, accompanied by Consul Parkes, to meet them at Tien-tsin. With them went a division of five gunboats. On being told that Sang-ko-lin-son had passed the previous day, Hope decided to occupy the treaty city with his small force. The British and French flags were hoisted over the east gate. The local people met the foreigners with smiles, having been told by proclamation that the barbarians had been defeated and there was nothing to fear from them. Negotiations with the imperial commissioners proved inconclusive, however, and the rest of the allied force pushed up-river to join Hope.

Elgin swiftly became frustrated with imperial prevarication and gave notice that he would push onwards to Tang-chow, 65 miles closer to Peking. Some 5 miles short of his target, it was agreed that a convention would be signed at Chang-tsin-wan. The allies' agreed campsite was found to be occupied by a large force of Chinese cavalry and infantry. On 18 September Consul Parkes was sent to Tang-chow to negotiate with Prince I, a nephew of the emperor, to arrange for Elgin's reception and to protest at the proximity of the Chinese force. With him went an escort of Fane's Horse, under Lieutenant Anderson, Elgin's private secretary, Henry Loch, and several others including Bowlby of *The Times*. The party set off under a flag of truce.

Meanwhile the Chinese cavalry advanced on both flanks of the allied force. Within two hours the British and French were almost entirely surrounded. Grant was anxious not to engage the energy while Parkes and the others were behind Chinese lines, but the decision was taken out of his hands when the guns and matchlocks in the centre of the Chinese emplacements opened fire on a small party under Lieutenant-Colonel Walker as they galloped through their lines. Grant recalled:

> Colonel Walker reported that, while waiting for Mr Parkes, a French officer joined him, who was suddenly set upon and cut down by a Chinese soldier and, on his riding up to prevent him being murdered, his own sword was snatched from his scabbard and some men tried to throw him off his horse. Seeing that it was a deliberate attempt to assassinate the whole of them, Colonel Walker set spurs to his horse and galloped out with his party, under fire of the Chinese line.

One of his men was wounded and one horse had a spear thrust into its back, but they all returned safely to the British positions.

Parkes and his companions were not so lucky. The consul, Loch and a sowar carrying the flag of truce were taken to San-ko-lin-son who received them with 'rudeness and insult' and ordered them to be bound. The three foreigners and two French prisoners were paraded in an open cart 'of the roughest sort' through Tang-chow and, bound to the same vehicle, transported onwards to Peking. The remainder were also captured and bound tightly – Lieutenant Anderson, Captain Brabazon, Mr de Norman of the British Legation, the journalist Bowlby, an English dragoon and eighteen sowars. They were carried off into the interior where all the

Europeans and several sowars died of mistreatment. Their hands and feet were bound so tightly with cords that the flesh burst and mortification ensued. Captain Brabazon was beheaded near Peking, on the orders of a mandarin who had twice been wounded with shell-splinters. Private Moyes of the Buffs suffered the same fate when he refused to kow-tow, although Chinese authorities later claimed that the Scots veteran, a well-known hell-raiser, had died of drink. Moyes was immortalised in a poem by Sir Francis Doyle:

> Last night among his fellow roughs,
> He jested, quaffed and swore;
> A drunken private of the Buffs,
> Who never looked before.
> Today, beneath his foeman's frown,
> He stands in Elgin's place,
> Ambassador from Britain's crown,
> And type of all his race.

Brabazon had volunteered to go with Parkes in place of Colonel Garnet Wolseley, the future viscount and commander-in-chief of the British Army, who had lagged behind the column to do some sketching. Elgin and Grant were unaware of the imprisonment of the delegation but knew that treachery was involved and, immediately following Walker's report, formed their men into a line of attack. Despite the large numbers of Chinese cavalry, the battle was little more than a rout. The Tartars advanced to within 200 yards of the British line, a 'whole cloud of horse'. The 99th fired a volley too early and the Chinese cavalry wheeled around. The dragoons gave chase. One Marine, Captain Carrington, wrote: 'The Tartars waited until our men had neared them within fifty yards, and then they fired a volley, wounding a Captain rather badly and killing a trooper. They then turned about and moved smartly on.' The Chinese were on the other side of a broad ditch which the first line of dragoons leapt easily, but in doing so they raised a cloud of dust which prevented the second line seeing enough to follow them. There were enough dragoons, however, to lay into the enemy. With the British on the left and General Montauban's men on the right, they dispersed a Chinese army reckoned to be 20,000 strong. British and French guns blasted great holes in the massed Chinese ranks at short range and San-ko-lin-son's army fled. Several hundred bodies were left on the field. The British lost one man dead, seventeen wounded and one missing.

The allied forces cleared out and burnt four military camps. After taking a nearby village with no casualties the men were allowed to fill their empty water-bottles. Carrington later recalled: 'I assure you it is very hard and thirsty work charging cavalry about such a dry and unsupportable country. The millet is but lately cut, and you have a plain of stalks, standing about a foot and a half high, with sharp tops that pierce like spikes. Several of the horses have been lamed by these points.'

Elgin blamed the Tartar general both for the treachery and for the ensuing carnage. He said that San-ko-lin-son believed the imperial commissioners had compromised his military position by allowing the allies so close to his lines.

The French attacking the bridge at Pa-le-chiao, 6 miles from Peking. (Illustrated London News)

He sought to counteract the evil effect of this by making a great swagger of parade and preparation to resist when the allied armies approached the camping ground allotted to them. . . . I cannot believe that after the experience which San-ko-lin-son had already had of our superiority in the field, either he or his civil colleagues could have intended to bring on a conflict in which, as the event has proved, he was sure to be worsted.

The allies marched on towards Peking. Six miles from the imperial city they met another Tartar army at Pal-le-chiao. While the French infantry stormed across a narrow bridge to destroy the main Chinese emplacement which guarded the imperial high road, the King's Dragoon Guards charged the Tartar cavalry, inflicting heavy losses. Large bodies of the enemy advanced to within 200 yards of Grant's hastily unlimbered cannon before salvoes of cannister drove them off. On the left flank Fane's Horse, thirsting for revenge after the capture of their comrades, attacked another body of horsemen, supported by the 1st Sikh Cavalry. The charges were across fields where crops of maize and millet had recently been cut, leaving sharp-pointed stubble which gouged the legs and bellies of the horses and made rapid movement very difficult. Despite these handicaps the charges were 'most effective'. Grant reported:

The enemy, though defeated on the spot, yet still remained in front, in clouds of horsemen who, though constantly retiring from the advance of any party of our cavalry, however small, never allowed more than 1,000 yards between us, and showed a steady and threatening front. At this time I had with me the cavalry, the 4th Infantry Brigade, and three Armstrong guns; the rest of the artillery, with the 2nd Brigade, having been left in the centre . . . With the three Armstrong guns under Captain Rowley, we fired occasional single shots on their thickest masses. Those shots, fired singly at slow intervals, served admirably to illustrate the good quality of the Armstrong guns; not one failed to strike the thick masses of the enemy, at once dispersing them from the spot.

The 99th Regiment took and burnt the headquarters camp of the imperial princes; seeing the flames and losing heart, the Chinese army retreated to Peking. Forty-three guns were taken in the action. In the centre of the field small piles of dead showed the effect of Grant's measured artillery fire. Allied losses were 2 dead and 29 wounded, most of them only slightly.

Meanwhile, in Peking Harry Parkes was separated from his companions and brought before a board of examiners who ruled that he be placed in a prison for common criminals. Parkes wrote in his memoir:

I found myself in a throng of 70 or 80 wild-looking prisoners, most of them offensive in the extreme, as is usual in Chinese gaols, from disease and dirt. I was again carefully examined and searched by the gaolers, who also saw that my chains were properly secured, and bound my arms with fresh cords, not so tightly as to prevent circulation or to occasion serious inconvenience. At the same time they removed, to my intense relief, the cords from my wrists which, being very tightly tied, had caused my hands to swell to twice their proper size, and were now giving me great pain. They then laid me on the raised boarding on which the prisoners sleep, and made me fast by another large chain to a beam overhead. The chains consisted of one long and heavy one, stretching from the neck to the feet, to which the hands were fastened by two cross chains and handcuffs, and the feet in a similar manner.

Parkes was repeatedly interrogated because of his knowledge of the language but refused to give useful information on Elgin's intentions. His gaolers may have been rough but he was well treated by his fellow prisoners.

It was only from the prisoners that I obtained sympathy or a hearing . . . Many of these unfortunate men were glad, when so permitted, to come round me to listen to my story, or any description that I would give them of foreign countries and usages. Instead of following the example set them by their authorities, and treating me with abuse or ridicule, they were seldom disrespectful, addressed me by my title, and often avoided putting me to inconvenience when it was in their power to do so. Most of them were men of the lowest class, and the gravest order of offenders, as murderers, burglars, etcetera. Those who had no means of their own were reduced by prison filth and prison diet to a shocking state of emaciation and disease; but those who could afford to fee the gaolers, and purchase such things as they wanted, lived in comparative fullness and comfort.

After only a few days in such primitive conditions Parkes was removed from the common prison to a separate cell which measured 8 feet square, with four gaolers appointed to watch him. He was frequently visited by Hang-ki, a Mandarin he had known in Hong Kong, who was sent by Prince Kung, the emperor's brother, to extract information and make use of him to obtain the most favourable terms from the British. He told Parkes he was to be taken out of prison, but Parkes bravely refused to leave unless Loch was released also. After a short stand-off, and after eleven days in captivity, both men were taken to a temple where quarters were provided and they were treated well. On 5 October, however, they were told they were to be executed that evening, but the order was countermanded by Prince Kung after the defeat at Pal-le-chiao.

Elgin and Gros refused to negotiate with the Chinese authorities until all the British and French prisoners had been released. They were still unaware of the deaths of most of the hostages. On 25 September Elgin gave Prince Kung notice that Peking would be bombarded and taken by force unless, within three days, the prisoners were surrendered, the convention signed at Tang-chow and the ratifications exchanged in Peking. Kung used his diplomatic wiles to delay and evade the ultimatum, and on 6 October the allies closed on the city.

The French column lagged behind, claiming later they had lost their way, and made straight for the Yueng-min-yeun, or Summer Palace of the emperor. Around twenty poorly armed eunuchs offered brave but hopeless resistance and were cut down by the rifles of the French. They began looting its treasures on a massive scale. One observer described the scene shortly afterwards:

> The public reception-hall, the state and private bedrooms, anterooms, boudoirs, and every other apartment has been ransacked; articles of vertu, of native and foreign workmanship, taken or broken if too large to be carried away; ornamental lattice-work, screens, jade stone ornaments, jars, clocks, watches and other pieces of mechanism, curtains and furniture – none have escaped from destruction. There were extensive wardrobes of every article of dress; coats richly embroidered in silk and gold thread in the Imperial Dragon pattern; boots, headdresses, fans, in fact, rooms all but filled with them . . .

Montauban, the commander-in-chief, obtained a magnificent diamond necklace. General Grant later succeeded in getting a small share of the booty for his own army. In the subsequent auction he gave his own share to be distributed among his men, for which he was rebuked by the Russell Government. Queen Victoria signalled her approval of his action. In total every British private received around a £4 share of the Summer Palace loot.

Two days later Parkes, Loch and the other surviving prisoners were released. Parkes wrote:

> We were placed in covered carts, without being able to see each other, and were escorted by a large party of soldiers and mandarins through streets which wore a deserted appearance to the Se-che, or north-western gate of the city. We soon

The King's Dragoon Guards closing with Chinese cavalry at Pa-le-chiao. (Illustrated London News)

saw, with grateful hearts, as those great portals opened and then immediately closed behind us, that we were already free men, for our guard, not daring to follow us out of the city, had left to ourselves the pleasant task of finding our own way to the allied camp.

What they did not know then was that fifteen minutes after the gates shut behind them, an express message was received from the emperor ordering their instant execution.

The British and French guns were lined up to bombard the imperial city and the Chinese authorities were told that the cannonade would begin at noon the following day unless Peking was surrendered and one of its gates placed in allied hands. The emperor, just twenty-nine years old but already dying of dropsy and debauchery, had abandoned the city and fled to Manchuria on the pretext of a hunting expedition, and it was left to Prince Kung to capitulate unconditionally. A gate was opened and for the first time in history the British and French flags flew above Peking's walls.

As part of the surrender terms it was agreed that the city be spared. Elgin did not know the fate of all the hostages: he had been told that they were all safe and comfortably lodged. When the truth emerged Elgin was understandably furious. He wrote to Kung, upbraided him for deception and added:

Of the total number of twenty-six British subjects seized in defiance of honour and of the law of nations, thirteen only have been restored alive, all of whom carry on their persons evidence more or less distinctly marked of the indignities and ill treatment from which they have suffered, and thirteen have been barbarously murdered . . . Until this foul deed shall have been expiated, peace between Great Britain and the existing dynasty of China is impossible.

Some advised Elgin to burn down the Imperial Palace but he felt that such action would only drive Kung and the rest of the Chinese Government to evacuate the city and threaten the allied forces from the countryside. Elgin learnt that several prisoners had been tortured in the Summer Palace, now largely gutted by both French and Chinese looters. He proposed to Baron Gros that it should be burnt down in retribution for a 'great crime'. The French ambassador refused to take part, even though his own forces had plundered the place, and Elgin resolved to carry it through on his responsibility alone. Although Parkes negotiated the surrender of Peking, he played no part in this decision, although he later said it was just punishment for the cruelty shown towards the prisoners.

It took a detachment of British soldiers to burn every building to the ground, as the Summer Palace occupied a large area of ground and consisted of some two hundred separate structures laid out in the style of the Trianon at Versailles. Wolseley compared it to 'a city composed only of museums and Wardour Streets'. The buildings themselves were set among gardens, temples, small lodges and pagodas, groves, grottos, lakes, bridges, terraces and artificial hills. Charles George Gordon, a 27-year-old captain in the Royal Engineers (and later to meet lasting fame and death at Khartoum), helped organise the destruction. He wrote to his mother:

We went out, and, after pillaging it, burned the whole place, destroying in a Vandal-like manner most valuable property which would not be replaced for four millions. We got upward of £48 apiece prize money before we went out here, and although I have not as much as many, I have done well. The people are civil, but I think the grandees hate us, as they must after what we did to the Palace. You can scarcely imagine the beauty and magnificence of the places we burnt. It made one's heart sore to burn them; in fact, these places were so large, and we were so pressed for time, that we could not plunder them carefully. Quantities of gold ornaments were burnt, considered as brass. It was wretchedly demoralizing work for an army. Everybody was wild for plunder.

The only consolation for the Chinese was that British and French looters preferred porcelain – much of which still graces English country houses whose present owners do not normally admit to handling stolen goods – and neglected the bronze vessels locally prized for cooking and for burial in tombs. Many such treasures dated back to the Shang, Zhou and Han dynasties and were up to 3,600 years old.

Once the Summer Palace was reduced to a charred desert a sign was raised on the site with an inscription in Chinese, reading that this was the reward of perfidy and cruelty. It was the last act of a bloody war.

★   ★   ★

General Sir Robert Napier, with Parkes at his side, marched into Peking on 13 October 1860. The Summer Palace was still burning. Eleven days later Elgin made his official entry into the city as a conqueror, not as an emissary. His escort consisted of 600 soldiers and 100 officers led by a cavalry detachment. Elgin was seated in a chair of state carried by sixteen Chinese in crimson robes. As he was carried into the Hall of Ceremonies a band played 'God Save the Queen'. His Lordship treated Prince Kung with a haughty politeness. The prince was alarmed when the lens of Signor Beato's camera was pointed at him, until reassured it was not a weapon. The photography intended to mark the historic occasion, however, was bungled.

The Treaty of Tien-tsin was ratified and further humiliations were heaped on the Quing Dynasty with the signing of the Convention of Peking. The war indemnity to be paid by the Chinese was increased by eight million taels. Tien-tsin itself was opened up to foreign trade, Kowloon was ceded to the British and foreign ambassadors were allowed to reside in Peking. The emperor was forced to apologise for the 'treachery' of the Taku garrison in firing upon Hope's squadron. The Allied forces stayed until reparations were paid and finally retired on 5 November.

Lord Elgin returned to England the following April, having stopped at Java on the voyage home. There was much criticism of his burning of the Summer Palace which many saw as an act of 'unintelligible and unpardonable' vandalism. The need to avenge the murder and ill-treatment of British subjects was not under question, merely the manner of that vengeance. 'Would any act of treachery committed by a Spanish sovereign justify the destruction of the Alhambra?' one critic asked. Elgin argued, with some force, that to demand the punishment of the actual murderers would have been absurd. The Chinese would simply have handed over as many victims as he asked for, or executed as many as he demanded should pay the price. But there would have been no guarantee that they were the actual perpetrators. That argument was accepted by at least one commentator who added: 'It is somewhat singular that so many persons should have been roused to indignation by the destruction of a building who took with perfect composure the unjust invasion of a country.'

Elgin and Grant may have delivered a victory, but political feelings in Britain were divided over both the cause and the conduct of the war. Earl Grey called a House of Lords debate in

Thomas Bowlby, *The Times* correspondent in China. (Illustrated London News)

which he accused Elgin of abusing the various treaties with China, of promoting the opium trade instead of stifling it, and of allowing an even more pernicious trade – the export of coolies – which, he said, was a slave trade in disguise. Lord Ellenborough asked whether 'Sir John Bowring's war' was really over and said that the Chinese had suffered great injustices. For the government, however, Lord Wodehouse claimed they had done everything to discourage both the opium and coolie trades. On the need for military action he added: 'If the Chinese once entertained the idea that we would depart from the words of the treaty, they would circumvent us by their tricky diplomacy, and oblige us at last to cut the matter with the sword.'

Barely a month after landing in England Elgin was appointed viceroy and governor-general of India. He arrived there in March 1862 and for twenty months threw himself into the task with his customary energy, despite frequent bouts of heat sickness. While travelling in the Himalayas he crossed a twig bridge over the River Chandra, a structure so battered by the rainy season that he over-exerted himself in getting across and suffered a heart attack. He died, aged fifty-two, at Dharmsala on 20 November 1863 with his wife and youngest daughter beside him. One obituary complained:

> In China and in India, where he was brought into contact with Englishmen and other Europeans settled among Asiatic populations, he seems to have formed a strong, and some persons thought an exaggerated, impression of the tendency of Europeans to ill-use the inferior races, his letters, both public and private, containing frequent and indignant allusions to this subject.

Thomas Bowlby's body was given up by the Chinese and buried in the Russian cemetery outside Peking's An-tin gate on 17 October. *The Times* took responsibility for the education of his eldest son.

General Grant returned to Britain a hero, having conducted what many regarded as a textbook campaign. After serving briefly as commander-in-chief of the Madras army he was made quartermaster-general at the Horse Guards and camp commander at Aldershot. He reformed army manoeuvres, introduced war games and military lectures, and greatly influenced his successor. Lord Wolseley said in 1872: 'If I have attained any measure of military prosperity, my gratitude is due to one man, and that man is Sir Hope Grant.' The subject of his admiration died, aged sixty-seven, in 1875 of an internal malady aggravated by active service in tropical climates.

Admiral Hope stayed on in China to help his erstwhile enemies fight off Taiping rebels. In the spring of 1862 he cooperated with the Chinese imperial troops under the American General Ward to clear the insurgents from the neighbourhood of Shanghai and Ningpo. In one attack, which he led in person, Hope was again wounded by a musket-shot. He then served in the West Indies but his retirement in Linlithgow was plagued by ill-health and pain from his numerous wounds. He died, aged seventy-three, in 1881.

Of the VC heroes of the Taku forts, Robert Rogers rose the highest. The Dublin-born lieutenant commanded the 90th Cameronians in the Zulu War and became a major-general before dying at Maidenhead, aged sixty, in 1895. Private John McDougall was just twenty-nine when he died in his home city of Edinburgh in 1869. Lieutenant Edmund Henry Lenon had a long military career, reaching the rank of lieutenant-colonel; he died at Lambeth in 1893, aged sixty-two. Lieutenant Nathaniel Burslem was promoted captain in the 67th, which later became the Hampshire Regiment, but he died just five years later, aged twenty-seven, drowned in New Zealand's Thames River. Private Thomas Lane, a Cork man, died in Kimberley, South Africa, in 1889 at the age of fifty-two. Ensign John Chaplin rose to the rank of colonel and died, a heavily whiskered eighty-year-old, at Market Harborough in 1920. Apprentice Andrew Fitzgibbon became an apothecary and died in Delhi in 1883, a few weeks short of his 38th birthday.

Sir Frederick Bruce did not stay long in China, despite the efforts and lives expended to get him to Peking. In 1865 he was made Britain's representative in Washington. He died in Boston two years later. His remains were embalmed and sent to Scotland, where they were interred in Dunfermline Abbey.

Sir Michael Seymour received much praise for his naval leadership during the earlier stages of the China War. One biographer said: 'The invariable success which attended his operations in the war in China was entirely due to his calm foresight and careful attention to the minutest of details.' China merchants presented him with a handsome service of plate. For three years, from 1859 to 1862, he was MP for Devonport. He died, a full admiral on the retired list, in 1887.

Sir John Bowring's passage home aboard *Alma* was not an easy one. The ship struck a rock in the Red Sea and sank; Bowring, the crew and his fellow passengers were marooned for three days on a coral reef where they suffered greatly before being rescued. The rest of his life was relatively quiet. He was sent on a trade mission to Italy but in Rome was struck by illness aggravated by the effects of the arsenic poisoning he had suffered in Hong Kong three years before. After a long convalescence he concentrated on translating, lecturing and writing poems and hymns, including the classic 'In the cross of Christ I glory'. Aged almost eighty he addressed a crowd of 3,000 at Plymouth in 1872. Weeks later, after a brief illness, he died at Exeter, just yards from the house where he was born.

General Charles Montauban was awarded the title Comte de Palikao in recognition of his services in China. He was best known by that title when he became prime minister of France at the start of the Franco-Prussian war.

The career of Sir Harry Smith Parkes and the opening up of China and the Orient continued to be inextricably linked. After acting as interpreter when Bruce was formally introduced as the first British minister to the court of Peking, Parkes returned to his duties as commissioner at Canton. Later he established consulates at Chinkiang, Kiukiang and Hankow, and orchestrated the opening up of the Yangtse to foreign trade, a move which added 3.5 million dollars a year to Britain's export trade. Admiral Hope ascribed the success of the dangerous and delicate operation to Parkes's 'unwearied zeal and thorough knowledge of the Chinese people and language'. In 1864 he was consul at Shanghai and then diverted his attention and energies to Japan. There he used his diplomatic skills to maintain British interests through years of turmoil and civil war, persuaded the Mikado to embrace western technology – such as a Mint, railways and lighthouses – and mediated in disputes with other nations. During his years in Japan he was attacked by a two-sworded warrior, assaulted by several swordsmen who wounded twelve members of his escort, and was waylaid by two fanatics who cut at him with blades. Parkes, unscathed throughout, captured one of the latter assailants.

In 1883 Parkes was appointed minister to China. After negotiating a successful Anglo-Korean treaty, he returned to Peking in time to encounter a new wave of anti-foreign feeling caused by the French attack on Tonking. The Chinese made no distinction between Britons and French in the ensuing riots, but Parkes kept a cool head and forced the Chinese to withdraw their proclamation to the Chinese population to poison the French where and when they found them. Worn out by overwork, he died in 1885. His death was ascribed to Peking fever.

Emperor Hien-feng died a year after his defeat and the entry of foreigners into Peking. He was succeeded by his five-year-old son T'ung-chi; during the child's minority the regency was held jointly by his mother, the former concubine Tsz'e Hsi, and the Empress Tsz'e An. The end of the war with the barbarians gave them the chance, with British, French and American help, to crush the Taiping rebels. But the power of the emperors never fully recovered, and the 'Unequal Treaties' were a constant reminder of their humiliation. The jealously guarded isolation of the emperors was shattered. Marx wrote: 'Isolation having come to a violent end by the medium of England, dissolution must follow as surely as that of any mummy carefully preserved in a hermetically sealed coffin, whenever it is brought into contact with the open air.'

China was condemned to a century of further revolts, disastrous wars, famine and then permanent revolution. Shanghai and Hong Kong became boom ports. And the fruit of the poppy spread across the globe.

★　　★　　★

CHAPTER SEVEN

The Shortest War – Zanzibar, 1896

'The suspense was intense . . . as the hands of the clock crept on.'

The bombardment of Zanzibar by British warships was probably the shortest war on record, and arguably the most one-sided. Within 40 minutes hundreds of people died under the impact of high explosives. It was little more than mass murder using the latest military technology. Like most such 'policing' actions it was intended to crush any opposition to Britain's imperial might and to protect lucrative trading and political interests. Yet it cannot be dismissed simply as just another cynical massacre, another stain on the reputation of the British Empire. One factor in the events which led to the slaughter was Britain's ultimately high-minded determination to stamp out, by the end of the nineteenth century, the institution of slavery. That does not, however, excuse the actions of one of Britain's most brutal and ruthless commanders.

★   ★   ★

The island of Zanzibar, like the nearby coastal areas of East Africa, was first settled by Persians and Arabs who intermingled with the native population. It was fertile and well-cultivated land, producing cloves and other tropical spices, using slave labour. It quickly became the hub of the flourishing eastwards slave trade. Other exports from the 'Great Land' – ivory, copal, skins, grain, local cloves and coconut – were sold through the ideally positioned island port, but it was the market in human beings that flourished and allowed the island to prosper. Those slaves snatched from the vast hinterland were dispersed across the Musselman territories bordering the Indian Ocean. Caravans penetrated deep into the mainland bearing both Oriental and European goods – glass, copper wire, cotton, pickaxes and guns – to be exchanged for human cargo. Through a network of trade routes and local pacts the Sultanate of Zanzibar wielded massive influence across large parts of the African continent – areas that became increasingly coveted by the European powers.

Vasco da Gama took possession of Zanzibar and the neighbouring island of Pemba for Portugal in 1499 and founded an Augustinian convent there. The Portuguese were expelled in 1698 by the Arabs of Muskat and Oman but missionaries, traders and explorers continued to foster foreign interest in the region. Zanzibar and Pemba were under the nominal control of Oman and in the early part of the nineteenth century became the region's trade capital, through which up to sixty thousand slaves were sold annually.

Rear-Admiral Sir Harry Holdsworth Rawson by C.W. Walton. (National Maritime Museum, Greenwich)

Britain's interests were largely due to Zanzibar's position on the world trade routes. It was roughly equidistant, around 2,400 miles, from the Cape and Bombay (and later the Suez Canal) and was the 'key to the ocean front door' of East Central Africa. Together with Mombasa and the proposed Uganda Railway, it allowed access to the vast, rich interior of the Dark Continent. Zanzibar town contained many British and European residents, as well as Arab and Indian Quarters, a variety of mosques and an English Universities Mission cathedral. There were several fine buildings, towers and libraries and a busy waterfront. The most important houses featured massive brass-studded doors with lintels and doorposts elaborately carved with Arabic and Indian motifs. The central streets were narrow and winding. The harbour was on an open roadstead on the western shore.

In 1858 Seiyd Madjid, Sultan of Zanzibar, declared himself independent of Oman, with the agreement of Britain. In 1873 and 1875 his successor, his brother Barghash, signed treaties with Britain declaring illegal the sea traffic in slaves. In 1886 the Sultan's sovereignty over Zanzibar island, Pemba and a substantial strip of the mainland coastline was recognised by Britain, France and Germany. In return Barghash's successor Khalifa granted to the German East African Company a lease, later bought by the German Government, of the coastline of what later became Tanganyika. A similar lease granted to Britain covered land to the north of the German concession. The transfers antagonised some sections of the local population, especially those rich Arab traders whose family fortunes were built on slaves.

The Germans, somewhat arrogantly, refused to fly the Sultan's flag in their territory. Twice German troops were landed from men-of-war to tear down such flags raised by the outraged populace, while German seamen in landing parties were fired upon. A commentator remarked at the time: 'The actions of the Germans had for some time past been rough and high-handed, showing an utter want of tact in their dealings with the natives, and betraying their ignorance of the Arab nature.' After one clash a German gunboat shelled the town of Tanga, landed an armed force and drove Arab troops into the jungle, killing twenty of them.

The Sultan sent in troops under General Sir Lloyd Mathews, a Briton who had won the trust of coastal natives over fifteen years and who now commanded Zanzibar's military forces, to restore order. This was done but anti-German feeling sparked more conflict at Bagamoyo in which German forces cut down 150 natives. At the same time, at Ketwa, several German officials and their servants were attacked; after killing some of their assailants, they were themselves murdered. Local tribesmen seized the town and re-hoisted the Sultan's flag. British missionaries in the area were left unharmed, confirming that the uprisings were not directed against foreigners or Christians in general, only against the Germans.

In 1888, at the height of the troubles, the Sultan granted the British East African Company exclusive trade rights over a territory of 50,000 square miles. The territory comprised a strip of mainland coastline 10 miles broad and 150 miles long, including the valuable harbour of Mombasa. The Company was required by its Charter to 'discourage and, so far as may be practicable with existing treaties, to abolish any system of slave trade or domestic servitudes within its territories'.

The British and German governments, with the concurrence of the ailing Sultan, agreed to a joint naval blockade against the slave ships and others carrying war contraband. Over 1,400 runaway slaves were discovered in hiding at three English mission stations near Mombasa and set free. France was reluctantly forced to take action against slavers flying their tricolour and to allow British and German warships to search suspect French vessels.

Meanwhile Khalifa was growing increasingly sick in mind as well as in body. He ordered the street executions of four untried murder suspects – the first instances of capital punishment in Zanzibar for twenty-five years. The brutality with which the sentences were carried out aroused much public anger. The Sultan ordered that the spectacle be repeated every day for a week, with the executions of twenty-four men and one woman previously sentenced to life imprisonment. British officials protested against such 'barbarous proceedings' and the prisoners were reprieved.

Khalifa died suddenly in 1890 and his brother Seyyid Ali was elected unanimously by the leading Arabs to succeed him. The new Sultan ordered the release of untried prisoners and suppressed insurgents with the help of British officers. In June he declared Zanzibar a British Protectorate and abolished all slave trading within his dominions, although that did not prohibit slave ownership. The following year a regular government was formed in which a British representative would serve as first minister. The British also had a veto on the succession and appointment of future Sultans. Britain's grip on Zanzibar continued after the death of Seyyid Ali in 1893 and the succession of Hamid-bin-Thwain. But dissent was growing within the Sultan's court, members of which saw their powers taken by British-run government institutions, and their wealth undermined by the suppression of the slave trade. The Sultan was permitted to raise a body of soldiers as a personal bodyguard, which was distinct from the British-controlled Zanzibar army. Numerous complaints were made about their swaggering behaviour.

At 11.40 a.m. on 25 August 1896 Hamid died suddenly and in very suspicious circumstances. He was almost certainly poisoned. His cousin Sayid Khalid, a 'rash and wilful' young man of twenty-five, was ready to act swiftly. It can never be proved conclusively that Khalid murdered his kinsman, but he very quickly took command of 1,200 of the late Sultan's troops and seized the Palace with the obvious intention of proclaiming himself the new Sultan.

General Mathews and Basil Cave, the British diplomatic agent to Zanzibar, had arrived at the palace within ten minutes of the old Sultan's death and were greeted by Khalid and his retainers a few minutes later. The British were brushed aside in their attempts to persuade Khalid to think carefully about his actions, and the two men retired to the New Custom House as Khalid's supporters, all heavily armed and well prepared, streamed into the Palace Square. Shortly after noon there were 900 men, under the command of the former Sultan's Captain Saleh, lined up in the square behind field guns that had been presented to Zanzibar by the German Emperor. Within a few hours their numbers had swelled to 2,500, with several Maxim guns ready for action. One Zanzibari machine-gunner sat in a chair behind his weapon, which was sighted steadily on the English Club. Their artillery also included a Gatling gun and a seventeenth-century bronze cannon. In the harbour Khalid's men took over the entire Zanzibar Navy – which consisted of the former British frigate *Glasgow*, a creaking, out-dated wooden hulk which had been presented to Zanzibar in 1878.

Mathews and Cave were joined by Zanzibar *askaris*, troops loyal to the government, and 150 naval men from Her Majesty's ships *Philomel* and *Thrush*, providentially anchored in the harbour. The *London Gazette* reported that officers and crew reacted 'with a promptness characteristic of the British Navy'. The shore parties 'landed, ready armed and equipped within 15 minues of the first signs of the disturbance'. The naval contingent was commanded by Captain O'Callaghan, while the askaris were under their own General Raike. All the British women and children were sent to the consulate which was guarded by bluejackets under Lieutenant Watson of *Thrush*. Another British ship, *Sparrow*, entered the harbour and was ordered to anchor alongside *Thrush* at moorings opposite the palace, their guns aimed at its frontage.

The former British frigate *Glasgow*, Zanzibar's only warship. (Illustrated London News)

During this time many messages were sent from Cave to Khalid warning him against any defiance of the 'protecting power' – Britain – and calling on him to leave the palace, disperse his troops and return to his own house. Khalid replied by giving notice that at precisely 3 p.m. he would proclaim himself Sultan. He was told in turn that such a move would be regarded as an open act of rebellion.

At 2.30 the Arabs in the palace buried the old Sultan and thirty minutes later Khalid, true to his threat, proclaimed himself the new Sultan and ordered a royal salute from his guns. Cave informed all the other foreign consuls that there was no new sultan and all flags remained at half-mast, save for a large red flag flying from the Palace Square. The news was also telegraphed to the London administration of Lord Salisbury; nothing further could be done until an answer was received.

The night of the 25th passed in uneasy peace. The majority of the womenfolk remained in the consulate building, although several moved to a British steamship and the German consulate. At 10 a.m. another British warship, *Racoon*, arrived and berthed in line with *Thrush* and *Sparrow*, threatening the palace. The day dragged on with no reply from London and both sides remained warily watching each other but doing nothing to provoke bloodshed. At 2 p.m. a steamer signal went up on the clock tower and to British surprise and delight the flagship *St George* joined the armoured armada in the harbour. On board were enough men to protect the town, under the command of Rear-Admiral Harry Rawson, commander-in-chief of the Cape and East Africa station.

Rear-Admiral Rawson's 7,700-ton flagship *St George* with the *Philomel* in the background. (Illustrated London News)

Sir Harry Holdsworth Rawson was well known as the successful commander of a punitive expedition against the Arab chief Mourah a year earlier. The son of a Surrey JP, he was born in Lancashire in 1843, educated at Marlborough College, and joined the Navy in 1857. As a midshipman he served with distinction in the Chinese War of 1858–60, commanding 1,300 Chinese troops at the defence of Ningpo and being commended for jumping overboard at night to save the life of a drowning Marine. As a lieutenant he was one of the officers who took the gunboat *Empress* to Japan, after it had been presented by Queen Victoria to the Mikado in 1863 to form the nucleus of his navy. As a captain he was principal transport officer in the 1882 Egyptian Campaign. He proudly wore the silver medal of the Royal Humane Society, awarded for saving life, but when it came to suppressing impudent challenges to the British Crown and its representatives across the globe he was utterly ruthless.

As Rawson was rowed to shore the eagerly awaited reply from London arrived. Broadly, it gave the British authorities on the spot permission to act as they saw fit. Further brief negotiations were held through emissaries but Khalid still refused to leave the palace. Rawson sent him an ultimatum – haul down the royal flag and leave the palace by nine the following morning, or be blasted out.

During the afternoon all merchant vessels steamed around to the south harbour so that the British frigates would have a clear line of fire. All foreign consuls were informed of the ultimatum and British subjects were instructed to put themselves in places of safety. Most European residents barricaded themselves in their homes to protect their property from looting. Thirty ladies were taken on board *St George* while girls of the Universities' Mission took refuge on the British India Steam Navigation Company's steamship where 'everything was done for their comfort' by Captain J. Stone. The night passed quietly and very slowly.

At 8.00 on the morning of the 27th there was no sign of capitulation from the palace and the signal was hoisted from the flagship to prepare for action. At 8.30 Khalid sent an envoy to Cave to ask what the British intended to do, and the ultimatum was sternly repeated. A Reuters correspondent present wired home: 'The suspense was intense during the last quarter of an hour, as the hands of the clock on the tower gradually crept on towards 9 o'clock.'

Two minutes after the hour *Racoon*, *Thrush* and *Sparrow* opened fire simultaneously. *Thrush* dismounted one of the Arabs' 12-pounders at the first shot. The palace was raked with shellfire, buildings were pounded into dust, and people were buried under falling debris. The palace, together with its adjoining harem, were just yards from the waterfront. It was no great stone citadel, but a flimsy wooden structure made up of spindly balconies and verandahs. The impact of high explosive and shell splinters on up to 3,000 defendants and servants packed inside the palace's narrow alleys and courtyards, and behind hastily erected barricades of baled goods, crates and bags of rubber, is all too easy to imagine. The Reuters man wrote: 'Khalid, in spite of his saying that he would rather die in the Palace than leave it, fled at the first shot with all the leading Arabs, who left their slaves and followers to carry on the fighting. This they did most pluckily, fighting to the last, probably from fear of being cut to pieces by their masters afterwards if they ran away.'

The gunship *Racoon* with *Sparrow* (left) and *Thrush*. (Illustrated London News)

The *Illustrated London News* reported:

Some fighting on land took place at the barriers of the approaches to the palace, the enemy firing on local Askaris from behind the stockades; but the greatest loss of life was in the palace, when it was knocked to pieces and set on fire by the guns of our ships. The palace and harem buildings, with their lofty wooden balconies and open upper floors, would seem likely to be consumed by a conflagration with frightful quickness; and if it be a fact, as it now said, that nearly five hundred men perished in the burning of that flimsy edifice, crowded together without a chance of escape, we can understand how that happened.

In the harbour the rickety, wooden *Glasgow* was sunk at its moorings, having had the effrontery to fire one of her little brass cannon at *St George*. She hoisted the British flag in token of surrender, and British launches were sent to pick up her crew, all of whom survived. Two small steam launches were also swiftly sunk after their Arab occupants aimed ineffectual rifle and musket shots at *Thrush*.

The bombardment ceased at about 9.40 a.m. when the older portion of the palace caught fire, the enemy artillery was silenced and the usurper's flag had been cut down by a stray shot. One British seaman, a petty officer on *Thrush*, was severely wounded in the pathetically unequal artillery duel but later recovered. The casualties on the opposing side topped 500, of whom most died in the scorched wreckage of the old palace, which was totally gutted.

The Times correspondent wrote:

No-one believed for a moment that Said Khalid would be so foolish as to defy us, and the only regret over the occurrence is that he should have escaped . . . and that more of the leading Arabs were not killed instead of their unfortunate slaves. It is acknowledged by everyone that the bombardment was unavoidable owing to Khalid's open defiance, and it is trusted that the Arabs who supported him with their advice, and whose names are believed to be known, will be made to bear the expense of the bombardment and pay claims for loot, which already amounts to three lakhs of rupees.

Khalid and his leading followers took refuge in the German consulate. The German consul refused to hand him over because an extradition treaty with Britain stipulated that a fugitive should not be given up for a political offence. On 2 October Khalid was smuggled on board a war vessel and taken to German territory. Cave protested but Khalid was granted asylum in German East Africa. He was finally apprehended by British forces in 1917. He suffered exile in the Seychelles and on St Helena for his challenge to the might of the British Empire. After several years he was permitted to return to East Africa but never posed a threat again.

Zanzibar's townspeople had largely stayed loyal to the British but there was a great deal of looting in the Indian Quarter. The steamer *Kilwa* brought 150 Sikhs from Mombasa to help restore and maintain law and order. Rawson sailed off to colonial glory, as we shall see.

On the afternoon of the 27th the new Sultan, 45-year-old Hamud-bin-Mahomed, was proclaimed with British support and much reduced power. The *Illustrated London News* described him as 'an elderly gentleman, respected for his prudent and peaceable conduct, acceptable to the better class of the Musselman townsfolk and trusted as a ruler likely to preserve the traditional policy of the realm'.

The British could have abolished the Sultanate and created a Crown Colony but did not want the expense of running a direct administration. They chose instead to keep the Sultan as a figurehead while tightening their own control on all military, financial and executive affairs.

Within months the legal status of slavery was finally abolished in Zanzibar. But this was no consolation to the dead, many of them slaves, buried after the ironclad firepower of the British Empire was turned against the balconies of a ramshackle Muslim palace.

★   ★   ★

CHAPTER EIGHT

The Benin Massacre, 1897

'Now this is white man's country.'

In 1884 the American Hiram Maxim set up a company to manufacture a battlefield weapon of mass destruction. The machine-gun that bore his name was able to discharge 600 bullets a minute, using energy captured from each successive detonation. The British Army enthusiastically adopted the weapon for use not against massed ranks of troops but to police the Empire's most unruly lands. Its firepower, properly used, showed natives the industrial might that could and would be used against anyone who dared challenge the authority of Queen Victoria.

A punitive expedition against bloodthirsty 'savages' who had murdered white men offered an excellent opportunity to demonstrate the superiority of civilised technology over pagan superstition. The outcome was inevitable because, in the words of a contemporary ditty:

> Whatever happens, we have got
> The Maxim gun, and they have not.

*   *   *

Benin was already well established as an important kingdom when the Portuguese first reached the Nigerian coast in the fourteenth century. A small city-state to the east of Lagos, it dominated the Yoruba country and the land that forms the south-west region of present-day Nigeria. The terrain inland from the coast was flat, criss-crossed by numerous creeks, and covered by dense forest. One European visitor recorded: 'Lagoons traversing the country connect Benin with Lagos, but the waterways are only fit for the passage of native canoes.' Another wrote: 'The climate appeared much healthier than at the coast, as there were numbers of bullocks and goats grazing on the common, and all were fat, well-conditioned, and therefore very different from the poor skinny creatures to be seen in the coast towns.' The subordinate people of Benin were of the Sobo, Mahin and Jekri tribes, the latter being regarded by Europeans as 'the most active and warlike'.

Trade, mainly in slaves, flourished between the Portuguese and the Beni people, adding to the wealth of the nation. The region was fertile and agriculture provided abundant crops of banana, yam and palm oil. Benin City became a true capital of commerce and tribal power, with fine buildings that rivalled any in West Africa. The most coveted western goods bartered for slaves and palm oil were gin, rum, tobacco, cotton goods, silk handkerchiefs and, most prized of all, guns and gunpowder.

The religion was fetishism, or ju-ju, based on the worship of the spirits of ancestors. One missionary publication said it involved 'ridiculous and cruel practices often admitting of human sacrifice'. But enlightened missionaries conceded that 'purer religious elements are found beneath all these superstitions', in particular a firm belief in God, the survival of the soul and the distinction between good and evil. Human sacrifice undoubtedly took place but some visitors confused fetish practices with simple Benin justice. On one occasion, a witness reported, 'Twelve men were taken with 12 cows, goats, sheep and chickens. The animals were killed near the altar, and the blood from them sprinkled on big ivories and brasswork.' The human prisoners, gagged and each held by four men, were led to a well and beheaded. But the human victims turned out to be convicted criminals, and at least some of the ju-ju practices relied on victims who were already condemned.

For two centuries European explorers were drawn to the River Niger and the surrounding lands, most famously Mungo Park's expeditions between 1795 and 1805. By then the power of the Beni Oba, or king, had been undermined by a loose theocracy of fetish priests who increased the practice of wholesale human sacrifice and discouraged contact with Europeans. As tales of barbarity – many of them doubtless exaggerated – spread, trade dwindled and Benin lost much of its influence over the region.

In contrast British influence grew immeasurably during the first half of the nineteenth century, curbing the slave trade in the Niger delta and on the Oil rivers. Britain encouraged the export of palm oil to replace the lost business. John Beecroft was appointed British consul for the Bights of Biafra and Benin in 1849 to further encourage legitimate trade. He used force to halt the slave trade through Lagos and imposed a treaty on the people which included abolition of human sacrifice. The authority of the consul was gradually widened, by negotiation and diktat, to cover most of the nations abutting the Niger. The region was declared a British Protectorate.

Fetish rules, however, continued to interfere with trade. The Oba exacted stiff taxes from Benin merchants trading with the outside world and the fetish priests ruled that certain valuable products should never be touched, including gum copal and palm kernels. Trading licenses were withdrawn with no warning and no explanation. One European complained: 'Of ivory the king claims one half of all that is obtained in his dominions, and declines to trade with the Europeans, keeping all that he receives for the purpose of purchasing slaves. When the supplies are less plentiful than he desires he raids the caravans and seizes their produce.'

In 1886 the Royal Niger Company was authorised by charter to administer the delta and the countryside through which flowed the rivers Niger and Benue. The company set up courts of justice and raised an armed constabulary. It was kept busy. In 1894 the constabulary aided a naval force in capturing the town of Brohemie on the Benin River, the headquarters of the Jekri chief Nana, who traded in slaves in defiance of British orders. Nana fled to Lagos where he gave himself up, claiming that five hundred of his followers had been killed in the operation. Spoils taken from his headquarters included 7,000 cases of Rotterdam gin and 600 cases of tobacco. Nana was tried and deported, and a British military post was established at Sabele.

At Akassa natives objecting to anti-smuggling measures and the high duties imposed on spirits attacked the Company's factory and killed several black employees. According to British reports they celebrated their 'victory' with a cannibal feast on Sacrifice Island. Constabulary and Marines attacked and burned the town of King Koko in retaliation.

This left Benin as the one nation adjoining the Protectorate not to submit to British commercial rule. An article in *The Times* said: 'In other parts of the back country the policy of controlling the more turbulent chiefs and developing direct trade with the interior has been successful, but in the Benin district advance has been rendered impossible by the attitude of the king of Benin and the savage system of pagan theocracy of which he is the representative.'

Benin's virgin forests were especially attractive to the Company, which was deeply involved in the booming rubber trade. They had a champion in the Protectorate's governor, Ralph Moor, a former inspector in the Royal Irish Constabulary. He argued long and eloquently that Benin should be opened up to trade, by force if necessary. Stories of cannibalism and other horrors helped in the propaganda, although it is undisputed that Benin was by then the centre of the illicit slave trade. The *Annual Register* for 1896 noted tersely: 'The tyrant of Benin, on the border of the protectorate, was causing obstructions to British trade, and repelled all friendly negotiations. Great cruelties were practised by this King, including human sacrifices.'

The 'tyrant' was forty-year-old Oba Overami, a pragmatist caught between the competing demands of the British and his fetish priests, and a patriot determined to keep his kingdom independent. The long-time trader D.P. Bleasby described him: 'As to the appearance of the King, he is, for a negro, a very pleasant-faced man. His eyes, though rather small, have a laughing expression. He has a short, curly beard, and altogether his face shows remarkable intelligence.' Bleasby said that he believed Overami would not authorise the execution of white prisoners but added that as the king was confined to his royal compound he did not always know what his chiefs were doing. He continued: 'There is in Benin no regular army. The inhabitants are natural huntsmen and every man, when he can raise the money, buys a flintlock gun. That is about the first thing he does. It is understood that every man in the country is the king's slave and under his orders, so that they would have to come to his aid when he commanded.'

British merchants who claimed to have visited Benin fed the public appetite for horror stories about the 'cannibal kingdom'. James Pinnock, who traded mainly from Sierra Leone, described a visit in which he saw 'a large number of men all handcuffed and chained to a longitudinal pole running around the building, standing about three feet from the ground, all with their ears cut off with a razor'. Another traveller, T.B. Auchterlonie, said that when he and his party approached the city they walked through a lane of large trees with between thirty and forty dead bodies on each side in all stages of decomposition, 'the idea being to impress those approaching the town with the power of the King'. He added: 'After passing the lane of horrors the approach to the city is across common, covered with good grass, and practically free of all trees or brush, but thickly strewn with the skulls and bones of sacrificed human beings.'

In 1892 Overami had signed a treaty agreeing to the abolition of both the slave trade and human sacrifice, but it was clear that he could not implement it even if he wished to. Negotiations with an increasingly exasperated Moor dragged on inconclusively, until in 1896 Moor returned to Britain on home leave. The matter was left in the hands of his eager subordinate Lieutenant James Phillips, who became Acting Consul General.

Phillips was a young man in a hurry. He was educated at Uppingham and Trinity College, Cambridge, where he graduated in 1886. He was appointed Sheriff of the Gold Coast and in charge of prisons in 1891, and an Acting Queen's advocate in 1892. Phillips apparently hoped to make his mark while his superior was away and opened his own 'goodwill' negotiations with the Oba through emissaries. Privately he wired the Foreign Office asking for permission, which was not forthcoming, to 'depose and remove the King of Benin'. He sent a message to the Oba announcing an impending visit to his kingdom. It would be an unarmed, he said, and peaceful mission, to discuss trade, not war.

Without waiting for a reply, Phillips left the coast for Benin City via Sapele on 2 January 1897. With him went Deputy Commissioner Major P.W.G. Copeland-Crawford, Captain Alan Boisragon, commandant of the Niger Coast Protectorate Constabulary, Captain A.J. Malings, wing officer of the same force, Robert Locke and Kenneth Campbell of the Consular staff, medical officer Dr R.H. Elliott, two civilian trading agents, Powis and Gordon, and around 250 native porters, servants and guides, all accompanied by a drum and pipe band.

Confusion still surrounds the purpose of Phillips' mission and the reason why he chose to take such large numbers with him. A column of that size suggested military intent, even though its European members were armed only with revolvers – a standard item of bush traveller's attire. The *Daily News* later commented: 'One of the strangest circumstances surrounding this unlucky enterprise, and one which will have to be fully explained, is why the march was made in the Consul-General's absence on leave.' If the expedition was meant to convey the impression of peace, then the fewer people the better – on previous occasions small numbers of British officers had been allowed to enter Benin City without any difficulty or danger. If it was meant to demonstrate the potential power of the British Empire, it should have been armed to the teeth. Instead it was strong in numbers but almost defenceless in arms. The newspaper said: 'The most mysterious part of the whole story is that, whereas the number of Mr Phillips' band was large enough to excite the suspicions and arouse the hostility of the natives, they were not prepared to resist anything like an organised attack. Nine or ten official whites and two or three hundred native followers provoked assault without inspiring alarm.'

Phillips' timing was bad, too, as his arrival in Beni territory coincided with a religious festival. The Oba, faced by what he took to be an invasion force, called a national emergency which brought tribesmen from all corners of his kingdom. The outcome was, to modern eyes, horribly predictable. It was, however, an enormous shock to a generation weaned on the notion of imperial invincibility.

On 12 January *The Times* reported: 'The Press Association states that alarming news reached the Foreign Office yesterday from the West Coast of Africa, to the effect that a party of British officials had been captured and possibly murdered in Benin City.' It proved to be a laconic understatement.

★   ★   ★

Phillips and his column were ferried by steamer 25 miles up-river, then took boats up the Gwato Creek. Men and supplies were landed on the riverbank and set off on foot towards Benin City, about 25 miles away, on 4 January. By the next day they had travelled half the distance and, according to later reports, 'were received in every town and village which they passed on their way to Benin with friendly greetings from the people and kindly messages from the King himself'. They marched through swampy forest in blistering heat. After stopping to confer with envoys from the Oba the party pushed on. Most of the revolvers were locked up in boxes carried by native porters. Commissioner Locke later told reporters:

> As soon as we had passed a fallen tree the natives, who were in ambush, fell upon us. Some were armed with long Danish guns and others with hatchets. A place had been cleared in the bush, and the men with guns were lying down with the muzzles of their long flintlocks nearly touching the path. They fired upon the white men indiscriminately.

Major Copeland-Crawford, being carried in a chair, was the first to be hit and wounded. Phillips, Dr Elliott and Captain Maling fell dead on the spot. Locke was luckier – he had been in the leading party with them but had fallen behind when he stopped to tie a bootlace. Copeland-Crawford was picked up by Locke and Captain Boisragon amid a shower of musket balls fired by mostly unseen attackers. The major was wounded again, this time fatally. Before he died he urged his comrades to leave him and save themselves. Powis, who spoke the Benin language, called out to the hidden warriors, trying to pacify them, but before he could say more than a few words he and Gordon were shot dead. Locke and Boisragon, both wounded, crawled into the bush and hid themselves. The bodies of the white men that they left behind were all decapitated in the ensuing blood frenzy.

A vanguard of natives had already been butchered, unknown to the main party, and the Beni attackers continued to slaughter the rest of the native porters. All but seven of them died. One of the survivors was a servant of Mr Powis, who found his master's headless body on the track before escaping to take the news back to the coast. Campbell was captured and taken to the city. The Oba refused to allow him to be brought within its boundary and he was taken to an adjacent village where he was beheaded. Phillips' finger rings were sent back to Overami, an act taken to indicate defiance of the British Crown.

Locke and Boisragon, a tough veteran of the Royal Irish Regiment who had seen action on the Nile and the Gold Coast, wandered for five days in the swamp-ridden bush, aided by Copeland-Crawford's dropped compass. They survived by eating cassava leaves. The only water they could drink was dew. Locke was still armed with a revolver and shot several natives during their odyssey. Boisragon was again wounded while beating off a band of natives with a stick. Eventually, half delirious and dressed in bloody rags, they reached a Beni village whose inhabitants treated them kindly. They were ferried down the creek in a covered canoe and delivered safely to the consulate, which was installed on a floating hulk at Sapelle.

Locke had four wounds, two in his right arm, one in the forearm and one in the abdomen. Despite their deprivations both men were reported to be in 'fairly good health'. Locke was sent home aboard the steamer *Volta* to recover fully. Boisragon sent his wife a telegram with just one word: 'SAVED.'

In Britain public opinion was inflamed. Reuter's Special Service reported: 'The King of Benin was carrying out an annual butchery of slaves, and did not want to see the white men, who had been received at Gwato with a friendly welcome, and who, under the impression that matters were all right, had proceeded on their journey. They simply intended to remonstrate with the King against these fearful butcheries.' The MP and historian Justin McCarthy wrote:

> The greatest devotee of peace could hardly expect that the English Government would take no steps to avenge the deeds of the King of Benin. It seems impossible to believe that there was not deliberate treachery on his part; for no company of sane Europeans experienced in the ways of that region of Africa would have ventured on an unarmed movement to the city of Benin without some assurance of peaceful welcome from the sovereign. The bravest men do not go out to die for no purpose whatever, and these men who died so bravely must have set out with some assurance that their peaceful offers were to be met in a peaceful way. [It was] absolutely essential that the Imperial Government should take the quickest and the sternest measures to punish the King of Benin for a course of treachery and murder which apparently had not all the sympathy of even his own subjects.

The Times thundered:

> The power of the fetish customs is so great that until it has been abolished it is believed that trade with Benin cannot materially be advanced. The rule of the king is one of terror. The most barbarous customs prevail, and the people are brutalized by the habits of human sacrifice, torture and cannibalism . . . These conditions, apart from the cruelty and savagery of his rule, naturally dispose the surrounding tribes to view without displeasure any measures which may tend to control his power and to enable them to pursue their profitable avocations of peace. His country is the most barbarous spot of the whole Protectorate, and the outrage which he has not feared to commit upon the British expedition renders inevitable the speedy end of a system which has been allowed to endure too long. The King of Benin must now share the fate of Nana, Ja-Ja, and other savage potentates who have mistaken the patience of the British Government for weakness which could with impunity be defied, and when his stronghold of brutality has been destroyed British authority will most effectively be vindicated by the opening of an important district to civilised intercourse.

Lord Salisbury, after meeting with Moor, immediately authorised a punitive expedition against the Oba. Nine men-of-war were summoned by telegraph from their African and Mediterranean stations. West Indian troops were brought by yacht from their quarters in Sierra Leone. The cruisers *Theseus* and *Forte* were ordered to the region. The former carried 12 guns with a complement of 544 officers and men under Captain Charles Campbell. The latter carried 10 guns and a complement of 318 under Captain R.F.O. Foote. At a press conference before embarking for the Niger, Moor said that the King of Benin was certainly a barbarian who knew little, if anything, of Britain. It was within the bounds of possibility that he would, when in a frenzy worked up by the priests, encourage his people to any act of massacre. He said he was confident that the forthcoming expedition would achieve its objects and 'lead to the completion of the administration in the Niger Protectorate'.

At Lagos, Moor was joined by Rear-Admiral Sir Harry Rawson, the commander-in-chief of the Good Hope station, who took charge of the expedition. Just a few months earlier Rawson, as we have seen, supervised the bombardment of Zanzibar. He reckoned on another pushover. His 500-strong naval brigade, comprising Marines and landing parties from the warships, was backed by 500 men of the Niger Coast Constabulary under Lieutenant-Colonel Bruce Hamilton of the East Yorkshire Regiment. A detachment of Hausa troops and local levies brought the entire force to be landed to 1,400 men. They were to be supported by 1,700 native bearers brought from Sierra Leone, Bonny and other places along the Gold Coast. The warships included Rawson's flagship *St George* and the cruiser *Philomel*, which had also taken part in the pounding of Zanzibar. A Liverpool company lent the expeditionary force the twin-screw, light-draught steel steamer *Kwarra*, which was ideal for navigating the intricate and shallow creeks up to Gwato.

Rawson had no shortage of advice. Sir Alfred Jephson, a veteran of the Nana expedition who had toured Benin lands, said:

> Owing to the massacre the King will know that an expedition will be sent against him and he will strain every nerve to put his place into a state of defence. I do not anticipate that there will be any great difficulty in getting at him. The principal difficulty will be the want of roads and the large amount of bush fighting involved. It has always been recognized that eventually Benin City must be taken and trade allowed to flow towards the sea, but it was clearly understood that the King could not be smashed without the employment of a properly prepared force. There can be no doubt that he has plenty of weapons of various sorts. We found that Nana had a quick-firing gun, and no doubt the King of Benin has plenty of arms, good, bad or indifferent.

A correspondent signing himself 'Old Calabar' warned:

> The natives of the Bight of Benin have been in trading communications with Europeans for a number of years, and a large number of, comparatively speaking, modern weapons have been sold to them – ten years ago Sniders were

quite common articles of commerce – so that our troops must not expect to have only the Birmingham-made flintlock gun to fight against.

The ill-fated Phillips expedition had taken a circuitous route from Sapele, but this time local traders advised a forced march overland to Benin City, a route only 18 miles long as the crow flies. What roads there were consisted entirely of forest tracks leading over a soil of red clay. The thick brush interspersed with jungle and swampland made it ideal territory for ambush.

Rawson's force sailed up the Benin River in hired steamers on 10 February and travelled in relative comfort along 55 miles of winding creeks and tributaries. A correspondent aboard one of the steamships wrote:

> The river was at places very narrow and, as the ships steamed along, the trees on either side could almost be touched. The luxuriant vegetation, the huge trees, the thick foliage, and the sharp bends of the river, all combined to make one of the most entrancing scenes that the eyes of man have ever beheld. Animal life was not wanting, the birds were singing on every branch, the alligators and crocodiles were basking in the sun on the low river banks, hundreds of flies darted about, and lastly, on board the steamer lived a pet monkey, which kept up a continued squirming and squeaking in his pleasure or his disgust at his home being invaded by so many human beings.

They landed at Warrigi on the following morning and marched directly to Siri, about 7 miles away, to make camp. The writer continued: 'For some time after our start the journey seemed exactly like a stroll in the early morning along an English country lane, but affairs were soon to wear a different aspect; the sun came up and temperatures quickly reached 130 degrees in the shade, and all began to gasp for breath, many men falling out.'

On the 12th a naval unit and Hausa troops under Lieutenant-Colonel Hamilton attacked and occupied Ologbo, a riverside village which Rawson intended to use as a base-camp, after a short skirmish in which one officer and three native troops were wounded. A Reuters correspondent reported that Maxims on board the launch *Primrose* swept the bush before the troops landed and 'the enemy fought stubbornly, firing repeated volleys, which were effectively returned'. The enemy occupied the perimeter of a clearing 'firing, shouting and playing tomtoms'. Skirmishers lay down and fired volley after volley for over an hour until the tribesmen pulled back. The attacking force followed closely behind and the enemy were driven on to the village, which was then shelled remorselessly, rushed and captured. Thirty enemy bodies were found next day, which must have been only a portion of their casualties.

Two smaller naval units attacked and took Gwato and Sapoba with heavier British losses. At Sapoba the commander, Lieutenant C.E. Pritchard, was shot dead and Private Colin Mill of Plymouth died of sunstroke. These early skirmishes showed that the battle for Benin was not going to be a pushover. The Oba's generals were adopting classic African tactics against a European force – allow them to move deeper and deeper into the disputed territory before trying to cut off supply lines.

The first fight at Ologbo, as depicted by H.C. Seppings Wright. (Illustrated London News)

The population of Benin was hostile to the invaders and so was the blisteringly hot and humid terrain. The greatest difficulty faced by Rawson was the provision and transport of water for such large numbers of men. Anything that could hold water was requisitioned, including large, basket-covered glass demi-johns. Hundreds of benzine oilcans, each holding four gallons, had been supplied. But Rawson still found it necessary to ration officers and men to two quarts per day on the march.

The Reuters man wired home: 'At Abou, which was reached about 11 a.m., a party of black troops, with two Maxims, one seven-pounder, and one rocket tube, supported by a party of bluejackets, rushed the enemy, after firing volleys into the bush for nearly an hour. The first village on the road to Benin was shelled and taken.'

The British troops placed great reliance on their new machine-guns. Naval surgeon Felix Roth described one action: 'We shelled the village, and cleared it of the natives. As the launch and surf-boats grounded, we jumped into the water . . . at once placed our Maxims and guns in position, firing so as to clear the bush where the natives might be hiding.' He noted 'no white men were wounded, we all got off scot-free,' adding: 'Our black troops, with the scouts in front and a few Maxims, do all the fighting.'

Rawson decided to keep garrisons at the captured towns and split his attack force in two. The native Scouts and Protectorate troops were to spearhead the advance on Benin City. The naval brigade columns would follow later. The black troops would again bear the brunt of the casualties and test the enemy's defences. In fact both columns were to face a gruelling march along narrow tracks, in sweltering heat, and under almost constant sniping and regular ambush.

British and Hausa troops in West Africa were well aware of the perils of bush-fighting, following early campaigns against the Ashanti and other impressive foes. Military historian Lawrence James explained the tactics that had been developed by the time of the march on Benin City:

> The officers in command relied on the drill and training of their men. As it moved through the bush, the column was in three sections . . . The first was the advance guard which was followed by one and a half companies (150 men) with a Maxim gun and seven-pounder, both dismantled and carried in pieces on the heads of porters. The rearguard comprised fifty men, who protected the remaining porters with their loads of ammunition, food and medical supplies. When the trackway was narrow, the whole column proceeded in single file and was at its most vulnerable. To meet ambush in these conditions, a special drill had been devised by which the front rank halted, turned right and fired volleys into the bush at the commands of an officer, and the second rank turned leftwards and did likewise. Where the bush was less dense, it was possible to send out flanking parties which fanned out ahead to draw fire or give warning of an ambush.

Rawson's columns faced additional horrors. Their path was marked by hundreds of corpses, men and women disembowelled on the orders of the fetish priests to appease the Beni gods and encourage them to drive back the invaders. Captain

'In Quest of Water'.

The Advance Guard on the march to Benin City. (Illustrated London News)

Maxim machine-guns defending the field hospital outside Benin City. (Illustrated London News)

Boisragon, who accompanied the expedition but was too ill to fight, recorded: 'Everywhere sacrificial trees on which were corpses of the latest victims.' Grisly remains were spread-eagled on lattices tied to the tree-tops and dangled by their ankles from plaited ropes. Another witness said: 'We came to a human sacrifice, lying in the path, a poor native female slave who had a piece of stick tied across her mouth, and her entrails cut out. As we proceeded these sights became quite common, so I shall forbear from remarking on them.'

The correspondent for the *Illustrated London News* described the column's tense progress through thick bush and jungle:

The path now got much narrower, and on account of the trunks of trees which barred the way our progress was necessarily very slow. Every now and then a halt had to be made, and rounds of Maxims and volleys to be fired, to prevent the enemy, who were hovering all around, closing on us, and thus doing damage with their rain of bullets and slugs . . .

The advance party fired all the way, to clear the enemy out of the bush, and drive them on. At every clearing, evidences of their proximity were found in the fires which had hardly burnt out and the gourds and other things left behind in their haste . . . The camp was lined and volleys were fired at the enemy, who could be seen running from tree to tree all around. More shots were fired, but

View of Benin City from one of the sacrifice trees.

the natives, warned to keep out of the way of our volleys, did not take aim, so the slugs that reached us were nearly all spent, and only inflicted trivial wounds.

The march was punctuated by both tragedy and lucky escapes. Sydney Ansell, the torpedo-instructor on the *St George*, who was in charge of the demolition parties clearing obstructions, was shot three times in the chest and died. He was buried in a clearing by his crew-mates. A consular official was surprised by a native who jumped out from behind a tree and fired at him, the muzzle of his gun just inches from his face. According to an observer, 'The rush of air bowled him completely over, but he suffered no damage, his helmet only being blown to atoms.'

Rawson's ninth telegram of the expedition said simply: 'Advanced from Ologbo 14th in two columns, joining up on 16th. Benin city taken afternoon 18th. Distant 24 miles. Running fight entire route. Great difficulty with carriers getting up water. Considerable resistance taking city. Entire force brought up numbers 540 men.'

The 18th saw an epic eight-hour running battle which was described in greater detail by Reuters:

We left Awakon with our whole force at 6 o'clock in the morning of the 18th inst. and came to a clearing in the bush near Benin city at 1 in the afternoon. All the way volleys were fired at us from right and left. At one place a stockade containing a large gun was blown up with guncotton.

When we reached the clearing the enemy gave considerable trouble, but after firing rockets and seven-pounders in the direction of the city and again advancing we suddenly emerged from the bush into the main thoroughfare. Here we met with a most determined resistance from the enemy, who were massed in the thoroughfare in front and also fired upon us from the thick bush on the opposite side and from behind the trees. There is no doubt they used repeating rifles. They then charged the road, which was flanked on each side by dense bush.

Our division opened out into skirmishing order. The Maxims soon disposed of the enemy in front, but a harassing fire was kept up on the right flank in spite of the volleys we discharged in that direction. Two hundred yards from the King's compound, or clearing, the enemy fired a big gun, after which our troops charged with a cheer and we met with no further opposition.

Another reporter described the same action: 'About two hundred of the enemy were seen, and many were shot down, but the wounded and the bodies of the killed were in nearly every case dragged into the bush and carried off. The war-rockets and the Maxims did their work well, and the force rushing on, headed by the Admiral, captured the principal compounds.'

The burial under fire of torpedo-instructor Sydney Ansell. (Illustrated London News)

Four whites were killed in that action, including naval surgeon C.J. Fyfe of *St George*, who was shot while tending the wounded. Sixteen were injured. A black sergeant, one scout and one carrier were also killed. Three protectorate soldiers, a messenger, three carriers and a guide, all black, were wounded. No estimate is given for enemy casualties. Reuters continued: 'All the troops, both white and black, behaved splendidly. They had to keep up a continual running fight for eight hours in the tropical heat and to undergo what is one of the most demoralizing forms of warfare – namely bush-fighting.'

The Oba, his chiefs and the fetish priests fled the city, leaving behind much grisly evidence which helped to feed the British propaganda machine and to justify the terrible revenge inflicted by machine-guns on the people of Benin. On the principal sacrificial tree facing the main gate of the king's compound were two crucified bodies. Rawson's telegram reported: 'City now deserted. Neither King nor Ju-ju men captured. A few natives from Phillips' party have come in from the bush. Dreadfully mutilated human sacrifices met en route and in city, crucifixions and mutilations. Ju-ju houses, compounds surrounding them, reek with human blood. Several deep holes in compounds filled with corpses.' Another witness recorded that the city was 'full of dead men's bones and all uncleanness'. The Reuters report said: 'The whole town reeks of human blood, and the bodies of many sacrificed and crucified human beings have been found about the place. This afternoon the forces have been occupied in the destruction of 'crucifixion trees' and Ju-ju houses, thereby breaking the power of the fetish priests.' The *Illustrated London News* report said: 'Benin is indeed a city of blood, each compound having its pit full of dead and dying; human sacrifices were strewn about on every hand, hardly a thing was without a red stain . . .' In the king's palaver house troops found possessions taken from the whites in Phillips' party – their sporting guns, helmet cases and cameras, together with merchandise brought by traders.

On the morning of the 19th a large party was sent out to procure water. They found a stream with good, fresh drinking water. About 3 miles from the city walls, they heard moaning; drawn to investigate they found a servant boy from Phillips' party still alive in a well piled high with dead.

Benin city was laid out in a uniform pattern in the shape of a cross with two principal roads, each 100 feet wide, crossing each other. Many of the mud-brick houses had been built by the Portuguese, although some were derelict. The king's compound was enclosed by strong mud walls 7 feet high and the royal throne was carved from red clay. Almost every house in the city had a more modest compound, at one end of which was a raised platform for fetish worship, decked out with carved figures of ivory, brass and bronze. Outside the city walls was a large clearing carpeted in human bones. This was where the dead were routinely brought and left on the ground to decompose in the sun, 'tainting the air for miles around, and making one of the most horrible sights that has ever been seen'.

The first task of the troops was to dismantle the palace and loot its treasures. The booty included 900 bronzes depicting important events in the history of the Benin people and quantities of carved ivory. Ju-ju houses were torched and on the third day of occupation the fires got out of control and began to engulf the entire city and the billets of the troops. *The Times* reported:

No-one was injured, this being chiefly due to the energetic action which was promptly taken by both officers and men, but a considerable quantity of personal effects, as well as provisions, was lost. The wounded in the hospital had a narrow escape. There were barely five minutes available in which to secure their safety, but the rescuers worked with a will and all were successfully removed from the hospital before it was seized by the flames.

The fire raged for two hours before it was brought under control. The arms and ammunition were saved, but large numbers of valuable ivory tusks and other curios stored in the palaver house were destroyed. So too were most of the troops' personal possessions and any clothing they were not actually wearing.

Rawson, his staff and the naval brigade returned to their ships. Messengers came in from the fugitive Oba to 'beg the white man' for clemency. On 25 February seven chiefs arrived to ask that a palaver with Moor be put off for a week. The consul-general released four of the chiefs to convey his agreement to the Oba, the remainder being detained as hostages.

British and Protectorate troops spent six months scouring the countryside for the Oba, burning villages as they went, but it was not until August that the king was cornered and brought back to his ruined city. Overami suffered ritual humiliation in front of an immense throng of his people. He was forced to kneel in front of the British Military Resident and eat dirt. With two other chiefs he had to make obeisance three times, grinding his forehead into the dust, and was told he had been deposed. Several weeks later he and his chiefs faced a show trial orchestrated by Moor. The consul-general told him: 'Now this is white man's country. There is only one king in this country, and that is the white man.'

*   *   *

Queen Victoria sent a telegram congratulating the victors. The newspapers echoed her praise. One said: 'The blood of our countrymen has been avenged, and a system of barbarism rendered hideous by the most savage, horrible and bloodthirsty customs that even Africa can show has been effectively broken up.' Overami's life was spared and he was exiled to Calabar, but six of his chiefs were condemned to death. Sentence was swiftly carried out on five of them. The sixth, Ologbosheri, remained at large and for two years waged a guerrilla war against the British until he too was captured and hanged.

Overami was replaced as Oba by a British puppet, Oba Seki, who controlled villages in rubber-producing areas. Much of that forest land was quickly sold to European firms supplying rubber to the empire. A council of chiefs was established under the direction of a British Resident to administer the territory. After a further minor expedition in 1899 Benin was completely pacified and added to the Niger Protectorate. The trade in indiarubber multiplied many times over and by the turn of the century the land was so civilised to the white man's taste that several golf links were created.

Rawson went home to a hero's welcome and an extra clasp for his KCB. He had pacified a bloody kingdom for the loss of just 11 men killed in the naval brigade, 5 dead from sunstroke, and 45 wounded. Other casualties in the ranks of the black Protectorate troops were not reported. A remarkable feature of this short expedition was that no troops in the field died from malaria and other fevers endemic in the region, although scores began to show the wasting symptoms during the march. On the voyage home 7 officers and 70 men did contract the fever, and Sergeant M'Kettrick died, while Sergeant Bruce died of 'heat apoplexy'.

The number of Benin casualties can only be guessed at. In the fighting along the road to Benin machine-guns constantly raked villages and forest and those hit would generally lie undiscovered where they fell or crawled deeper into the bush to die. A much smaller policing operation in 1898 left 150 natives dead. It would be a fair guess to suggest that Rawson's men and machine-guns accounted for ten times that number or more.

Rawson commanded the Channel Squadron from 1898 to 1901 and was Governor of New South Wales from 1902 to 1909, his term being lengthened by a year owing to his popularity. He returned to London to preside over the Interview Committee for Naval Cadets, a role model for young men. In November 1910 he died, aged sixty-seven, after an operation. Moor committed suicide in Barnes in September 1909. He drank potassium cyanide bought to kill wasps in his garden.

The Protectorate saw several further wars before it was truly colonialised. At the same time as the Benin expedition the Royal Niger Company also invaded the Islamic state of Nupe in the north. Just 30 officers and 50 Hausa troops of the Royal Niger Constabulary defeated a force of 3,000 at Bida using artillery and the murderous Maxim guns. They went on to subdue the neighbouring land of Borin. Troops were sent to wipe out slave-traders at Kano in 1903 and Sokoto later the same year. In 1906 a small force of the Northern Nigerian Regiment was defeated at Satiru by rebels whose leader claimed to be the Mahdi. The rebels were wiped out by artillery and machine-guns in an action in which the British suffered no losses – but as many as 2,000 rebels were killed.

The 900 looted Benin bronzes, some caked with dried animal and human blood, were auctioned by the Admiralty to offset some of the costs of the expedition. Most were bought by German museums, but around fifty went to the British Museum where they are still displayed on the hall-landing of the main staircase. Numerous attempts by successive Nigerian governments to recover them for their nation have been rejected.

Overami died, still a prisoner in Calabar, in January 1914. Over the next four years at least some of the men who had so successfully deployed machine-guns against his followers would see their own sons cut down in the same way in the muddy fields of another continent.

★   ★   ★

CHAPTER NINE

The Tirah Campaign, 1897–8

'Stiff climb, eh, Mackie?'

The north-west frontier held a particular glamour for armchair generals and schoolboys fed on a regular diet of Boy's Own stories of adventure in the rugged mountains, of gallantry against a cruel foe, of songs sung round campfires and medals won by the chestful. But for the real veterans the strips of coloured ribbon did not ease the loss of comrades who never came home, nor remove the stain of barbarous warfare in which the British Empire, at the height of its power, behaved like brigands and arsonists in a land which was not their own.

★　　★　　★

Afghanistan is a cruel, inhospitable country of savage mountains and arid plains where hardly a tree grows. Its people were hard, proud and independent, quick to avenge the mildest slight with a blood feud. The great beauty of the high country was matched by the terror of travellers lost inside its vastness. But to the Victorian Raj the value of Afghanistan was immense. Its mountains provided a natural battlement protecting India from an avaricious Russia. Invaders from the north and west could only negotiate a few narrow passes through the ice-covered barrier of the Hindu Kush.

British attempts to dominate and occupy the land were met with ferocious resistance and fanatical uprisings. The almost continual military and diplomatic skirmishing which spanned most of the nineteenth century was known as the 'Great Game', and Britain twice invaded Afghanistan with bloody consequences on both sides. The north-west frontier inspired Kipling and generations of adventurers, and the battle honours won there adorn most old regimental museums.

The British referred to the tribesmen who lived on the Indian side of the Afghan border as 'Pathans' but there was little ethnic distinction on either side of it. Herodotus referred to them as subjects of Darius the Great, men who wore 'cloaks of skin and carried the bows of their country and the dagger'. In the fourteenth century the Arab traveller Ibn Batuta wrote: 'They hold mountains and defiles and possess considerable strength and are mostly highwaymen.' The British observer Mountstuart Elphinstone described them as a people 'whose vices are revenge, envy, avarice, rapacity and obstinacy; on the other hand they are fond of liberty, faithful to their friends, kind to their dependents, hospitable, brave, hardy, frugal, laborious and prudent'. Dr Hugh Luard said of some Afridi elders: 'They were grim, earnest serious men, in dirty clothes, but with piercing blue eyes, firm strong mouths, strength of character firmly marked on their weather-beaten faces. It is absurd to call them savages.' More ominously Lady Sale wrote in 1842: 'Here every man is born a soldier, every child has his knife, every Afghan is armed complete with some three or four of these knives of different sizes, pistols and a jesail.' The latter, she said, was a flintlock rifle much superior to the British muskets, having a longer range.

Although friendships and alliances were formed with the British, most Afghans regarded the foreigners as infidels and any period of peace was uneasy and short-lived. A major problem was defining the southern boundary of Afghanistan with India. Much of the territory was barely explored, and was occupied by warlike tribes who laughed at the idea of owing allegiance either to the rulers in Afghanistan or to those in British India. In 1893 Sir Mortimer Durand and the Amir of Afghanistan agreed a line on the notional map which passed through areas that were completely unmapped. Sir Ambrose Dundas said: 'It is a vague sort of line, sometimes following watershed, and sometimes not. There is the same mountainous tangle of country on both sides of it, and nowhere is there anything artificial or natural to tell you when you have reached it.' Another man who knew the country better said maps were no use anyway and when shown one said: 'It is all wrong. I know, I have been in those places. Your maps are guesswork.'

Bordering Khyber, on the British side of the invisible line, was Tirah, the land of the Afridis. The tribesmen levied tolls on the Khyber Pass and Elphinstone described them as 'the greatest robbers among the Afghans'. Their homeland was almost completely unknown to foreigners, being within what the Afridis themselves called the 'Purdah nashin' – 'concealed behind the curtain'. The 'curtain' was the range of high mountains which ringed it on all sides. Tirah was closed to all foreigners and the Afridis maintained an isolation which was jealously guarded. One tribesman told a later traveller that foreigners were only admitted as prisoners. Colonel Sir Robert Wharburton, who made friends with many Afridis during eighteen years on the frontier, wrote:

> The Afridi lad from his earliest childhood is taught by the circumstances of his existence and life to distrust all mankind: and very often his near relations, heirs to his small plot of land by right of inheritance, are his deadliest enemies. Distrust of all mankind and readiness to strike the first blow for the safety of his own life have therefore become the maxims of the Afridi. If you can overcome this distrust, be kind in words to him, he will put up with any punishment you like to give him except abuse.

Winston Churchill, then the correspondent for the *Daily Telegraph*, described the Afridis as 'amongst the most miserable and brutal creatures of the earth . . . Their intelligence only enables them to be more cruel, more dangerous, more destructive than wild beasts.' Generally the Indian Government left the Afridis alone and the furthest any expedition went was the Samana Range, which guarded the southern side of the Afridis' summer home, the Tirah Maiden. A valley covering some 900 square miles, this was the only part of the land fertile enough to sustain the tribesmen's flocks.

The demarcation of the Durand Line caused unrest all along the Afghan border. In 1897 tribes from Malakand to Tirah answered a call from the mullahs to revolt in a *jihad* or holy war against the British. Foremost among them was Saidullah of Swat, known to the British as the 'Mad Mullah'. Churchill compared him to the medieval monk who preached the First Crusade: 'Civilisation is face to face with militant Mohammedanism. What Peter the Hermit was to the regular bishops and cardinals of the Church, the Mad Mullah has been to the ordinary priesthood of the Afghan border.'

It is likely that the Amir of Afghanistan, Abdurrahman Khan, encouraged the unrest because he regretted the extra influence granted to the British by the Durand Line. Lieutenant T.P. Dowdall wrote:

Three months ago the Amir sent agents all over Afghanistan telling all to be ready for the *jihad*. This was all in the papers but of course it never occurred to anyone that it could be directed against us, though there is absolutely no-one else against whom he could possibly proclaim a *jihad*. He then sold 80,000 rifles (made in Cabul under English supervision) to the frontier tribes at 2/6 each . . . he could afford this as we give him a large subsidy yearly to insure his friendship.

Whether such widespread suspicions were well founded or not, the Amir gave no further help to the rebel tribes.

Open warfare broke out in the Tochi valley in June 1897 when the commander of a small party escorting a British agent was killed in an ambush. A field force under Major-General G. Corrie Bird occupied the valley, meeting little resistance. Much more serious was an attack later that month on forts in the Swat valley. In a counter-action at Chakdara 60 Bengal Lancers and 180 Sikhs of the 45th killed over 2,000 tribesmen for the loss of five dead. The tribesmen from then on avoided committing large numbers in conventional battles. A punitive expedition under Brigadier-General Sir Binden Blood inflicted more bloodshed on the Swat tribes. In August Shabkadr Fort was attacked by the Mohmands but the police garrison held out until a relief column arrived a month later.

In Kohat district on the borders of Tirah the Afridis and their neighbours the Orakzais joined forces and closed the crucial Khyber Pass. Then, in September, they attacked the much-resented British strongholds built earlier in the decade along the Samana Ridge. The small Saragarhi fort, held by just twenty-one men of the 36th Sikhs, was wiped out. The cleric Dr Theodore Pennell, who was camped on the range and who had read the Sunday service before the attack, watched from far away: 'The Sikhs knew that the Pathans would give them no quarter, so they prepared to sell their lives dearly. The Afridis worked nearer and nearer, and many of the brave defenders fell . . . So the noble garrison fell at their posts to a man.' The Afridis admiringly told of one Sikh who, refusing to run or surrender, killed twenty of them while defending the guardhouse and only perished when the building was burnt down around him. The dying hero, whose name was never known, had his throat cut. Two other forts, Lockhart and Gulistan, held out until relieved. *The Times* roared:

Afridi sharpshooters. (Illustrated London News)

With minds inflamed by the preachings of their mullahs, the Afridis recklessly broke a faith they had kept for 16 years, and, throwing prudence to the winds, put to the sword their own kinsmen – levies in our pay who gallantly resisted their assaults – and declared war to the knife against a Government which has ever treated them in the past with forbearance and with generosity.

A correspondent wrote that the most worrying aspect of the attack on the forts was that the Afridis, despite a war-like past which had made them 'notoriously vain', had for sixteen years stayed aloof from the revolts of their neighbouring tribes. The Afridi chiefs and their allies demanded the withdrawal of all British forces from the Samana Range and the Swat region, together with the release of all Pathan prisoners and hostages. These terms were unacceptable to the British, while the attacks on the forts were considered outrages that must not go unpunished. Now it was Tirah's turn to face an expeditionary force.

Colonel Warburton wrote: 'My mind is very heavy over this hideous disaster, which I feel could have been staved off even up to the day of mischief. It makes me quite sad to think how easily the labour of years – of a lifetime – can be ruined and destroyed in a few days.

*   *   *

Two well-equipped divisions left Kohat on 11 October 1897 to punish and subdue the Afridis and the neighbouring Orakzais in the Tirah heartlands. The majority of the troops were Indian and Gurkhas but there were also four British battalions, with each man carrying the new bolt-action Lee-Metford rifles. The columns were completed by two squadrons of cavalry, four mountain batteries, a machine-gun detachment and Pioneers. The mobile field hospital possessed an X-ray camera. Another brigade was mustered to keep open lines of communications while the Rawalpindi Brigade was kept in reserve. In total the Tirah Field Force numbered 35,000 combatants and around 20,000 followers, making it the largest single force ever to be committed to the frontier. For baggage all mounted officers were allowed one mule each, while in native regiments the allowance was one mule to two officers. To aid mobility no bakeries were allowed in the vanguard and troops were rationed to biscuits.

The force was commanded by General Sir William Stephen Alexander Lockhart, an experienced soldier and veteran of the Indian Mutiny, who was regarded as a disciplinarian. He had previously led similar punitive missions against the Orakzais. Born in 1841, the son of a clergyman, he joined the Bengal Native Infantry as an ensign when barely eighteen. Promotion followed swiftly through the Indian Mutiny and the Bhutan campaign where he distinguished himself in reconnaissance. His skill at scouting and outpost duty was noted in dispatches along with his 'keen eye for ground' which was particularly useful in hill warfare. He was again commended during the Abyssinian campaign which culminated in the capture of the Magdala mountain fortress in terrain just as rugged, if rather warmer, than the Himalayas. More campaign ribbons were pinned to his tunic after further service in India but

General Sir William Lockhart. (National Army Museum)

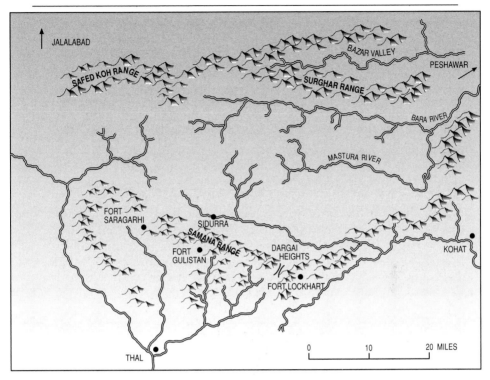

The Tirah Valley, 1897–8.

he was especially proud of the bronze medal of the Royal Humane Society, won for rescuing two women from drowning in a Gwalior lake. Lockhart's service as quartermaster-general in Bengal was interrupted by a bout of malaria which almost killed him. During the earlier 1878 Afghan campaign he commanded British forces at the Khyber Pass who successfully kept the Afridis in check. During the early 1880s he was an effective intelligence officer and envoy and during the 1890s he commanded the Punjab Frontier Force. Most of his time was occupied in hill warfare, including the Waziristan expedition. He was a grizzled old soldier who had earned the respect of his men. His deputy commander, leading the Second Brigade, was General A.J. Yeatman-Biggs, who did not always enjoy the same esteem among the rank and file. Yeatman-Biggs had served in China (where he was slightly wounded during the storming of the Taku forts), South Africa and Egypt before his Indian Army service.

The combined active manpower facing them in the two tribes was estimated at 50,000. The mullahs circulated a story intended to stiffen the resolve and religious ardour of the warriors. They said that hundreds of years before a venerable prophet called Sheikh Mali Doba blessed and buried a red and green flag enclosed within an earthenware pot. His prayer was that in any time of great tribulation the flag would show the Afridis whether or not they would emerge safely from their troubles. The pot was dug up as the British army approached and at a great public ceremony presided over by their religious leader, Said Akbar, nine cows were slaughtered and their blood sprinkled over the vessel, which promptly burst open to reveal the flag. When it was hoisted on a pole, all the standards of the clans bowed down to it of their own accord. This was interpreted as an omen that the Afridis would be victorious.

The first difficulty the British encountered was the lack of accurate information about the terrain, or even the direction of their target. The available maps were almost blank and the little information they did contain was inaccurate. One private complained: 'As no white man has ever been in the country, so there is nothing definitely known.'

The British forces set off from Kohat to Shinwara on the southern edge of Tirah in October 1897. Gunner subaltern George MacMunn described the spectacle:

> The roads in every direction were full with gathering troops. Highland regiments, Gurkhas, Sikh corps, long lines of Indian cavalry, their lances standing high above the acrid dust that they stirred. By the side of the roads strings of laden camels padded on beside the troops, the jinkety-jink of the mountain guns, the skirling of the pipes, all contributed to the wild excitement and romance of the scene.

After a week's march into increasingly hostile country the first clash of arms occurred when the 3rd Gurkhas cleared out a small village at Dargai at a cost of 2 dead and 13 wounded. The King's Own Scottish Borderers and the Gurkhas then took the commanding Dargai Heights, which dominated the left flank of any force descending the Chagra valley, with minimal casualties. But no supply arrangements had been made to allow them to consolidate their position and they were forced to withdraw owing to inadequate stocks of food, fuel and ammunition. It took a further two days for pack mules to bring the necessary supplies up from the main army and by then the Heights had been reoccupied by Afridi tribesmen. It was to prove a costly mistake.

Nineteen standards were counted on the ridge top, representing the principal Afridi clans, as well as their Orakzai allies, with a total of 8,000 men defending what looked like an impregnable position. The British officers pinned their hopes on the eighteen guns of the mountain batteries and the toughness of the gun-crews.

On the morning of the 20th the British nine-pounders began to shell the enemy positions from 1,800 yards. The bursting shrapnel did little damage among Afridis shouting defiance from behind rocky parapets. They waved their standards and kept up a hot fire on the slowly advancing Second Division. After three hours the bombardment succeeded in forcing the tribesmen's heads down, allowing some Gurkha scouts to cross the open ground and form up in new positions sheltered from Afridi sniper fire. Their colleagues were too slow to follow, however, and the main Gurkha force was badly cut up by tribesmen armed with breech-loading Sniders and Martini-Henry rifles. The survivors were pinned down behind what little cover they could find below a sheer cliff. Several companies of the Dorset and Devonshire regiments tried to support them but also came under withering fire. The situation looked desperate as the well-positioned tribesmen threatened to halt the Field Force at its first major obstacle.

Lieutenant-Colonel Mathias of the Gordons was told that the ridge must be cleared 'at all costs'. He told his men, to ringing cheers, 'The Gordon Highlanders will take it!' He ordered his officers and pipers to the front and the ensuing charge across bullet-swept open ground became one of the most famous military exploits of the late Victorian age. The pipers played 'Cock of the North' as the kilted Highlanders roared up the exposed neck of rock under heavy and accurate fire which left sprawling heaps of bloody tartan. Piper Milne was shot through the lung and fell unconscious. Piper George 'Jock' Findlater was shot in both ankles but calmly sat himself down on a boulder and, after catching his breath, carried on playing. His coolness won him the Victoria Cross. Colonel Mathias was in the thick of his men and told his colour-sergeant: 'Stiff climb, eh, Mackie? Not quite so young as I was.' Mackie gave him a resounding clap on the back and said: 'Ye're gaun verra strong for an auld man.' The battalion lost thirty-two men dead but crossed the open ground as ordered and bounded up the rocky heights, quickly followed by the Gurkhas, Sikhs and the Dorset and Devonshires. The combined forces, better sheltered from the Afghan marksmen, then scaled a precipitous goat path weaving through outcrops and crevices. During the mêlée Private Edward Lawson of the Gordons, Private Samuel Vickery of the Dorsets and Captain Henry Singleton Pennell of the Sherwood Foresters also won VCs. The Gordons reached the ridge crest first, their bayonets fixed, but the enemy had already melted away. Total casualties among the attacking force topped 200, most of them wounded. Colonel Mathias was grazed but other men had even narrower escapes. A bullet passed through one major's helmet without injuring him, while Lieutenant Dingwall was hit four times without suffering more than scratches – one bullet struck his revolver, and another his cartridge case, exploding the ammunition within.

Reuters reported: 'It is impossible to speak too highly of the gallantry of the Gordon Highlanders . . . As they were led down the slopes back to camp after their splendid and successful charge, they were spontaneously cheered by all the other regiments.' Special mention was also made of the Gurkhas and their commander, Captain Robinson: 'He led his men across the exposed ground to cover and, finding that the force there was insufficient, he returned alone over the fire-swept space and was wounded leading a second rush in support of the first contingent.' The reporter added: 'Individual instances of conspicuous bravery among the troops were numerous, and many men lost their lives in heroic attempts to save their wounded comrades.'

In that action, like many on the Afghan border, many casualties were incurred while carrying off the wounded. The reason was simple enough: the tribesmen had a fearsome reputation for torturing and mutilating their injured foes, and burial parties had often seen the sickening results. The rule was that no one still breathing should be left behind. Rudyard Kipling wrote:

> When you're wounded and left on Afghanistan's plains
> And the women come out to cut up what remains,
> Just roll to your rifle and blow out your brains
> And go to your Gawd like a soldier.

Queen Victoria telegraphed from Balmoral: 'Please express my congratulations to all ranks, British and Native troops, on their gallant conduct in actions. Deeply deplore loss of precious lives among officers and men in my army. Pray report condition of wounded, and assure them of my true sympathy.'

The victory was achieved by late afternoon, but once again it was marred by the incompetence of staff officers who failed to make proper provision for supplies. In failing light the men were ordered to bivouac on the crest without greatcoats, blankets or fuel for fires in temperatures which swiftly fell below zero. Their only food and water was what they carried into battle on their belts and in their haversacks. Six miles away officers neglected to look after several hundred mules. They were left without food and water, and their full loads were not removed as they were tethered for the night. The following morning most of the mules died as they climbed towards the base camp up the Khanki valley. The whole expedition was halted for a week as patrols were sent out to gather the 3,000 camels needed to bring up 600 tons of stores.

At last, on 29 October, the army began to move against the 6,700-foot Sampagha Pass. This gorge was quickly taken with only token resistance, and the Arhanga Pass also fell before the Pathans had recovered from their surprise. A correspondent wrote:

> When from their eyries in the rocks they note the General's skilful dispositions, the quiet businesslike way in which they were carried out, the steady unwavering advance of the men, the numbers launched against them, the menace to their flanks, the searching fire of the guns, and the deadly precision of our artillery fire, their hearts fail them, and they go.
>
> The strength of the enemy on this occasion or their losses it is impossible to estimate. It was expected they would muster in thousands for the defence of this particular pass, and that here if anywhere they would make a great and gallant stand. But it may be doubted if more than 1,000 of them were actually in line when attacked. The remainder were probably more concerned in removing their families and flocks and herds to places of safety and refuge than in meeting us in fair fight. It may be supposed that as they have had weeks of warning they might have done this sooner . . . possibly they could not bring themselves to believe, until literally the eleventh hour, that after centuries of inviolate seclusion we should dare, or should be able, to lift the purdah and penetrate into their sacred valley. Blood splashes were found in many places along their line of defence, and some of them were killed and others wounded, chiefly by artillery fire.

The Field Force could now look down on the Tirah Maiden, the first foreigners ever to have seen it. Colonel Hutchinson wrote to *The Times*:

We have all been very much struck by the appearance of this valley. It is wide, well-watered land even here at its head, fairly timbered with apricot and walnut trees about the houses, which are very numerous and well built. A great deal is under cultivation, the fields are carefully terraced and signs of plenty and comfort are abundant . . . the Autumn tints remind me of England.

The contrast with the arid, treeless country around this huge hidden valley was dramatic. Hutchinson reported two-storey stone houses and barns stocked with Indian corn, barley, potatoes, beans, walnuts and onions. The colonel gloated: 'It has been the proud boast of the Afridis from time immemorial that no enemy of whatever race or creed has ever attempted to cross the mountain barriers which shut them in. Well, we have changed all that.' Another correspondent wrote: 'Here we are in the promised land at last. A land not exactly flowing with milk and honey, but extensive, fertile, highly cultivated and capable of much development under a settled Government.' The Field Force descended into that green lushness and began to plunder the abandoned food stores.

The main camp was established about 3 miles from Arhanga, in the centre of the Tirah Maiden, close to the hamlet of Nureddin. *The Times* correspondent wrote:

There are no villages but there are innumerable houses dotted all over the country. They occur every quarter mile or so, and are large, strong, substantial buildings, generally including a tower or keep, and capable of mounting a strong defence so long as artillery is not brought against them. In each of these houses lives a family, or a group of blood relations; in one, for example, several brothers, with their wives and children, and fathers and mothers; in another, a petty chief with his immediate followers, his sisters, cousins and aunts, and so on. But, needless to say, they are all empty now. With one accord the people have fled before our approach, and we have the valley to ourselves.

The tribesmen had not deserted their valley, however, merely vanished into the surrounding hills and ravines, from which they emerged to ambush supply columns and pick off unwary patrols. They cut telegraph wires and at night crept close to the British camps to snipe at figures marked out by the firelight. Hutchinson said: 'It is extremely unpleasant, this whizz and spatter of bullets while you are at dinner or trying to enjoy a pipe round a camp fire before turning in.' Private Walter Ware wrote to his parents after counter-measures were taken:

Afridis used to come down on the low hills in the night. Thousands of them, and fire in our camps, in fact we had to sleep in our trenches all night long. I say sleep, but it was very little of that. . . We are being fired on every night now but they can't hurt us much as we have built fortifications all round the camp and they won't come too near us so we don't take any notice of them.

Dispatches reflected the growing frustration of the British:

During the last two nights the firing into camp by prowling marauders has been very bad, but no casualties have been incurred. Last night the 5th Gurkha scouts stalked a firing party, and a *mêlée* ensued, with the result that eight Afridis and one Gurkha [were] killed. It was a very plucky and creditable performance of the Scouts who, under Lieutenants Lucas, Bruce and Tillard have done excellent service since the expedition started. The nights are extremely cold now, with hard frosts, but the sun is hot in the day time. The health of the troops is good, and the wounded are doing well. . .

General Kempster's Brigade destroyed the home of the Mullah Said Akbar, a prominent leader of the revolt. Incriminating correspondence was found there, which has been taken charge of by the Political Officer for examination. Our foraging parties were today fired on and more or less seriousiy engaged in several directions. There were a few casualties among the men, but none among the officers . . .

A party, while engaged in fixing a site for a new camp and signalling station, were treacherously fired on at short range by Afridis. Nobody was touched, but the party had a miraculous escape . . . Major O'Sullivan, of Sir William Lockhart's staff, and three other officers narrowly escaped being cut off. Some of the enemy, concealing their rifles, sauntered up with apparently friendly intentions. Major O'Sullivan, however, suspected treachery and whistled to the other officers as a signal to them to return. The enemy immediately opened fire but the officers, who escaped unhurt, took shelter in a neighbouring house. Luckily a company of the 3rd Gurkhas were close at hand and were able to rescue them. It is expected that the object of the enemy was to capture them alive. A similar attempt was made in the case of some of the infantry, but owing to the careful precautions taken it proved futile.

Among the papers discovered in the Mullah's house were letters written by the 'Mad Mullah' stating that the Turks had beaten the Greeks and seized the approaches to India, and that, with the British army isolated, now was the time to strike a blow for Islam.

A steady stream of supplies flowed through the Arhanga Pass and the baggage trains were in constant danger of ambush. The Afridis knew to attack when both men and animals were exhausted. In one raid the Queen's Royal West Surrey Regiment lost 3 men killed and 4 wounded, 10 boxes of Lee-Metford ammunition – a total of 11,000 rounds – 3 rifles, 350 kits and 71 baggage ponies which stampeded away into the darkness as soon as the firing started. On another night nine drivers were killed or wounded and 188 kits belonging to the 15th Sikhs were carried off. The Afridis had a well-deserved reputation as craftsmen and they became adept at making booby-traps from captured supplies. In Mastura an armoury was found containing anvils, mechanical appliances, 150 Nobel dynamite cartridges, Lee-Metford bullets with the lead withdrawn from their nickel cases, and dozens of Curtis and Harvey red powder tins.

The artist Melton Prior, attached to the Field Force, described a 'spirited affair' when a body of King's Own Scottish Borderers stormed an enemy position above

Camp at Bagh showing low stone fortifications to protect the tents from snipers, drawn by the artist Melton Prior while attached to the Field Force.

the camp at Datoi: 'Our men had to climb almost precipitous rocks and then rush the enemy's position under a fire so close that not more than five yards' distance lay between the English officer in command and the foremost Afridie. After a brief stand the tribesmen retreated down a wooded ravine.' This action was untypical in that the Afridis allowed the British to get so close.

One of the most frustrating aspects of this sort of warfare was that many of the tribesmen were either former sepoys themselves or had been trained by sepoys. They also used modern rifles, in many cases stolen from the British, which used smokeless powder, making it almost impossible to pinpoint snipers in the rugged hills. Surgeon-Captain Pollock observed: 'They never show and don't stand up to be killed.'

Lockhart decided that if he could not beat his invisible enemy in pitched battle he would force them to negotiate by destroying their own Eden. He ordered the systematic burning of farms and homes across the Maiden. Entire hamlets were dynamited and the wreckage torched until nothing was left but ashes and rubble. Orchards were cut down and wells filled with sand. Grainfields were trampled by horses' hooves and the ground laced with salt. The troops were given free rein to loot anything from food and firewood to tribal keepsakes and the few personal possessions left by the fleeing tribesmen. It was a scorched-earth policy exacerbated by vengeance for the innumerable pinprick ambushes on the British forces. The Reuters correspondent Lionel James reported: 'One of the most magnificent sights one could wish to see was the destruction of the valley by fire and sword as the evening waned into night. The camp was ringed by a wall of fire – byres, outhouses, homesteads and fortresses one mass of rolling flame, until the very camp was almost as light as day.' Hutchinson, writing in *The Times*, said: 'Whether these measures will have the effect of making them yield their submission, or whether it will exasperate them into making a big attack on our camp, time alone can show.'

Lockhart was convinced that stern measures were necessary to bring in chieftains willing to negotiate. 'Seeing us in possession, occupying their land, devouring their stores, and noting our determination and our power to punish, with the winter, too, coming on while they are wanderers on the bleak mountain sides, they must see the hopelessness of prolonged resistance.'

Lockhart's scorched-earth policy was heavily criticised by some fellow officers and politicians. After the campaign Lord Roberts said in a parliamentary debate: 'Burning houses and destroying crops, necessary and justifiable as such measures may be, unless followed up by some form of authority or jurisdiction, means starvation for many of the women and children . . . and for us a rich harvest of hatred and revenge.' But Sir Neville Chamberlain wrote in favour: 'To have to carry destruction, if not desolation, into the homes of some hundreds of families is the

The King's Own Scottish Borderers storming Afridi positions above Datoi. (Illustrated London News)

great drawback to border warfare; but with savage tribes to whom there is no right but might, and no law to govern them in their intercourses with the rest of mankind, save that which appeals to their own interests, the only course as regards humanity as well as policy is to make all suffer, and thereby, for their own interests, enlist the great majority on the side of peace and safety.'

The stripping of the land continued, and with it the officially sanctioned looting. *The Times* correspondent noted:

Strings of mules go out every day, with sufficient escorts, and return in the evening laden up with forage, which abounds, and with sacks of potatoes, wheat, Indian corn, pumpkins, walnuts . . . The foragers not infrequently find odds and ends of booty, which they annex for themselves, old *jezails*, swords, daggers and Korans. These are retained by the finders as mementoes of the campaign. Of Korans there are two kinds – one printed in Peshwar or Lahore, and of no particular interest or value, the other hand-written and generally illustrated and illuminated. These are rare and are very precious finds indeed. A few have been taken.

The mosques, as religious establishments, were spared the torch. But one at Bagh, reputed to be where the Mullahs had hatched the revolt, was the target of a punitive column. The building itself was untouched, but the stately trees surrounding it were 'ringed', the bark sliced round by Gurkha kukris so that they would die in a year. This petty act was to leave a permanent reminder of British wrath and to reduce the site's religious importance and sanctity.

With no towns to occupy and no formal army to beat, the campaign became a war of attrition with columns spiralling out in different directions. Repeatedly the enemy melted away before them, only to re-form and harry the soldiers as they returned to their scattered camps. One reconnaissance sortie on 9 November by General Westmacott and the Dorsetshire and Northamptonshire regiments and the 36th and 18th Sikhs is typical. Their target was the Saran Sar ridge in the west range of the valley, where enemy positions had been spotted. Sharp-shooters peppered the column as it approached but when the soldiers scaled the ridge they found it deserted. Reuters reported:

The retirement was slow and difficult. When it had been proceeding about an hour, the enemy, who had meanwhile had time to collect and choose points favourable for an attack, were again in great force and opened fire upon the troops.

It was seen that the five companies of Northamptons on the summit of the cliff were making no progress. In reply to inquiries which were heliographed they signalled back, 'Several wounded; cannot carry them down; need support.' General Westmacott then ordered up the 36th Sikhs to the support of the Northamptonshire men. They went up like greyhounds as soon as they understood that the rearguard was in difficulties, and all were withdrawn without further loss to the foot of the hill under cover of the guns.

But the necessity of transporting the wounded still greatly retarded the retirement of the force. Between the hill and the camp lies a stretch of quite the worst country over which a general could be called upon to withdraw his force in the face of a strong enemy skirmishing on over-hanging crags, consisting as it does of deep and broken *nullahs* intersecting the line of march every hundred yards or so. It was here that the enemy concentrated their attack. Their knowledge of the country enabled them to creep up the ravines to within short range of the retiring British force. The Northamptons fought with great bravery, and most of their casualties occurred while they were engaged in saving their wounded. Owing to the nature of the country and the broken formation in which they arrived at the foot of the hill, they were obliged to retire in groups. All the wounded were brought into camp as darkness was setting in, but an officer, Lieutenant Macintire, and 12 men, appear to have been cut off. It is hoped that they may yet come in.

The enemy followed their usual tactics, and during the fighting in the ravines displayed wonderful audacity. Considering the force in which they gathered, it was only the dispositions made by General Westmacott which saved the rearguard from annihilation. General Westmacott personally held his men together and saw all the wounded sent on before him on the road to the camp, himself coming in with the rearmost party.

The day's operations cost the general 7 dead, 13 missing and 45 wounded. More severe casualties were suffered by General Francis Kempster's Brigade when their flanks were attacked as they crossed the Teeri Kandao Pass. The rearguard, comprising Gordon Highlanders, Sikhs, Gurkha Scouts, two companies of Dorsetshires and a mountain battery, left the Waran valley long after the main body had set out. They reached the summit of the pass in mid-afternoon, exhausted and constantly harried by enemy snipers. A young lieutenant was killed, shot through the head. His death marked the start of a serious attack by a large body of Afridis who swarmed down the mountainside. Hand to hand fighting was hardest in thick woods abutting the trail. In one bayonet charge the Sikhs killed up to sixty of the tribesmen, whose marksmen were hampered by the trees and foliage. The Sikhs were in a precarious position, however, and their commander, Colonel Abbott, was painfully wounded in the neck and face. Another officer was shot through the heart. Other Sikh units and the Dorsetshires came to their support and all were able to retire down the pass. One report of the engagement said:

It was now nearly dark and the enemy, getting round the flank, were found to be holding a cluster of houses directly in the path of the retreating column. Colonel Haughton at once formed up the whole force with fixed bayonets and, with loud shouts and cheers, the Afridis were driven out, many being shot and bayoneted.

Darkness had now fully set in, so Colonel Haughton decided to stay during the night in the position gained. Half a company of the Dorsetshire Regiment here joined his party. The remaining company and a half seem to have missed the direction and, getting separated, were attacked by the Afridis in the

'A sniping affair by the camp'. (Illustrated London News)

gathering gloom and suffered the disastrous loss of two officers and 13 men killed and 11 wounded. Several rifles were also lost. The enemy in this action have lost very heavily.

Meanwhile one company of the 36th Sikhs rushed another village in the dark and took possession of two blockhouses from which they steadily repulsed an Afridi attack. The enemy were so close that they could be heard abusing the defenders and in particular Gul Badshah, the Orakzai orderly of an officer.

The following day, as the dead were buried, General Lockhart commended all units for their heroism and stamina. He went on:

We must remember that we are opposed to perhaps the best skirmishers and best natural rifle shots in the world, and the country they inhabit is the most difficult on the face of the globe. Their strength lies principally in their intimate knowledge of the ground, which enables them to watch our movements unperceived and to take advantage of every height and every ravine. Our strength lies in our discipline, controlled fire and mutual support, and our weakness in our ignorance of the ground and the consequent tendency of small parties to straggle and get detached. The moral, therefore, is that careful touch must be maintained; and if small bodies do from any cause get separated from their regiment they should, as far as possible, stick to the open and not enter ravines or broken ground where, with such an enemy, they at once place themselves at a terrible disadvantage.

I hope that before long we may obtain an opportunity to meet the enemy on such terms as will enable us to wipe out old scores, and I am confident that when the time comes you will all conduct yourselves with steady courage worthy of our best traditions. In the meantime there is no occasion for depression because some of us have been surprised, outnumbered and overwhelmed on bad ground.

Later, addressing the Sikh and Gurkha regiments he praised their endurance, courage and resolution and said that he was proud to have such battalions under his command. He told them that the Queen-Empress was personally watching their performance.

The Tirah Maiden was healthier than most of the frontier region, but as winter set in the army of occupation regularly sent back sixty or seventy men a day, some wounded in action but most suffering from pneumonia, frostbite or dysentery. While the British and Indian soldiers shivered in their billets, however, the approach of the winter snows also affected those tribesmen who had watched their means of winter survival destroyed. The first tribal leaders to come down from the hills to talk peace were the *maliks* of the Orakzais. These 'venerable old greybeards' listened with quiet dignity as Lockhart spelled out tough terms. All captured British arms were to be returned along with 300 of their own breech-loading rifles plus a fine of 50,000 rials. The Orakzai chiefs agreed these terms on hearing that the British would not occupy their lands permanently. Churchill watched the arms handover, writing: 'These tribes have nothing to surrender but their arms. To extort these few had taken a month, had cost many lives, and thousands of pounds. It had been as bad a bargain as ever was made.'

The Afridis, freezing in the snow-laden hills, refused to follow the Orakzai surrender. Their hit-and-run guerrilla tactics increased the toll of casualties. Hutchinson told his readers:

They have absolutely nothing to learn from us, these Afridis. Contrariwise, their dashing and bold attack, the skill with which they take advantage of ground, the patience with which they watch for a favourable moment, and their perfect marksmanship – all these qualities have again and again won our admiration.

It was now December and the British, unequipped to suffer the deepest winter, left the fire-blackened valley. In icy sleet, biting winds and dense mist they began to march down the 40-mile Bazar valley. Lockhart's aim was to use the withdrawal to reopen the Khyber Pass and thus achieve his military objectives. That involved

A sketch by Melton Prior showing the bodies of dead officers being taken down country for burial, escorted by Bengal Lancers. (Illustrated London News)

crossing the Bazar River, a boiling stream with steep banks and dangerous overhangs. Men's moustaches and horse's tails froze solid. The fields along the banks were ice-encrusted bogs which swallowed up mules and their packs. Most of the army's tents were lost and the men spent the nights huddled around spluttering camp fires, risking the light which made them targets for Afridi snipers in return for meagre warmth.

The tribesmen launched sporadic night attacks on isolated parties and occasional daylight attacks on the rearguard of the main column. The most determined of these was on 13 January while the 4th Brigade was packing up the remaining camp equipment. The Afridis' target was the baggage train and their heavy fire swiftly killed ten pack animals. The native drivers panicked and ran between the lines. Many fell during the confused firefight while the British and Indian troops fought back as they carried their wounded to cover. A stand was made near a ford in the river and the defenders were only saved by a mountain-gun battery and Peshawar pickets who turned back to hammer the attackers. By then the Afridis had cut down many men and beasts. Casualties among the British soldiers topped 40 but the main carnage was inflicted upon the baggage train. The official history recorded that 'upwards of 100 followers and about 150 animals seem to have been lost that night'.

Churchill wrote:

People talk of moving columns hither and thither as if they were mobile groups of men who had only to march about the country and fight the enemy wherever found; and a very few understand that an army is a ponderous mass which drags painfully after it a long chain of advanced depots, rest camps and communications . . . In these valleys, where wheeled traffic is impossible, the difficulties and cost of moving supplies are enormous.

It took Lockhart five days and nights to fight through the Bazar valley and his army suffered 164 casualties, but he was now on more familiar ground and could concentrate on the Khyber Pass. His men began to systematically locate and capture or destroy the tribal flocks of sheep and goats. The Afridis continued to put up stout resistance and there was a tough fight at the Shinkamar Pass in January. In a repeat of the earlier Dargai blunder, British troops first held, and then abandoned, rocky heights above the main column. Several companies were ordered to retake the position. One, led by Lieutenant Thomas Dowdall, succeeded but in the very 'moment of triumph' he and several others were killed by snipers. His commanding officer told the young man's mother: 'There was nothing of the drawing room or carpet soldier about him, only a plucky desire to be in the thick of the fight and share the danger with his men by whom his loss will be deeply regretted.' In all, 6 officers and 20 men were killed and 31 wounded in the last major action of the war. Also among the dead were Lieutenant-Colonel John Haughton, who had so bravely commanded at the Saran Ridge engagement, and Lieutenant Arthur Turing whose obituary recalled his youth at Bedford School 'where he distinguished himself both as a scholar and as an oarsman'.

The loss of their flocks finally persuaded the Afridis to abandon the struggle. As the snows began to melt in the weak spring sunshine, the fighting petered to an end. One Afridi chief pledged that British forts on the borders of their lands would be safe from attack. 'Leave us alone,' he said. 'We will fight the Russians or any other European armies that come against India.'

★   ★   ★

Sporadic fighting continued in some areas but gradually all the tribal *maliks* tendered their submission. Lockhart issued an ultimatum that all fines must be paid by 23 February but an extension was granted because of snow clogging the passes. In March the Afridis gave up seventy hostages, and the final surrender of arms was completed on 1 April. The Afridi chieftains were surprised that Lockhart did not take more vindictive action and when the general left Peshawar on 5 April their entire *jirgah* assembled at the station to bid him farewell.

Lockhart returned a conquering hero. He received the thanks of the government, was showered with further honours and quickly succeeded Sir George White as commander-in-chief of India. He died suddenly in Calcutta two years later. One obituary referred to his command in Tirah: 'He showed exceptional skills in handling his force of regulars in an almost impracticable country, in a guerrilla warfare, against native levies of sharpshooters, who were always trying to elude him, but he outmanoeuvred them and beat them at their own tactics.' Another said that he had brought the Tirah campaign to a 'rapid and successful conclusion'. The price had been heavy. The Tirah Field Force took five months to subdue an elusive enemy at a total cost of 287 dead, 853 wounded and 10 missing. Among the dead was 67-year-old Sir Henry Havelock-Allen, who had won the Victoria Cross at Cawnpore and was once described as the bravest man in the British Army. He had accompanied the expedition as a newspaper correspondent, but ignored repeated advice to stay close to the column and his butchered body and that of his horse were eventually found by a search party.

General Yeatman-Biggs came in for particular criticism for the logistical blunders and delays, and for failing to adequately support the other columns. He was swiftly beyond such criticism, however, as he died of dysentery at Peshawar, his body weakened by exposure and fatigue. Lockhart, in his final set of dispatches, said that his fellow-officer had been in poor health from the start of the campaign. Gossip sent back to Britain by Churchill suggested that General Kempster had been reported as 'no longer possessing the confidence of his troops'.

Winston Spencer Churchill, a young officer heartily despised for his vaunting ambition, missed most of the action in Tirah but that did not stop him offering a critical opinion. 'I am afraid the Tirah campaign has ended disastrously,' he wrote to his 'Mamma'. 'The troops have done what they were ordered – but they were disastrously led. The last retirement to Peshawar has been a most terrible blunder. Whatever the inconvenience of wintering in Tirah, it was preferable to the chance of the Afridis thinking they had driven us out. All the officers who have come down here sick and wounded show a most unsoldierlike spirit, declaring that it is not good enough and they are glad they are out of it.'

In another letter he wrote:

The troops have done all that was asked of them. They have marched freely into all parts of Tirah and have burned and destroyed everything that came to hand. The tribesmen have been powerless to stop them but have been able to make them pay heavily in men and officers.

The whole expedition was a mistake because its success depended on the tribesmen giving in when their country was invaded and their property destroyed. This they have not done. We have done them all the harm possible and many of them are still defiant. Had they cannons we could have captured them. Had they towns we could have destroyed them. Had they any points of strategical or political importance we could have occupied them. But regular troops cannot catch or kill an impalpable cloud of skirmishers. It is because we have no real means – except by prolonged occupation – of putting the screw on these tribesmen and making them give in – that it is a great mistake to make the attempt.

In public, however, Churchill could not risk such forthright views and in a letter to *The Times* he toadied to his superiors and, with no hint of self-irony, condemned the grumblings of armchair generals:

I daresay you meet many in England . . . who imagine that the Field Force is sulking in its tents, quivering with anger, and quaking with fear. To such a visit to the scene would be an education. They would observe in the Khyber Pass or along the Bara river, the camps of five brigades of men, hardened by war, proud of their experience, confident in their strength, ready and eager to advance against the enemy. They would see at Jamrud that enemy, begging only for time to collect their fine, fighting amongst themselves to gather the *tale* of rifles, anxiously offering hostages, and abjectly imploring that whatever may happen, the soldiers shall not come back.

I suppose that on all military operations there must be a proportion of cases of cowardice and incompetency and a much larger proportion of errors of judgement. Outpost affairs may be disastrous, troops may be exposed to unnecessary hardships, supplies and commissariat will at times go wrong, many tempers must be tried. When civilised forces collide one side or the other wins the battle, and a victory covers everything. The peculiar difficulty which attends mountain warfare is that there are no general actions on a great scale, no brilliant successes, no important surrenders, no chance for *coups de theatre*. It is just a rough hard job, which must be carried through. The war is one of small incidents.

Churchill's praise of the Tirah Field Force and its commanders may have been faint, but the force had beaten, for the first time, frontier guerrillas fighting in their own homeland, and, by example, curbed the warlike tendencies of other tribes. General Sir George White said that no campaign had ever been conducted in India in more arduous and trying circumstances: 'The country was physically most difficult, and the enemy were well-armed and expert in guerrilla warfare. Severe punishment was, however, inflicted on them. The officers and men conducted themselves in a manner thoroughly befitting the traditions of the Queen's Army.'

The campaign also added to the battle honours of the regiments which took part. Around 200 officers and men were mentioned in dispatches and no fewer than seven Victoria Crosses were won, four of them on the Dargai Heights. Piper Jock Findlater and Private Vickery received theirs personally from Queen Victoria while recovering in Netley Hospital. Findlater tried to hobble to his feet but was waved down by the monarch. As she left the hospital corridor he played 'Haughs of Cromdale'. Findlater was promoted to Pipe-Major and fêted across Britain. He died in Turriff, near his birthplace, in 1942. Vickery, from Somerset, was made up to sergeant and died in Cardiff in 1952. Private Lawson, a Geordie, also witnessed two world wars before his death in Northumberland in 1955. Captain Pennell, from Dawlish in Devon, did not enjoy a similarly long life. He died in St Moritz early in 1907, aged thirty-two. These men, and many others, felt that equal honours should have gone also to Sikhs and Gurkhas who had borne the brunt of the initial assault on the ridge. But it was not until 1911 that Indian Army officers and men were made eligible for Britain's foremost award for valour.

Three more VCs were awarded for bravery during the early part of the uprising: Brevet Lieutenant-Colonel Robert Bellow Adams, a staff officer and Indian Army Guide, led two officers and five men under heavy and close fire to rescue a lieutenant of the Lancashire Fusiliers lying disabled by a bullet wound and surrounded by enemy swordsmen at Nawa Kili. While he was being brought to cover, the lieutenant

Queen Victoria conferring the VC on Piper Findlater and Private Vickery at Netley Hospital. (Illustrated London News)

was shot again and killed. Four horses, including the colonel's, were shot. Adams was later knighted and promoted to major-general. Punjab-born, he died in Inverness in 1928 and his body was cremated in Glasgow. Lieutenant Hector Lachlan Stewart MacLean's VC was posthumous. He died of wounds suffered during the action at Nawa Kili, not too many miles from the place of his birth twenty-eight years earlier. His Kent family erected a memorial in St Alban's Church, Marden. The third officer involved, Lieutenant Alexander Edward Murray Fincastle of the Queen's Lancers, received his medal from Queen Victoria at Buckingham Palace. He later became a major and the Earl of Dunmore. He served in the early part of the Boer War and the first half of the First World War. He died in London in 1962, aged ninety.

Churchill, who had not reached the Tirah army until the hard fighting was finished, wanted a medal to further his military, literary and, above all, political career. In a letter to a more senior officer whom he had befriended he said: 'I am entitled to a medal and two clasps for my gallantry, for the hardships and dangers I encountered. I am possessed with a keen desire to mount the ribbon on my breast.' In another letter to his mother he boasted that as a result of the campaign he had made 'a great many friends in high places – as far as soldiering is concerned'. He also reckoned that he was entitled to three months' leave on full pay. His subsequent career does not need to be recounted here.

The mixed victory in Tirah committed ever more numerous troops to garrison the forward positions along the frontier and this was questioned in both India and Britain. Secretary of State Lord Hamilton wrote: 'If we can conciliate and attach to us these tribes, then from a military point of view we are greatly the gainers. If we only make them more hostile, whatever benefit we gain theoretically in strategy, by occupying their country, we lose tactically by the forces locked up in maintaining our communications.'

Such sentiments were echoed strongly by Lord Curzon, who in 1899 became the new Viceroy of India. The 39-year-old statesman hit upon a political solution – to remove the frontier from within the jurisdiction of the Punjab and turn it into a province in its own right which would act as a buffer between the Raj and the unruly regions to the north. The frontier was to be defended by the tribes themselves, formed in local militias trained by British officers and, ironically, given the terms of the Tirah capitulation, armed by the British. Minor tribal uprisings, banditry and kidnapping continued to flare up but the strategy largely succeeded into the following century in holding firm the boundaries of British India. Typically, the Afridis continued to behave independently and at the turn of the century carried on a gun-running trade, while the 1923 kidnapping of a seventeen-year-old English girl, Molly Ellis, caused outrage. There was great relief when she was freed unharmed.

Across the border there was cooperation from Abdurrahman Khan and relative peace continued after his death in 1901. Unrest in India and calls for a new holy war sparked the third major Anglo-Afghan conflict in 1919 and sixty years later Soviet tanks opened another chapter in Afghanistan's bloody history. The blood shed since then dwarfed Britain's earlier invasion of a paradise valley hidden high in the mountain fastness.

★   ★   ★

The War Correspondents

A substantial number of the first-hand accounts of the distant wars included in this book have been gleaned, in the safety and warmth of my home, from the contemporary accounts of war correspondents who generally shared the discomfort and danger suffered by nineteenth-century soldiers and sailors. Their courage and tenacity has too often been neglected. They were a motley crowd: full-time professional reporters and enthusiastic amateurs; tradesmen, adventurers and failed businessmen; commissioned soldiers, with a talent for words which could supplement their army pay; scholars and missionaries; distinguished writers and hacks; glory-hunters, charlatans and heroes.

At first they were generally despised, and regarded as dangerous meddlers at worst and lickspittle propagandists at best. Wellington's view dripped contempt: 'every man who can write, and who has a friend who can read, sits down to write his account of what he does not know, and his comments on what he does not understand'. Much later Kitchener referred to a posse of professional reporters as 'drunken swabs', while Wolseley referred to 'those newly invented curses to modern armies'. But with the dramatic rise in literacy as the century progressed – between 1841 and 1900 the rate rose from 63 to 92 per cent – and the reduction and then abolition of newspaper tax, generals and politicians began to appreciate the power of a mass circulation press.

Its power to wreck reputations and reform absurdly redundant practices was proven by the reports from the Crimea of William Howard Russell (1821–1907) of *The Times*. His reputation is so firmly set that it does not need to be enhanced here, other than to quote one general's verdict: 'An honest truth-telling man.' Russell may be the 'father' of war correspondents, but many others followed him to feed the public's appetite for news and sensation with equal integrity and zeal. Some of them were driven by self-aggrandisement and bravado; most by the desire to earn an honest crust by informing, enthusing and entertaining the public.

The best of them, then as now, were always found as close to the action as possible, sharing the privations of the front-line troops rather than the fine wines of a general's table far from the sound of gunfire. They too suffered dysentery, rotten food, seasickness, malaria and the range of other tortures which often proved more dangerous than an enemy's bullet or spear-thrust. Robert Furneaux wrote of Russell's successors:

Without a continental war, or even one of great historical significance, for them to chronicle, they galloped their horses and rode the trains, through many campaigns in the mountains and valleys of the Balkans, the frontiers of India, the plateaux of Central Asia, the veldt of Zululand and Natal, the sands and deserts of Egypt and the Sudan, in fever-ridden Cuba and the Philippines, while a new and eager newspaper-reading public clamoured for their stories.

Their reports often had important consequences. When the American reporter J.A. MacGahan was engaged by the *Daily News* in the Balkans he exposed the mass murder of Bulgarian Christians by the Turks. The global outcry that ensued led to Bulgarian independence.

Sometimes the way news was brought out of war zones was as heroic as the military actions themselves. MacGahan's colleague on the *News*, Archibald Forbes rode 140 miles in thirty hours on a succession of post horses over the Carpathian mountains to bring news of the Russians' failed assault on Plevna. After further reportage in the Balkans and India, Forbes was sent to cover the war with the Zulus. Having witnessed Cetewayo's defeat at Ulundi he rode all night through enemy-infested and unknown territory to the nearest telegraph station and, having wired his story, rode on a further 175 miles to Durban to mail war artist Melton Prior's sketch of the battle.

At least one correspondent became the story. When the *Morning Post*'s Winston Churchill was captured by Boers he remarked: 'This will be good for my paper.' His escape and evasion of his pursuers became an epic avidly lapped up by the British public. He returned a national hero and his accounts, in both newsprint and book form, netted him £10,000, earnings which laid the foundation of his political career.

Most correspondents were listed as non-combatant observers but that did not stop them carrying arms and, on occasions, using them. The *Daily Telegraph* reporter Bennet Burleigh, a Glaswegian by birth who fought on the Confederate side in the American Civil War, was mentioned in dispatches for helping to steady the line at Abu Klea. During that action he was hit in the neck by a spent bullet but calmly asked a colleague to pluck it out as he continued firing. His scoops included the first reports of Gordon's death at Khartoum, the safety of the relief column and the victory at Omdurman.

Men such as Burleigh escaped death many times during long, illustrious careers. Others weren't so lucky, as we have seen with the grisly fate of Thomas Bowlby, *The Times* correspondent in the China War. They never came home or filed their final report. The death toll included many veteran correspondents.

John Cameron of *The Standard* and St Leger Herbert of the *Morning Post* were shot dead at the battle of Abu Kru, the latter as he was opening a tin of sardines.

The Times correspondent Frank Power was captured and killed by the Mahdi's men as he tried to reach a telegraph station to appeal for help for the besieged garrison at Khartoum.

Another *Times* correspondent, the Honourable Hubert Howard, who also wrote for the *New York Herald*, was killed by a stray British shell at Omdurman, while Henry Cross of the *Manchester Guardian* died after the battle from a fever.

Reporters Edmond O'Donovan and Frank Vizetelly were killed at Tel-el-Kebir, sharing with the soldiers the hardships and hazards of desert warfare.

George Warrington Steevens covered colonial campaigns for the *Daily Mail* with an accuracy and eloquence which impressed even hostile old generals, but died of fever during the siege of Ladysmith. Steevens drank a hoarded bottle of champagne on his deathbed, surrounded by fellow correspondents. One colleague described his special talents: 'In a scientific age, his style may be described as cinematographic. He was able to put before his readers, in a series of smooth-running little pictures, events exactly as he saw them with his own intense eyes.' Another said: 'What Kipling did for fiction, [Steevens] did for fact.'

The names of these journalistic dead, and those of many others, are not recorded on regimental war memorials. But they, too, must not be forgotten.

★   ★   ★

Bibliography

General

Briggs, Asa, *The Age of Improvement 1783–1867* (Longman, London, 1959)

Brooks, Richard, *Naval Brigades from the Crimea to the Boxer Rebellion* (Constable, London, 1999)

Callwell, Colonel C.E., *Small Wars* (London, 1906)

Dictionary of National Biography (Oxford University Press, 1921–2)

Farwell, Byron, *Queen Victoria's Little Wars* (Allen Lane, London, 1973)

Featherstone, D., *Colonial Small Wars 1837–1901* (Newton Abbot, 1973)

Haythornthwaite, Philip J., *The Colonial Wars Source Book* (Arms & Armour Press, London, 1995)

James, Lawrence, *The Savage Wars – British Campaigns in Africa, 1870–1920* (Robert Hale, London)

Judd, Denis, *Empire – The British Imperial Experience from 1765 to the Present* (HarperCollins, 1996)

Lucas, T.J., *Camp Life and Sport in South Africa* (London, 1878)

Morris, James, *The Pax Britannica Trilogy* (Faber & Faber, London, 1968)

Mostert, Noel, *Frontiers – The Epic of South Africa's Creation and the Tragedy of the Xhosa People* (Jonathan Cape, London, 1992)

Pakenham, Thomas, *The Scramble for Africa* (Weidenfeld & Nicolson, 1991)

Spiers, Edward M., *The Late Victorian Army* (Manchester University Press, 1992)

Strawson, John, *Beggars in Red – The British Army 1789–1889* (Hutchinson, London 1991)

——, *Gentlemen in Khaki – The British Army 1890–1990* (Secker & Warburg, London, 1989)

Buenos Aires

Annual Registers, 1806–7

Auchmuty, General Sir Samuel, *Dispatches*

Backhouse, Lieutenant-Colonel J.T., *Dispatches*

Beresford, Major-General William Carr, *Dispatches*

Court-Martial of General Whitelocke (Official Papers, 1808)

Ferns, H.S., *Britain and Argentina in the Nineteenth Century* (Oxford University Press, 1960)

Graham-Yooll, Andrew, *Small Wars You May Have Missed* (Junction Books, London, 1983)

Marley, David F., *Wars of the Americas – A Chronicle of Armed Conflict in the New World* (ABC-Clio, California, 1998)

Murray, Admiral George, *Dispatches*

Pendle, George, *A History of Latin America* (Penguin, London, 1981)

Popham, Commodore Sir Hugh, *Dispatches*

Rock, David, *Argentina 1516–1982 – From Spanish Colonization to the Falklands War* (Taurus, London, 1986)

Scobie, J., *Argentina: A City and a Nation* (New York, 1964)

The Times

Whitelocke, General John, *Dispatches*

The First Burma War

Annual Registers, 1824–6

Sheppard, Eric, *A Short History of the British Army* (Constable, London, 1926)

Stewart, A.T.Q., *The Pagoda War* (Faber & Faber, London, 1972)

Tarling, Nicholas (ed.), *The Cambridge History of Southeast Asia, Volume Two* (Cambridge University Press, 1992)

The Times

Vincent, Frank, *The Land of the White Elephant* (Harper, New York, 1874)

The Black War

Bonwick, James, *The Daily Life of the Tasmanians* (London, 1970)

Calder, J.E., *Some Accounts of the Wars and Habits etc., of the Tribes of Tasmania* (Hobart, 1873)

Davies, David, *The Last of the Tasmanians* (Harper & Row, USA, 1973)

Dodd, Agnes F., *A Short History of the English Colonies* (J.M. Dent & Co., London, 1901)

Fenton, James, *A History of Tasmania from its Discovery in 1642 to the Present Time* (Hobart and London, 1884)

Robson, Lloyd, *A Short History of Tasmania* (Oxford University Press, Melbourne, 1985)

Younger, R.M., *A Concise History of Australia and the Australians* (Hutchinson, 1969)

The Opium War

Annual Registers, 1840–43

Bremer, Commodore Sir James Gordon, *Dispatches*

Burrell, Major-General George, *Dispatches*

Cotterell, Arthur, *China – A History* (Random House, London, 1988)

Ebrey, Patricia Buckley, *China – Cambridge Illustrated History* (Cambridge University Press, 1996)

Elliot, Charles, *Dispatches*

Fairbank, John *King, China – A New History* (Harvard University Press, 1992)

Gough, Major-General Sir Hugh, *Dispatches*

Gray, Jack, *Rebellions and Revolutions – China from the 1880s to the 1980s* (Oxford University Press, 1990)

Inglis, Brian, *The Opium War* (Hodder & Stoughton, 1976)

Low, Sidney, and Sanders, Lloyd C., *The History of England During the Reign of Victoria* (Longmans, London, 1913)

Martineau, Harriet, *A History of the Thirty Years' Peace* (George Bell, London, 1878)

Morton, W. Scott, *China – Its History and Culture* (Lippincott & Cromwell, New York, 1980)

Peyrefitte, Alain, *The Collision of Two Civilisations – The British Expedition to China 1792–4* (HarperCollins, London, 1989)

Pottinger, Sir Henry, *Dispatches*

Pratt, Major J.L., *Dispatches*

Roberts, J.A.G., *Modern China – An Illustrated History* (Sutton Publishing, 1998)

Twitchett, Denis and Fairbank, John K. (eds), *The Cambridge History of China, Volume 10, Late Ch'Ing 1800–1911* (Cambridge, 19??)

Webb, Frank, *A History of Hong Kong* (HarperCollins, 1993)

Wood, Frances, *No Dogs and Not Many Chinese – Trading Port Life in China* (John Murray, London, 1988)

Yong Yap and Cotterell, Arthur, *Chinese Civilisation – From the Ming Revival to Chairman Mao* (Weidenfeld & Nicolson, London, 1977)

The Persian War

Annual Registers, 1856–7

Illustrated London News

Jones, Felix, *Report to Secretary to Government in Bombay* (1856)

Outram, Sir James, *Dispatches to C-in-C, Bombay* (1857)

The Arrow War

Annual Registers, 1856–60

Bowring, Sir John, *Dispatches; Autobiographical Recollections* (1877)

Cotterell, Arthur, *China – A History* (Random House, London, 1988)

Ebrey, Patricia Buckley, *China – Cambridge Illustrated History* (Cambridge, 1996)

Elgin, James Bruce, Earl of, *Dispatches*

Fairbank, John King, *China – A New History* (Harvard University Press, 1992)

Grant, Sir James Hope, *Dispatches; Incidents in the China War* (with Major Knollys, 1860)

Gray, Jack, *Rebellions and Revolutions* (Oxford University Press, 1990)

Holt, Edgar, *The Opium Wars in China* (Putnam, London, 1964)

Hope, Admiral Sir James, *Dispatches*

Lane-Poole, S. and Dickins, F.V., *The Life of Sir Harry Parkes* (1894)

McCarthy, Justin, *A History of Our Own Times* (Caxton, London, 1908)

Osborn, Sherard, *Fight on the Peiho* (Blackwoods Magazine, 1859)

San-Ko-Lin-Son, *Memorial to the Emperor* (1859)
Seymour, Admiral Sir Michael, *Dispatches*
Spence, Jonathan D., *The Search for Modern China* (Hutchinson, London, 1990)
The Times
Yong Yap and Cotterell, Arthur, *Chinese Civilisation* (Weidenfeld & Nicolson, London, 1977)

The Shortest War

Annual Registers, 1880, 1890, 1896
Brooks, Richard, *Naval Brigades from the Crimea to the Boxer Rebellion* (Constable, London, 1999)
Illustrated London News
Reuters, *Reports from Correspondent* (1896)
The Times

The Benin Massacre

Annual Registers, 1888–9, 1894–8
Gott, Richard, Article in the *Independent*, 1997
Illustrated News, Special Supplement (1897)
James, Lawrence, *The Savage Wars – British Campaigns in Africa, 1870–1920* (Robert Hale, London)
Jephson, Sir Alfred, *Correspondence* (1897)
Keegan, John, *A History of Warfare* (Hutchinson, London, 1993)
McCarthy, Justin, *A History of Our Own Times* (Caxton, London, 1908)
Reuters, *Special Service* (1897)
The Times

The Tirah Campaign

Churchill, Randolph S., *Winston S. Churchill, Volume 1* (Heinemann, London, 1966)
——, *Volume 1 Companion, Part 2* (1967)
Churchill, Sir Winston, *Story of the Malakand Field Force* (London, 1898)
Hutchinson, Colonel H., *The Campaign in Tirah* (London, 1898)
Illustrated London News
Keay, John, *The Gilgit Game* (Murray, London, 1979)
Richards, D.S., *The Savage Frontier – A History of the Anglo-Afghan Wars* (Macmillan, London, 1990)
Schofield, Victoria, *Every Rock, Every Hill – The Plain Tale of the North-West Frontier and Afghanistan* (Buchan & Enright, London, 1984)
Shadwell, Captain L.J., *Lockhart's Advance Through Tirah* (Calcutta, 1898)
The Times

Index